Exalted and Assaulted

Exalted and Assaulted

Conflicted Sentiments about the Profession of Classroom Teaching in America

Michael F. Addonizio

2022

W.E. Upjohn Institute for Employment Research
Kalamazoo, Michigan

Library of Congress Cataloging-in-Publication Data

Name: Addonizio, Michael F., author.
Title: Exalted and assaulted : conflicted sentiments about the profession of classroom teaching in America / Michael F Addonizio.
Description: Kalamazoo, Michigan : W.E. Upjohn Institute for Employment Research, [2022] | Includes bibliographical references and index. | Summary: "This book examines the recent history and current state of the K–12 public school teaching profession in the U.S. Topics include the workings of teacher labor markets, teacher unions and collective bargaining, teacher evaluation, and the effects of the charter school movement on the teaching profession. Impacts of the COVID-19 pandemic on the teaching profession are discussed in an epilogue"—Provided by publisher.
Identifiers: LCCN 2021055207 (print) | LCCN 2021055208 (ebook) | ISBN 9780880996839 (Paperback : alk. paper) | ISBN 9780880996846 (eBook)
Subjects: LCSH: Teaching—United States.
Classification: LCC LB1025.3 .A3754 2022 (print) | LCC LB1025.3 (ebook) | DDC 371.1020973—dc23/eng/20220110
LC record available at https://lccn.loc.gov/2021055207
LC ebook record available at https://lccn.loc.gov/2021055208

The facts presented in this study and the observations and viewpoints expressed are the sole responsibility of the author. They do not necessarily represent positions of the W.E. Upjohn Institute for Employment Research.

Cover design by Carol A. S. Derks.
Index prepared by Diane Worden.
Printed in the United States of America.
Printed on recycled paper.

To my grandchildren, James and Eleanor. And to all children who are enriched by their public schools and their teachers.

Contents

Figures

Tables

Boxes

Acknowledgments

The genesis of this book dates back to 2007, when the Board of Governors of Wayne State University awarded me a Charles H. Gershenson Distinguished Faculty Fellowship to support my research and encourage me to widen my focus. So that's what I've tried to do. After decades of studying the theories and practice of public school finance and the workings and impacts of school choice policies across the states, I turned my attention to a new line of questioning: *How* do schools use resources? I soon focused on their most important resource—the teachers.

Early work with Wayne State colleagues Phil Kearney (formerly of the University of Michigan), Marytza Gawlik, and Fran and Will Sosnowsky examined the backgrounds, training, and credentials of classroom teachers and how these teachers were distributed across local school districts and types of schools (e.g., charter, traditional, elementary, secondary, etc.) in the Detroit metropolitan region. We managed to contribute a few articles to a then rapidly growing research literature on "teacher quality." As this work proceeded, my interest in public school teachers expanded to the profession as a whole, a profession that appears uniquely paradoxical—public school teachers in America are exalted as pillars of our communities and architects of our democracy, entrusted with our children's social and intellectual development while, at the same time, often assaulted as the source of children's educational failures and our economy's ills. Our public school teachers are viewed, at once, as the sole reason for our public schools' shortcomings and as the only people who can save them.

As I thought about this paradox and began to examine the profession of classroom teaching in the U.S., I recalled the smart, generous, funny, and inspirational teachers I had decades ago in public school. I grew up in Haverhill, Massachusetts, a midsize, largely blue-collar city about 30 miles north of Boston. I graduated from Haverhill High School, a large school of about 2,500 students, in 1966. Back then, public schools were generally seen as essential ladders of mobility and anchors of civic life. Teachers were respected and appreciated.

Since then, of course, much has changed. With this book, I have tried to understand what has changed for the teaching profession and why. In that effort, I needed a lot of assistance, and I want to thank all those who helped me bring this book to publication. Doug Whitman, Dean of the College of Education at Wayne State, and Assistant Dean Bill Hill, along with other Wayne State colleagues, provided a very supportive environment for this work. Special thanks goes to Ben Pogodzinski, who carefully read and critiqued drafts of each chapter. His insights made this a better book. Kate French, postdoctoral scholar extraordinaire, read a draft of the first few chapters, provided helpful comments, and suggested that I think more about *why* teachers have come to be so concerned with current education policy (generally not of their making) and that I consider the costs to students of excessive teacher turnover. Good advice I've tried to follow. Many thanks also to an anonymous reviewer who read my first complete draft of the manuscript and provided a wealth of ideas for its improvement.

I'm indebted to Kevin Hollenbeck of the W.E. Upjohn Institute for Employment Research, who encouraged me on this project and provided his trademark insightful comments and suggestions on the opening chapters. Thanks also to Brad Hershbein and Randall Eberts of the Upjohn Institute for their sponsorship and support. And a special thanks to Ben Jones of Upjohn for his superb editorial support, turning an unwieldy manuscript into this better organized and more readable volume. Thanks also to Erika Jones of Upjohn for her expert work on all the graphics.

Many thanks also to John Chamberlin, Alan Deardoff, and Brian Jacob of the Gerald R. Ford School of Public Policy at the University of Michigan for supporting my Visiting Scholar appointment in 2017 and giving me an ideal venue for launching this project. David Arsen and Tanner Delpier of Michigan State University provided valuable advice about Michigan data sources for Chapter 6, and Ruth Beier, Chief Economist for the Michigan Education Association, provided critical teacher salary data for that chapter. Jack Schneider of UMass–Lowell generously directed me toward data and information sources for the Bay State. Thanks also to Michael Griffith, then of the Education Commission of the States and now the Learning Policy Institute, for leads on data sources, and to Scott Adams for permission to republish his hilarious and telling art. He says more in three cartoon panels than I do in the rest of Chapter 5.

In addition, I'm indebted to the many researchers and educators I have cited throughout this book. As I noted earlier, the topic of public school teachers and their profession was a departure from my earlier work in public economics and school finance. Whatever contribution I have managed to make here sits atop the work and wisdom of many others.

I also need to acknowledge some special folks who came to mind as I undertook this project and, once again, inspired me in my work: Miss LoPresti, Miss Sullivan, Miss Morin, Miss Nadeau, Miss Tattersoll, Mr. Macul, Miss English, Mr. Mardekian, Mr. Cohen, and Miss Hanoian. You were the reasons I always liked school, and you helped steer me into this line of work.

And, finally, a huge thank you to Joan for sage editorial advice, unlimited patience, and unwavering support during this long project. Without you, this book would not have been possible.

—Michael Addonizio

1
Exalted and Assaulted

Conflicted Sentiments about the Teaching Profession

It is the supreme art of the teacher to awaken joy in creative expression and knowledge. —Albert Einstein

Public schools and classroom teachers both shape and reflect our societal values. They are both foundational institutions of civil society and barometers of the condition of civic life. They are considered both vital sources of equal opportunity in American life and impediments to that same fundamental goal. The teaching profession in particular has long seemed to foster a certain ambivalence in the minds of the American public. The profession itself is generally exalted as being among the highest of callings and the "great equalizer" envisioned by Horace Mann, while those who practice are often maligned as less than our best and brightest and not truly professional, in terms of not only their knowledge base and skill level but their dedication, which is often seen by critics as directed more toward job security than toward their students and their craft. The sociologist Dan Lortie, in his 1975 classic work *Schoolteacher*, succinctly captures this uniquely ambivalent public perception of the profession:

> Teaching seems to have more than its share of status anomalies. It is honored and disdained, praised as "dedicated service" and lampooned as "easy work." It is permeated with the rhetoric of professionalism, yet features incomes below those earned by workers with considerably less education. It is middle-class work in which more and more participants use bargaining strategies developed by wage-earners in factories. . . . Teaching, from its inception in America, has occupied a special but shadowed social standing. The services performed by teachers have usually been seen as above the run of everyday work, and the occupation has had the aura of a special mission honored by society. But social ambiguity has stalled those who undertook the mission, for the real regard shown those who taught has never matched the professed regard. (Lortie 1975, p. 10)

This conflicted view held by the American public of the teachers in their public schools has seemingly reached new levels of intensity since Lortie's landmark study. Americans' faith in education as a means to advance our society has never wavered, and our collective view of the educational imperative is stronger than ever as information expands exponentially, technology advances at an accelerating pace, and economic inequality widens. At the same time, while mounting evidence points to the classroom teacher as the most important resource in our public schools, criticism of public school teachers has reached new heights, with parent groups, civil rights activists, Wall Street investors, and political leaders of both major parties forming an unprecedented alliance against teacher unions and their "industrial style" job protections.[1]

Much of the American public has grown increasingly resentful of the teaching profession, which remains highly unionized during an era when job protections and defined-benefit retirement systems are now nearly nonexistent in the private sector. This growing resentment is fueled in large part by the widely shared view that the profession does little to deal with poor performers and, indeed, is generally hostile to any such efforts. As education scholar David Cohen observes, "With the exception of the National Board for Professional Teaching Standards (NBPTS), no organization of teachers has set standards of quality practice, devised means to discern whether they have been met, and used those means to regulate quality" (Cohen 2011, p. 59).

This popular critique of the teaching profession has given rise to policymakers' growing insistence on closely assessing individual teacher performance in order to weed out the union laggards and open the profession to nonunion members and graduates of nontraditional, nonuniversity teacher preparation programs. For example, the Every Student Succeeds Act (ESSA), signed by President Obama on December 25, 2015, provides for the creation of "teacher preparation academies" such as those funded by venture philanthropists, including Eli Broad and Bill Gates, and relaxes standards for teacher education programs that prepare teachers for high-poverty schools. And this is merely the latest in a long line of initiatives aimed at broadening access to the teaching profession and diluting union influence.

These efforts have taken a toll on both teacher morale and the profession's appeal to potential entrants, whether new college graduates or midcareer professionals. For example, a recent MetLife survey of teachers found that between 2008 and 2012, the proportion who reported being "very satisfied" with their current job plunged from 62 percent to 39 percent, the lowest in a quarter century (Goldstein 2014, p. 3). And a survey of a nationally representative sample of 3,328 public school teachers by the nonprofit Center on Education Policy found that about half of these teachers would leave the profession if they could get a higher-paying job. Furthermore, fully 46 percent of teachers cited state or district policies that hamper their teaching as being among their biggest challenges—double the percentage of respondents who cited classroom conditions, like large classes or economically disadvantaged students, as being among their greatest challenges. According to the center's report, most teachers feel excluded from education policy discussions at all levels of government (Wise 2016). At a time when our public school classrooms will need new infusions of talent as teachers of the baby boom generation retire and schools seek to restore teaching positions lost in the Great Recession, the embattled profession of classroom teaching appears much less appealing to aspiring or midcareer professionals than ever before.

Indeed, one could argue that the profession is in crisis. Enrollment in teacher preparation programs has declined sharply in recent years, falling from 691,000 in 2009 to 451,000 in 2014, a drop of 35 percent (Sutcher, Darling-Hammond, and Carver-Thomas 2016). And turnover in the profession is rampant, with between 40 and 50 percent of new teachers leaving the profession within five years. Furthermore, many mid- and late-career teachers who have honed their skills over years in the classroom are opting to leave the profession short of retirement, raising the prospect of critical teacher shortages in the years to come. A 2016 study by the Learning Policy Institute reveals that retirements generally constitute less than one-third of annual teaching exits. Of those who leave teaching voluntarily, most cite job dissatisfaction as a key factor in their decision. The study estimates a teacher shortage of approximately 64,000 teachers in the 2015–2016 school year, rising to about 112,000 by 2018 and remaining close to that level thereafter (ibid.).

A High Turnover Profession

As Lortie (1975) observes, teaching was institutionalized as high-turnover work during the nineteenth century, often requiring annual infusions of many new members to meet classroom demands. The profession continues in that vein to the present day. With an annual attrition rate of nearly 8 percent, the U.S. teaching workforce "continues to be a leaky bucket" (Sutcher, Darling-Hammond, and Carver-Thomas 2016, p. 2). It is because of this high turnover and the sheer size of the needed teacher workforce (five times as many people teach as practice either medicine or law in the United States) that the profession will never approach the elite status enjoyed by doctors or lawyers. As John Dewey observed in 1895, "Education is, and forever will be, in the hands of ordinary men and women" (Archambault 1964, p. 199). At the same time, no one can deny the importance of the profession for society's pursuit of democratic values and economic progress. The work of the classroom teacher is critically important to our social and economic well-being, and yet, teachers find themselves constantly having to navigate tensions between their low professional status, accountability measures imposed from outside the profession, and the autonomy and working conditions necessary for their effectiveness and success.

A Nation at Risk

Arguably the most impactful education report in U.S. history,[2] *A Nation at Risk* was authored by the National Commission on Excellence in Education, an 18-member group appointed by Terrel H. Bell, President Ronald Reagan's Secretary of Education. Completed in 18 months and released in April 1983, in the depths of a severe economic recession, the 36-page report created an immediate sensation with its blunt opening statement:

> Our Nation is at risk. Our once unchallenged preeminence in commerce, industry, science, and technological innovation is being overtaken by competitors throughout the world. . . . The educational foundations of our society are presently being eroded by a rising tide of mediocrity that threatens our very future as a Nation and a people. . . . If an unfriendly power had attempted to impose on America the mediocre educational performance that exists today, we might well have viewed it as an act of war. As it stands,

we have allowed this to happen to ourselves. . . . We have, in effect, been committing an act of unthinking, unilateral, educational disarmament. (National Commission on Excellence in Education 1983, p. 5)

The report cited declining SAT scores from 1963 to 1980, falling scores on standardized achievement tests, poor performance on international assessments, the increase in remedial math courses across college campuses, and the incidence of functional illiteracy among youth and young adults as evidence of U.S. educational decline—a decline that commission members asserted would impose substantial social and economic costs on the nation.

Regarding teachers, the commission report argued that American teachers were academically weak, drawn from the "bottom quarter" of college graduating classes, and particularly weak in mathematics and science. To improve teacher quality, the commission recommended higher base salaries, merit pay for superior performance, and more stringent evaluation systems for purposes of earning and retaining tenure. The report also called for new avenues into the teaching profession whereby new college graduates and career changers who had not studied education could obtain "alternative" teaching credentials in relatively short order.

Publication of A Nation at Risk set off what many have called the first wave of comprehensive public school reform across the states, focusing on such initiatives as boosting high school graduation requirements, making standardized achievement tests more demanding, and increasing the amount of instructional time in schools. Among the report's many recommendations, two resonated particularly strongly with the press and the public: strengthened high school graduation requirements and higher standards for entrance into the teaching profession. Regarding the latter, the commission reasoned that those entering the profession should be expected to meet high educational standards relating to both teaching aptitude and competence in an academic discipline. Teacher compensation should be increased and should be "professionally competitive, market-sensitive, and performance based." Decisions regarding salary, retention, tenure, and promotion "should be tied to an effective evaluation system that includes peer review so that superior teachers can be rewarded, average ones encouraged, and poor ones either improved or terminated" (National Commission on Excellence in Education 1983, p. 30). The contentious issue of tying individual teacher evaluations to student scores on standardized tests is not raised in the report. The topic began to emerge publicly in the early 1980s but did not assume center stage until decades later during the Obama administration. It remains a particularly contentious issue for the teaching profession, with neither policy nor practice enjoying much support in the research literature.

The states respond

The states' responses to the report were most dramatic with respect to high school curriculum and graduation requirements, as virtually all states increased requirements in academic subjects. However, the report also inspired changes in teacher compensation. When *A Nation at Risk* was released in 1983, teachers were rarely paid or promoted on the basis of performance, and there were few career advancement opportunities that did not require teachers to leave the classroom for administration. By the early 1990s, however, dozens of states and scores of school systems had established career ladders, mentorships, and other leadership opportunities that offered teachers increased status, higher salaries, and new professional challenges without requiring that they abandon the classroom.

New avenues into the profession

Policymakers responded to this call as well, creating alternative paths to certification in many states. The results of this expanded access to the profession, however, have been generally disappointing. Rather than stabilizing and strengthening school faculties across the states, graduates of these streamlined programs, which provide candidates with less pedagogical training than do traditional, university-based programs, have suffered from higher rates of annual turnover than regular pathway teachers. And while alternatively prepared teachers are disproportionately represented in hard-to-staff fields such as math and science and in schools serving primarily students of color, their high attrition rates have disrupted student learning and raised school costs. I examine the impacts of these nontraditional teacher preparation programs on the composition and mobility of the teacher labor force in our discussion of teacher labor markets.

A Nation at Risk produced little substantive improvement in measured student achievement because the reforms were both cosmetic and "top down"—that is, imposed on educators by politicians and bureaucrats and overly focused on school inputs (e.g., longer school day or year, increased graduation requirements, etc.) and basic skills. Many education leaders and scholars assert that these reforms failed to improve classroom instruction because teachers were excluded from the reform process. More specifically, the reformers' calls for a more rigorous academic curriculum, including increased coursework in English, math, science, history, and foreign languages, to be taught to a much broader student body, stood little chance of having a discernible impact on classroom teaching and learning without much more input from classroom teachers as to teacher preparation, curriculum content, pedagogy, and teacher supports. Indeed, policy has gone in the opposite direction, with new teacher evaluation schemes based on student test scores being designed and adopted over strong objections from classroom teachers as well as the education research community.

A flawed economic analysis

The education reforms triggered by *A Nation at Risk* were focused on the perceived needs of business and industry, emphasizing math, science, and technology-related curricula. This emphasis stemmed from the report's unmistakable linkage of school reform with the nation's economic growth.[3] This perceived linkage between economic prosperity and the quality of the public schools is most clearly stated in the report's section titled "The Risk":

> The world is indeed one global village. We live among determined, well-educated, and strongly motivated competitors. We compete with them for international standing and markets, not only with products but also with the ideas of our laboratories and neighborhood workshops. America's position in the world may once have been reasonably secure with only a few exceptionally well-trained men and women. It is no longer.

> Knowledge, learning, information, and skilled intelligence are the new raw materials of international commerce and are today spreading throughout the world as vigorously as miracle drugs, synthetic fertilizers, and blue jeans did earlier. If only to keep and improve on the slim competitive edge we still retain in world markets, we

must dedicate ourselves to the reform of our educational system. (National Commission on Excellence in Education 1983, pp. 6–7)

This alleged causal relationship between the anemic productivity growth of the U.S. economy in the late 1970s and early 1980s and the quality of the nation's public schools, while clearly the source of much of the report's public acclaim, was almost certainly mistaken. This flaw in the commission's theory became readily apparent a decade later. By 1994, the United States had become the most competitive economy in the world. Unemployment had fallen below 5.5 percent (down from the recession's peak level of 10.8 percent in December 1982), inflation was a mere 2.7 percent (down from 13.9 percent in January 1980), and productivity was growing at its fastest rate in more than two decades. Educational outcomes in U.S. public schools, on the other hand, had changed little between 1980 and 1994, years when the nation embarked on the longest peacetime economic expansion in its history.[4]

Certainly, as the workforce becomes more educated and work becomes more capital- and skill-intensive, productivity accelerates and the economy grows. But history has demonstrated that changes in the macroeconomy occur much too quickly to be explained by the quality of such a slow-to-change institution as our public schools. Most workers in the economy who exert the greatest impact on current levels of productivity were educated decades earlier. The lag between changes in school quality and effects on productivity and economic growth appears to be much longer than implied in *A Nation at Risk*. Nonetheless, despite its flawed analysis of the impact of school quality on economic growth, publication of *A Nation at Risk* was a landmark event in the history of U.S. public education. The report ushered in an unbroken period of intense debate, scrutiny, and reform of public schools that continues unabated to the present day.

The National Board for Professional Teaching Standards

In 1986, three years after publication of *A Nation at Risk*, the Carnegie Task Force on Teaching as a Profession helped establish a National Board for Professional Teaching Standards (NBPTS), whose mission is to "establish high and rigorous standards for what teachers should know and be able to do, [and] to certify teachers who meet these standards" (NBPTS 1989, p. 1). The NBPTS began with a 63-member board of directors, two-thirds of whom were teachers. Board members were tasked with establishing a voluntary process by which teachers could become certified through demonstrating mastery of an ambitious set of national standards.

The model adopted by the National Board is similar to that of other professions, such as medicine and law, in which accomplished members of the profession play a major role in setting standards for entry and advancement in the profession. After establishing the standards, the NBPTS worked with measurement experts to design the performance-based assessments that teachers would complete to earn certification. The first National Board–certified teachers (NBCTs) earned their credentials in 1994. By the end of the 2020–2021 school year, 128,500 teachers had earned National Board certification, including more than 36,500 in North Carolina and Florida combined (NBPTS 2021a,b).

The NBPTS awards certificates in 25 areas across 16 different subjects and spanning pre-K through grade 12. The assessment consists of a multimedia portfolio that demonstrates knowledge of content and pedagogy and evidence of student learning. The portfolio includes videotaped samples of teaching practice, samples of student work, and commentaries that explain how the evidence provided addresses each standard being assessed. Candidates also complete an online assessment. The entire process takes at least one year and costs $2,500. Candidates must hold a valid teaching license and have at least three years of teaching experience. Since the program's inception, about 30 states and some local districts have provided incentives and supports for teachers seeking National Board certification. Examples include full or partial subsidies for program costs, professional development resources, and increased compensation for NBCTs, with additional stipends for such teachers who work in high-poverty or low-performing schools.

The general effectiveness of NBCTs has been confirmed by solid research. In 2008, the National Research Council reviewed 25 rigorous studies and concluded that students taught by NBCTs had higher achievement test gains than students taught by comparable non-NBCTs, although the differences varied by state (National Research Council 2008). Some studies have found greater positive impacts for students of color and students from low-income families (Cannata et al. 2010; Harris and Sass 2009).

The Changing Landscape of Public School Teaching

Much has changed over the past two decades for the profession of public school teaching. The recent emphasis on teacher accountability based on student test scores, the creation of new avenues into the teaching profession (often involving little or no pedagogical instruction or clinical experience), the rise of privately run charter schools, and falling real financial support for K–12 education have changed the U.S. public education landscape and significantly altered the professional lives and working conditions of our classroom teachers. And these reforms often exert mutually reinforcing effects on the work of teachers, constricting their autonomy, discretion, and creativity and generally diminishing the profession's appeal for both new college graduates and career changers.

Consider, for example, the jobs of teachers in the growing number of charter schools run by charter management organizations (CMOs), private, nonprofit organizations largely motivated by the worthy goal of narrowing the achievement gap as defined by race or class. Unlike their traditional public school counterparts, teachers working in CMO-run public schools are at-will employees who work longer school days and years for relatively low compensation, must be available to their students evenings and weekends by cell phone for help with homework and other matters, and generally lack experienced colleagues to whom they can turn for counsel and support. Similarly, teachers in charter schools managed by for-profit educational management organizations (EMOs) lack the job protections afforded by union membership. Moreover, their work is further subject to management's efforts to cut costs by substituting capital for labor and replacing in-person teaching with online programs.

Full-time virtual schools

EMOs have been far more inclined than CMOs to utilize online instruction as a substitute for, rather than a complement to, traditional classroom teachers. This low-cost, technology-intensive approach to K–12 instruction by means of full-time virtual schools, also referred to as "cyber schools" or "online schools," has grown rapidly in recent years. The most notable example of this form of educational privatization is K12 Inc., a Virginia-based K–12 company founded in 1999 by one-time "junk bond king" Michael Milken and hedge fund manager Ronald Packard. K12 Inc. is the largest for-profit provider of precollegiate online learning and one of the few publicly traded companies in the K–12 marketplace. A second prominent example of K–12 online schooling is Connections Academy, a subsidiary of the publishing giant Pearson. Founded in 2001 and headquartered in Baltimore, Connections Academy enrolled more than 60,000 students across 29 virtual public schools in 25 states for the 2014–2015 school year.

These full-time virtual schools serve several purposes. Elite athletes seeking flexible schedules and academic workloads find these schools convenient, as do students who stay home for health or other reasons. More generally, cyber schools facilitate school choice, generally enrolling students from across local school districts within a state. Through advocacy and lobbying efforts by national organizations and prominent providers, 30 states and the District of Columbia have created cyber schools (Watson et al. 2011). Miron and Urschel (2012) report that by 2012, nearly a quarter of a million students were enrolled in full-time virtual schools.

This low-cost, technology-intensive form of educational privatization has grown rapidly in recent years while largely avoiding the glare of the public spotlight (save for some press reports of poor academic performance, financial mismanagement, and, occasionally, outright fraud).[5] In these cyber schools, the teacher's role is greatly circumscribed by management, often reduced to guiding students through a scripted online experience narrowly designed to prepare students for standardized reading and math assessments. This is not surprising for EMO management, whose objective is profit maximization, not the students' intellectual, emotional, and moral growth, aims that have historically been at the heart of good teaching.

This wide gulf between management's and faculty's missions has resulted in rampant teacher turnover and low-quality instruction, an entirely predictable outcome that is baked into the EMO business model, but an outcome that is anathema to the teaching profession and one that takes its toll on members. In his landmark study of the teaching profession, Lortie sought to identify occupational characteristics that attract people to teaching. Interviewing teachers in five towns in the Boston metropolitan area, Lortie asked them to describe the occupation's appeal, what made it more attractive than alternatives they seriously considered. Two themes that emerged from these intensive interviews were service and interpersonal exchange. Lortie concluded:

> Teachers are involved with knowledge and its diffusion; their work has also been described as an "art" requiring special sensitivity and personal creativity. Involvement with knowledge and the call for creativity could quite logically serve as foci for attraction to teaching. It is therefore interesting that neither of these aspects of the role receives as much attention as the interpersonal.

> Teachers have been perceived as performing a special mission in our society, and we see the continuation of that conception among those engaged in the work today. The idea that teaching is a valuable service of special moral worth is a theme in the talk of Five Towns teachers. (Lortie 1975, p. 28)

The importance that workers attach to belief in their mission cannot be overstated. As economists George Akerlof and Rachel Kranton observe, "Workers who identify with the mission of their leaders dedicate themselves selflessly to their work, whereas their opposites do the bare minimum of what is required and typically look elsewhere for employment" (Akerlof and Kranton 2010). This conflict of mission and vision between teacher and corporate management in an EMO-run cyber school is articulated in an online post by Darcy Bedortha, a teacher who resigned from K12 Inc. in 2013. "I became a teacher because I am an advocate for youth and social justice," Bedortha wrote. "However, this purpose was hard to fulfill working in a K12 Inc. school. With the kind of technology, systems and process management needed to keep the enrollment machine running (and the machine is priority), there is never much time to actually teach.

"I found it impossible to meet the learning needs of my students in that situation" (Bedortha 2014).

Full-time virtual schools may be an effective alternative for some students with a particular learning style and strong support at home, but research evidence provides little support for the widespread adoption advocated by special interests, usually those who would profit greatly. Whitney Tilson, a hedge fund manager and founding member of Teach for America, provides a telling perspective: "When K12 was small, it was mostly serving kids like mine, with at least one—if not both—college-educated parents working in the home with children. In those cases, it really works" (Molnar 2013, pp. 3–4). The research literature on cyber schools, however, cautions strongly against their more general use. Researchers Gary Miron and Jessica Urschel studied K–12 schools and reviewed the literature. They observe that "studies on full-time virtual schools in the charter sector have all found the performance of these schools to be lagging substantially behind brick-and-mortar schools and district schools. The new findings . . . on mean performance on state reading and math assessments, and on-time graduation rates, all found that K12 schools were performing at levels far below those of the states in which they operate" (Miron and Urschel 2012). Similarly, a 2016 report by the National Association of Charter School Authorizers and 50CAN, a national charter lobbying group, found that full-time cyber students made no significant gains in math and less than half the gains in reading compared to their traditional public school peers (National Alliance for Public Charter Schools 2016).

Teaching, Technology, and Baumol's Cost Disease

Broad-based efforts by EMOs, CMOs, and other educational entrepreneurs to cut school operating costs by substituting capital for labor have generally failed. Whether pursued by means of cyber schools or more broadly with the proliferation of smartboards, tablets, laptops, or other devices, these interventions have resulted not in lower costs, but lower quality—that is, an inferior educational service.[6] While technology can be an effective complement to in-person teaching, it is rarely an effective substitute. Kentaro Toyama, a professor at the University of Michigan's School of Information, has formulated what he terms technology's "Law of Amplification," writes Nicholas Kardaras: "Technology could help education where it's already doing well, but it does little for mediocre educational systems." Worse, in struggling schools, Toyama says, it "can cause outright harm" (Kardaras 2016, p. 5).

The chronic failure of efforts to substitute capital for labor in the classroom, documented in a large and growing literature, can be understood with an elegant theory posed decades ago by the economist William Baumol to explain stagnant productivity growth across certain sectors of the economy. This theory, which has come to be known as "Baumol's cost disease," holds that costs are destined to rise in certain sectors of the economy, including education, health care, and the performing arts, because it is difficult to reduce the labor required to supply these services. First enunciated in 1966, the idea is restated by Baumol (2012) in his book *The Cost Disease: Why Computers Get Cheaper and Health Care Doesn't*:

> Since the Industrial Revolution, labor-saving productivity improvements have been occurring at an unprecedented pace in most manufacturing activities, reducing the cost of making these products even as workers' wages have risen. In the personal services industries, meanwhile, automation is not always possible, and labor-saving productivity improvements occur at a rate well below average for the economy. As a result, costs in the personal services industries move ever upward at a much faster rate than the rate of inflation.[7] (p. xvii)

Our economy will always have a "low productivity" sector, where effective services depend primarily on skilled workers whose effectiveness can be enhanced by technology but whose skills, talent, wisdom, and judgment cannot be displaced by it. Baumol points to education and the performing arts as prime examples of industries that must absorb rising labor costs because they are limited in their ability to substitute capital for labor. For Baumol, education is more akin to a string quartet than an auto factory. Just as the quartet will always require four musicians, the successful classroom will always need a teacher. This should not be cause for concern or efforts to curtail the supply of labor-intensive services like education, the performing arts, or health care. Productivity rises across the entire economy, simply more slowly in some industries than others. And as overall productivity rises, so too does the purchasing power of consumers. As Baumol observes, "no matter how painful rising education and medical bills may be, society can afford them and there is no need to deny them to ourselves or to the less affluent members to our society, or indeed to the world. Overall incomes and purchasing power must rise quickly enough to keep these services affordable, despite their persistently rising costs" (Baumol 2012, p. xvii).

As overall productivity rises, even if it rises more slowly in some industries than others, the same or fewer hours of labor will produce more goods and services. Thus, in societies with competitive economies, education, health care, and other labor-intensive services will remain affordable despite their rising cost. And while technology can often effectively enhance (complement) human performance, wholesale attempts to substitute capital for labor in education and these other services do not lower cost. They lower quality. The centrality of teacher skills and human relationships generally in the educational process is eloquently described by University of California, Berkeley, professor and author David Kirp. "It's impossible to improve education by doing an end run around inherently complicated and messy human relationships," Kirp says. "All youngsters need to believe that they have a stake in the future, a goal worth striving for, if they're going to make it in school. They need a champion, someone who believes in them, and that's where teachers enter the picture. The most effective approaches foster bonds of caring between teachers and their students" (Kirp 2014, p. SR4).

The power of technology can be effectively harnessed in the classroom only through the unique capabilities of a skilled teacher, including creativity, intuition, empathy, and professional judgment. Technology serves the teacher, not the other way around.

A Dwindling Pipeline, Rising Attrition, and High Turnover

Enrollments in teacher preparation programs across the U.S. have fallen steadily in recent years. Between 2009 and 2014, enrollments in undergraduate and postbaccalaureate teacher preparation programs fell by 35 percent, a drop of nearly 240,000 candidates. And the number of program completers fell by more than 23 percent over the same period (Sutcher, Darling-Hammond, and Carver-Thomas 2016). Interest in the profession has also declined precipitously in recent years. In a 2014 survey of those taking the ACT college entrance exam, a mere 5 percent of respondents expressed interest in a career in education, down 29 percent from 2010 (ACT 2015). And in the 2016 report of an annual survey of college freshmen, a mere 4.2 percent of students cited education as their probable field of study, down from 9.2 percent in 2007 and the lowest proportion of students considering teaching as a profession in 45 years (Eagan et al. 2017).

Just as fewer aspiring professionals are now entering the teaching profession, more are leaving before retirement. For example, attrition rates for first-year teachers rose from 9.8 percent in 1988–1989 to 14.6 percent in 2000–2001, before settling back to 13.1 percent in 2008–2009.

And more than 41 percent of new teachers leave the profession within five years (Perda 2013). Moreover, cast in absolute numbers rather than percentages, our current teacher attrition problem appears even more daunting: following the 1987–1988 school year, about 6,000 first-year teachers left the profession; 20 years later, after the 2007–2008 school year, the number of first-year teachers exiting the profession soared to about 25,000 (Ingersoll, Merrill, and Stuckey 2014).

Why do they leave? Examining the most comprehensive data source on teachers available—the Schools and Staffing Survey (SASS) and its supplement, the Teacher Follow-Up Survey (TFS)—University of Pennsylvania researchers Richard Ingersoll, Lisa Merrill, and Daniel Stuckey found that about 20 percent of the first-year teachers who left following the 2007–2008 school year indicated they had been laid off or terminated. About 35 percent cited personal or family reasons, including health, pregnancy, change of residence, or caring for family members. A slightly higher percentage left teaching to pursue further education or another career. The foremost set of reasons for leaving the teaching profession, cited by more than 45 percent of those leaving (some teachers cited reasons in more than one category), concerned dissatisfaction with their school and working conditions, including salaries, classroom resources, student behavior, accountability measures, opportunities for professional development, input into decision making, and school leadership (Ingersoll, Merrill, and Stuckey 2014). Taken together, these findings depict a profession in flux and increasingly unstable, as the numbers of both those entering and those leaving have been increasing in recent years.

This trend of rising teacher attrition, or teachers leaving the profession, is damaging to teacher development, particularly among novice teachers. As I document in the following chapters, teachers hone their craft through classroom experience. Not only does careful research overwhelmingly confirm dramatic improvement in teachers' effectiveness over the first four or five years of their careers, but growing evidence reveals continued improvement well beyond these formative years (see, for example, Harris and Sass 2011). And this trend of rising attrition is part of a larger problem of teacher turnover, generally defined as the annual change in teachers at a particular school. While some turnover in personnel in any organization is typical and often healthy, high rates of teacher turnover are problematic for several reasons. First, rapid turnover exacerbates teacher shortages for many schools in hard-to-staff subjects such as math, science, and special education. Furthermore, turnover among minority teachers, who are generally overrepresented in schools serving economically disadvantaged communities, undermines teacher recruitment and efforts to diversify teaching faculties in these struggling schools. Finally, rapid turnover has been found to impair student learning (e.g., Hanushek, Rivkin, and Schiman 2016; Henry and Redding 2018; Ronfeldt, Loeb, and Wyckoff 2013; Sorensen and Ladd 2019).

The Failed Legacy of *A Nation at Risk*

New avenues and requirements for entry into the teaching profession, changes in the teachers' workplace, and reforms of teacher evaluation and compensation systems and career ladders have been instituted across states since publication of the commission report. Indeed, the debate over public school performance and teacher quality in particular has only escalated in the ensuing years. Top-down reforms adopted across state capitals following publication of *A Nation at Risk* produced generally disappointing results. First, tightening high school graduation requirements to include more coursework in mathematics and science merely increased the number of high school dropouts entering the labor force with weak cognitive skills (Hodgkinson 1985, cited in Murnane 1988). Furthermore, states' increased use of standardized tests emphasizing low-level computational skills instead of complex problem solving led to classroom emphasis on scripted drill and practice at the expense of more sophisticated and creative instruction addressing higher-order skills. As education researchers have observed, the "command and control" reforms triggered by this much-heralded federal commission report failed because they circumscribed the discretion and practice of classroom teachers, the very professionals best positioned to effect school improvement (Murnane 1988; Wise 1988).

The regimented and largely counterproductive reforms of the post-*Nation* period were followed by the launch of the choice and charter school movements in the early 1990s. The charter school movement, which began in 1992 with the opening of the nation's first charter school in Minnesota, has been particularly disruptive for the traditionally highly unionized profession of classroom teaching. Numerous published studies have documented the low salaries and the diminished fringe and retirement benefits and job protections of charter-school teachers, the vast majority of whom are unorganized (see, for example, Addonizio, Kearney, and Gawlik 2015).

"Top Down" Reform Comes to Washington

Another wave of reform was ushered in with the 2001 reauthorization of the 1965 Elementary and Secondary Education Act (ESEA), commonly known as the No Child Left Behind Act (NCLB). Under NCLB, schools that chronically failed to make "adequate yearly progress" (AYP) were subject to a widening set of reforms and sanctions that included the offer of transfer to another school for families that wanted to, the provision of supplementary educational services outside the normal school day, the replacement of school staff, and the conversion of the school to charter status. Teacher quality was a central focus of this landmark legislation. The law required that by 2006, teachers in schools receiving federal Title I funding be "highly qualified." Specifically, teachers were required to meet three criteria: 1) be fully certified by the state, 2) hold at least a bachelor's degree from a four-year institution, and 3) be proficient in the subject(s) they taught.

The drumbeat of reform rose several more decibels in 2009 with Race to the Top (RTT), part of a congressionally approved economic stimulus package that provided more than $4 billion in grants to states and school districts that adopted reforms of teacher accountability and teacher tenure rules and generally freed schools from job-security and working-condition policies traditionally found in teachers' collective bargaining agreements. The robust state and local responses to these incentive grants and NCLB waiver requests altered the landscape of the teaching profession in important ways. These responses created reporting systems that emphasized surveillance and accountability, while weakening institutional supports for teaching and learning. They also raised fundamental questions about the validity and reliability of teacher evaluation and performance assessment, particularly systems that link teacher evaluations to student performance on standardized achievement tests. A state-by-state analysis, released in November 2015 by the National Council on Teacher Quality (NCTQ), found that 42 states and the District of Columbia required that student growth and achievement on standardized assessments be considered in evaluations of public school teachers. In 2009, only 15 states had linked student achievement measures to teacher evaluations (NCTQ 2015).

This prominent strand of the school reform movement, however, has recently taken a new turn. The powerful RTT incentives for states to emphasize student test scores in their teacher evaluation systems—while introducing new, more demanding tests tied to Common Core standards—aroused strong opposition from both ends of the political spectrum. Teacher unions, citing serious concerns with the validity and reliability of teacher performance measures derived from student test scores, vigorously opposed these measures. And they were joined in this opposition by Tea Party adherents and other conservatives who viewed these Obama administration initiatives as another unwarranted federal intrusion into local public schools.

In response to these pressures from unlikely political bedfellows, and to widely reported difficulties in implementation, including evidence of cheating and clumsy implementation (e.g., school districts using reading scores to evaluate art and gym teachers), President Obama signed a new education law in December 2015 that largely abandoned the RTT teacher evaluation reforms. The new Every Student Succeeds Act (ESSA) effectively terminates the Obama administration's incentives for states and districts to adopt more stringent teacher evaluation programs and bans the U.S. secretary of education from promoting teacher performance metrics in the future. Whether this new federal law leads the individual states to relax their test-based, value-added teacher evaluation standards remains to be seen.

The Plan for the Rest of the Book

I examine major institutions and reforms that have shaped the profession of K–12 public school teaching in the United States, with emphasis on the period since the publication of *A Nation at Risk* in 1983. In Chapter 2, I discuss the workings of public-school-teacher labor markets and the factors that influence teacher supply and demand at the national, state, and local levels. I focus particularly on the root causes of the substantial inequality in the distribution of teaching talent across local schools and districts within states and assess the impacts of teacher compensation systems, including salary structures and retirement benefits, on teacher supply.

Chapter 3 chronicles the rise of public-school teacher unions in the 1960s and 1970s and contrasts the prominence of unions in public education with their dramatic decline in recent decades in the private sector. I examine recent state legislative efforts to curb union power and circumscribe teachers' job protections and assess judicial challenges to both these new state laws and to more long-standing union protections, such as public unions' authority to impose fees on nonmembers.

Chapter 4 traces the growth of charter schools in the U.S. and the evolution of this movement from the teacher-led reform envisioned by Al Shanker and other public education leaders in the late 1980s and early 1990s to a broad movement to privatize public education and greatly diminish the influence of classroom teachers in matters of curriculum, pedagogy, school governance, and working conditions. This privatization agenda, while enacted on a state-by-state basis, has been coordinated nationally to a great degree by the American Legislative Exchange Council (ALEC) and other organizations seeking to diminish the influence of teachers, and particularly union members, in public schools.

Chapter 5 traces the origins and the current state of the art of teacher evaluation and accountability. I review the rapidly expanding research literature on "value-added" modeling and the policy initiatives that have been spawned by this literature. I trace the origins of this movement back to the early 1980s, when a statistician studying the effects of radiation on farm animals for the Oak Ridge National Laboratory in Tennessee contacted the Tennessee governor's office with a proposal for measuring teacher effectiveness in the state. Although this offer was not pursued by the governor, the concept of "value-added" measurement came to dominate teacher evaluation and accountability policies at the state and federal levels.

In Chapter 6, I focus on the teacher workforce in two states, Michigan and Massachusetts, which have experienced very different educational outcomes since the early 1990s, when each state embarked on a series of substantial K–12 education reforms. Outcomes in Michigan have declined precipitously over the past two and a half decades, while Massachusetts has enjoyed such high and rising educational outcomes that the Bay State is widely considered to have the best public school system in the U.S. I consider how state and local policies impacting the work of classroom teachers have contributed to the wide and growing disparities in educational outcomes between the two states.

The concluding chapter, Chapter 7, explores a number of problematic trends that may discourage interested and talented candidates from entering the teaching profession or encourage the early exit of incumbent professionals. I also examine the recent and remarkable #RedForEd movement and what this newfound union muscle and public support may portend for the profession. I also offer some ideas and avenues for reform that hold promise for strengthening the most important resource in our public schools—our classroom teachers.

Finally, an "Epilogue" addresses the still unfolding impact of the COVID-19 pandemic on our classroom teachers. While the full impact on teachers, students, and families may not be well understood for some time, one outcome is now clear: the pandemic has brought the inequities between affluent and poor schools and communities into bold relief. The heightened stresses and increased workloads burdening teachers, their school colleagues, and their students and families are examined, with particular emphasis on the supply of teachers across our local schools. It concludes with some observations on how these stresses on teachers and schools may be mitigated by the one-time federal emergency aid already received and makes a case for more permanent state support.

Notes

1. The tide may now be turning, at least with the federal government. The generally antiteacher union policies of the early Obama administration began to be unwound in early 2016 with the signing of the Every Student Succeeds Act (ESSA) (see Chapter 5), and the Biden administration thus far has been much more union friendly than the two preceding administrations.
2. This section follows Addonizio (2014).
3. At the time of the report's release, the U.S. economy was in the depths of a recession that had begun in 1979. The unemployment rate had soared to 9.6 percent by 1983, with 10.7 million Americans looking for work and another 1.6 million having abandoned their search. Productivity growth, the source of improved living standards, was alarmingly low, having dropped precipitously from an average of 2.6 percent annually during the years 1962–1973 to an anemic 0.9 percent annually during the years 1973–1986. As a result, real wage growth nearly vanished, falling from a healthy 2.6 percent between 1962 and 1973 (tracking productivity growth) to a miniscule 0.3 percent during the latter period (Blinder 1987).

4. For a good analysis of U.S. macroeconomic performance during the 1970s and early 1980s, see Blinder (1987), especially Chapter 2. For insight into the relationship between education and economic productivity, with emphasis on this period, see Murnane (1988).
5. By one estimate, online instruction costs 36 percent less per student than traditional, face-to-face teaching. See Peterson (2010), p. 250, cited in Abrams (2016), p. 141.
6. According to Nicholas Kardaras, the flood of technology into classrooms represents an "educational" Trojan horse driven by profit motive, not education science: "Education technology is estimated to become a $60 billion industry by 2018. With the advent of the Common Core in 2010, which nationalized curriculum and textbooks standards, the multi-billion-dollar textbook industry became very attractive for educational gunslingers looking to capitalize on the new Wild West of education technology. A tablet with educational software no longer needed state-by-state curricular customization. It could now be sold to the entire country" (Kardaras 2016).
7. Baumol introduced his classic theory in 1967; see Baumol (1967).

2
Teacher Labor Markets in the U.S.

The Anatomy of Local Shortages

*Children are not a distraction from more important work. They are
the most important work.*

—C. S. Lewis

The U.S. teacher workforce is vast, having experienced decades-long growth that has only recently abated and reversed. According to the Census Bureau, pre-K–12 teachers make up one of the largest occupational groups in the United States (U.S. Bureau of Labor Statistics 2021a) and the growth in their numbers has far outstripped the growth in student enrollments. From 1987–1988 to 2017–2018, total K–12 enrollment in the U.S. (traditional public, charter, and private) rose by 22 percent, while the teaching force increased by well over twice that rate—fully 54 percent—indicating a lowering of average class sizes. For public schools, the percentage increases in enrollments and teachers over this period were 27 percent and 53 percent, respectively (Ingersoll et al. 2021). Class sizes have indeed fallen in our public elementary schools, where the average class size dropped by 20 percent—from 26.2 to 21.1 students—from the late 1980s to 2008, when the Great Recession brought teacher workforce expansion to a temporary halt. In contrast, typical subject-area courses at public middle and secondary schools saw little change in class size during this period.

While this growth in the U.S. K–12 teaching force in recent decades has been remarkable, it has not been constant. The teaching force increased by about 1.3 million from 1987–1988 to 2007–2008 and then declined by about 45,000 between 2007–2008 and 2011–2012 (Ingersoll, Merrill, and Stuckey 2014). By the 2015–2016 school year, U.S. public schools employed 3.8 million full- and part-time teachers, a 27 percent increase over 1999–2000. K–12 enrollments, by comparison, grew 7 percent over this period (National Center for Education Statistics 2019a). By 2017–2018, the public school teaching force had fallen to 3.5 million full- and part-timers, divided roughly equally between elementary and secondary schools (National Center for Education Statistics 2021a).

The Transformation of the Teaching Force

Over the past three decades, from 1987 to 2018, the U.S. elementary and secondary teaching force has not only grown substantially, but it has become older, less experienced, more diverse by race and ethnicity, more female, and less stable (Ingersoll et al. 2021).[1] This same period has also seen large differences in the growth rates of different teaching fields. Figure 2.1 presents the proportional increases in teachers by subject over these three decades.

These data, which include private schools as well as traditional publics and charters, reveal very uneven growth rates across subjects. In terms of sheer numbers, the greatest increase has occurred in special education, most assuredly in response to increasing requirements of the federal Individuals with Disabilities Act (IDEA), the centerpiece of federal special education legislation.

Besides special education and ESL (English as a Second Language) or bilingual education, other fast-growing fields have been the core

Figure 2.1 Percent Increase in Teachers by Field, 1987–1988 to 2017–2018

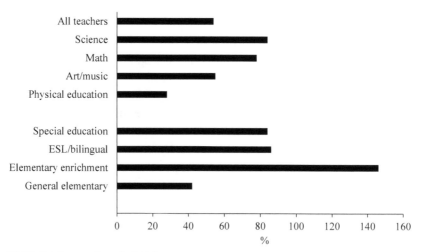

SOURCE: Ingersoll et al. (2021).

academic subjects of English/language arts, foreign languages, mathematics, and science. The number of mathematics teachers increased by 78 percent, while the number of science teachers rose by 84 percent. These combined increases account for about 20 percent of the overall growth in the teacher workforce over this period. In their 2021 study, Ingersoll and colleagues attribute the growth in the numbers of math and science teachers, who have been in short supply for decades in the U.S., to changes in secondary-school graduation requirements across the states. In their analysis of data from the Schools and Staffing Survey (SASS) and Teacher Follow-Up Survey (TFS) over the 25-year period from 1987 to 2012, Ingersoll, Merrill, and Stuckey (2014) find that enrollments in math and science courses rose by 69 percent and 60 percent, respectively. However, contrary to conventional wisdom, the new supply of qualified math and science teachers has been more than sufficient to accommodate student enrollment increases and rising teacher requirements in these core subjects. On the other hand, the main but often overlooked source of math and science teacher shortages is preretirement volunteer turnover (Ingersoll 2011; Ingersoll et al. 2021; Ingersoll and Perda 2010).

A less experienced teaching force

Because the teaching force has grown dramatically, our schools employ far more beginning teachers than in the past. For example, in 1987–1988, schools employed about 84,000 first-year teachers; by 2007–2008, there were over 239,000. By 2011–2012, despite several years of layoffs and little hiring during and following the Great Recession, there were still 147,000 first-year teachers in our schools. By 2017–2018, this number had grown to about 300,000 (Ingersoll et al. 2021). Similarly, in 1987–1988, approximately 1 million teachers (about 37 percent of all teachers) had 10 or fewer years of teaching experience; by 2017–2018, this number had grown to over 1.8 million teachers (about 44 percent of the teacher workforce).

A more female teaching force

School teaching, historically a predominately female occupation, has become even more so in recent decades. As Ingersoll, Merrill, and Stuckey (2014) observe, this is a surprising development, given that many professions historically dominated by males have opened up to women in recent decades. For example, data from the Bureau of Labor Statistics (2021b) reveal that in 1972, only 10 percent of physicians, 4 percent of lawyers, 2 percent of dentists, and 13 percent of pharmacists were female; by 2019, these proportions had risen to 41, 37, 36, and 63 percent, respectively. In light of these and other career choices increasingly open to women, one might expect that fewer women would be entering professions that historically have been predominately female. But this has not happened with teaching. Both the number of women entering teaching and the proportion of teachers who are female have risen steadily since the early 1980s. By the 2017–2018 school year, about 76 percent of public school teachers were female, with a lower percentage of male teachers at the elementary level (11 percent) than at the secondary level (36 percent) (National Center for Education Statistics 2021b). The steady rise in the proportion of female teachers is depicted in Figure 2.2.

Figure 2.2 Percent Female Teachers, 1980–1981 to 2017–2018

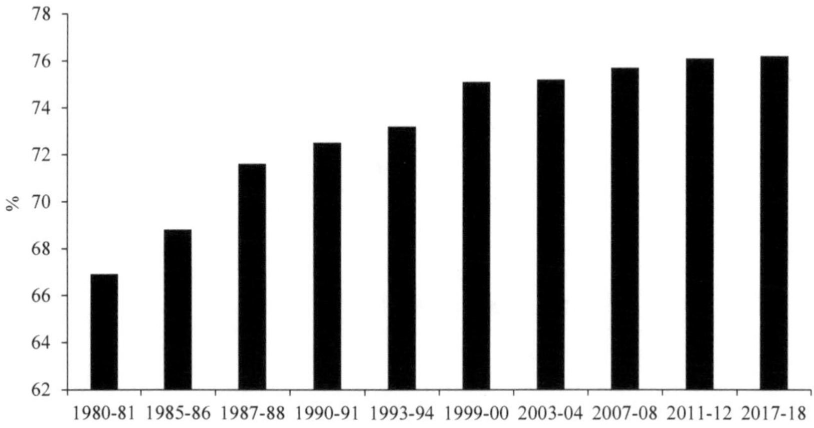

SOURCE: Ingersoll et al. (2021).

A more diverse teaching force

Teaching remains a largely white workforce, and the percentage of minority students continues to exceed the percentage of minority teachers in U.S. schools. The persistence of this gap, however, is not due to a failure in recruiting minority teachers. Rather, the gap has persisted largely because the proportional growth of minority students has exceeded the corresponding growth in minority teachers. The percentage of all teachers who were members of a minority group rose from 12.5 percent in 1987–1988 to 17.3 percent in 2011–2012 and reached 20 percent by 2017–2018. In sheer numbers, our schools employed about 327,000 minority teachers in 1987–1988 and more than 810,000 in 2017–2018, with most of the increase occurring in high-poverty public schools. However, although minorities have joined the teaching force at higher rates than whites in recent decades, they have also exited the profession at higher rates. In the decades from the late 1980s to 2012–2013, the annual rate of minority teacher turnover from public schools increased by 45 percent (Ingersoll et al. 2021).

A less stable teaching force

As noted earlier, elementary and secondary teaching has long been recognized as a high-turnover profession. Analyzing national data, Ingersoll et al. (2021) find that teacher attrition is similar to that of police officers and is higher than in nursing. Teaching has a far higher turnover rate than such prestigious, and much smaller, professions as law, engineering, architecture, and academia. And the teaching profession has become less stable in recent years. Between 1988–1989 and 2004–2005, the annual attrition from the teaching force rose by 50 percent, from 5.6 percent to 8.4 percent, before declining gradually to 7.7 percent in 2012–2013 (Sutcher, Darling-Hammond, and Carver-Thomas 2016). This trend of generally rising attrition is depicted in Figure 2.3.

While telling, however, these aggregate figures conceal substantial differences in teacher turnover across subjects, grade levels, and localities. Examining both components of teacher turnover—migration (teachers moving between schools and districts) and attrition (teachers leaving the profession), Ingersoll et al. (2021) document that nearly half of all public-school teacher turnover occurs in just one-fourth of the

Figure 2.3 Annual Attrition Rate (%)

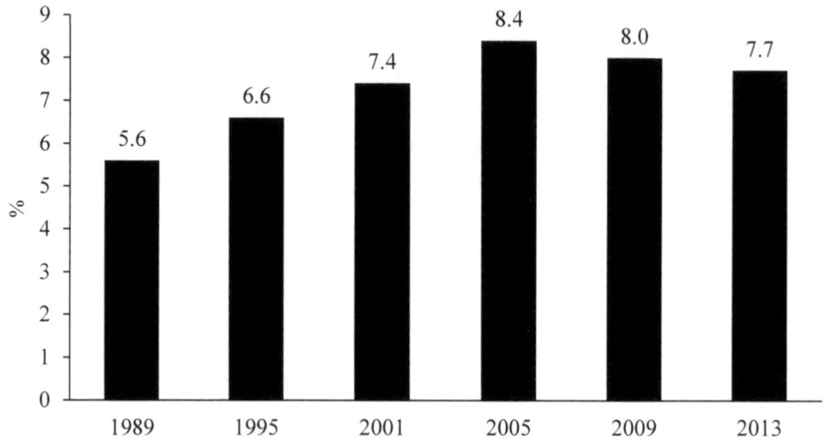

SOURCE: National Center for Education Statistics (2015), cited in Sutcher, Darling-Hammond, and Carver-Thomas (2016), p. 39.

public schools, with the highest turnover rates afflicting high-poverty, high-minority, urban, and rural public schools. Put another way, teachers in high-poverty, high-minority schools tend to have higher rates of attrition, as do teachers of color, who are disproportionately employed in these schools. Furthermore, teachers with little preparation (brought into the profession through alternative routes) tend to leave the profession at rates two or three times that of teachers with more comprehensive (traditional) preparation (Sutcher, Darling-Hammond, and Carver-Thomas 2016).

Beginning teachers (those with less than five years' experience) exhibit particularly high rates of turnover. Using national longitudinal data from the Baccalaureate and Beyond survey, Ingersoll et al. (2021) find that more than 44 percent of new teachers leave teaching within five years. Their estimates of cumulative beginning attrition rates are presented in Figure 2.4.

The high attrition rates for novice teachers have been generally holding steady or rising slightly since the late 1980s. For example, annual rates of leaving for first-year teachers in public schools rose from 8.1 percent in 1988–1989 to 11.1 percent in 2000–2001 before falling to 9 percent in 2012–2013 (Figure 2.5). And since the teaching force has

Figure 2.4 Cumulative Attrition Rates of Novice Teachers, 1993–2003

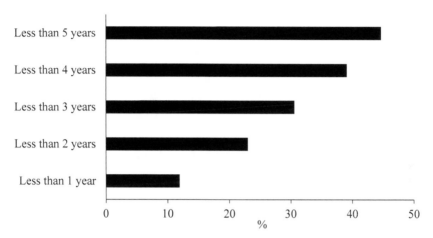

SOURCE: Ingersoll et al. (2021).

grown so dramatically in recent decades, the sheer numbers of public school teachers who quit the profession after one year has also soared, rising from about 7,500 in 1987–1988 to about 11,000 in 2012–2013. We now have more beginners teaching in our public schools, and these beginners are more likely to leave the profession than their veteran counterparts, strongly suggesting a growing instability in the teaching profession in the coming years.

The Unequal Distribution of Teaching Talent

Many educational leaders and policymakers characterize American public education's most pressing problem today as being the unequal distribution of high-quality teachers across U.S. classrooms (see, for example, Buddin and Zamarro 2009; Clotfelter, Ladd, and Vigdor 2005; Lankford, Loeb, and Wyckoff 2002; Murnane and Steele 2007). Both No Child Left Behind, signed by President George W. Bush in 2002, and Race to the Top, President Obama's $4 billion grant competition for the states, emphasized recruiting and retaining high-quality and effective teachers, particularly in disadvantaged schools and districts. This focus on effective teachers is prompted by mounting evidence that technological advances have increased demand for cognitive skills, par-

Figure 2.5 Annual First-Year Public School Teacher Attrition Rates, 1988–1989 to 2012–2013

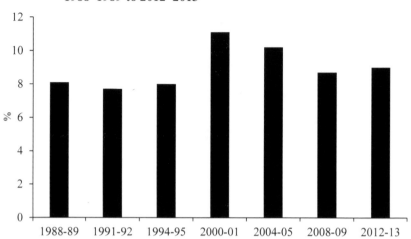

SOURCE: Ingersoll et al. (2021).

ticularly communication and problem-solving skills, and that widening economic inequality in the U.S. is increasingly driven by a widening skills gap.

This skills gap, in turn, is largely determined by variation in teacher quality across our public schools (see, for example, Aaronson, Barrow, and Sander 2007; Chetty et al. 2011; Chetty, Friedman, and Rockoff 2014; Hanushek and Rivkin 2004; and Rockoff 2004). And closing this skills gap would yield great economic benefits. Analyzing an extraordinarily rich data file for more than one million students from grades 3 through 8, linked to tax records on parent characteristics and adult outcomes, Chetty, Friedman, and Rockoff (2014) find that students assigned to effective teachers (i.e., teachers who succeed in raising student achievement test scores) are more likely to attend college, attend higher-ranked colleges, earn higher salaries, live in higher-socioeconomic-status neighborhoods, and save more for retirement. In short, good teachers create substantial economic value.[2]

This focus on teacher quality and concern over the unequal distribution of skilled teachers across classrooms, schools, and districts underscores the importance of understanding the workings of the

teacher labor market, particularly the market for *effective* teachers—
that is, teachers who are skilled at raising the achievement levels of
their students. Research on teacher sorting (i.e., the nonrandom distribution of teacher quality across students of varying racial and socioeconomic backgrounds and levels of educational disadvantage) finds
that low-income and minority students are more likely to have teachers
who are inexperienced and less qualified (e.g., graduates of a noncom-
petitive college, low certification test score, etc.) (Clotfelter, Ladd, and
Vigdor 2005, 2006; Lankford, Loeb, and Wyckoff 2002). The uneven
distribution of teaching talent is exacerbated by teacher mobility. Careful research finds that teachers who switch schools generally move to
schools with lower concentrations of low-income and minority students
and higher levels of achievement (Boyd et al. 2005; Hanushek, Kain,
and Rivkin 2004; Scafidi, Sjoquist, and Stinebrickner 2007).

THE WORKINGS OF THE TEACHER LABOR MARKET

Insight into the root causes of these disparities requires an understanding of the workings of supply (i.e., decisions by teachers and prospective teachers) and demand (i.e., decisions by the school leaders who
hire them) in teacher labor markets. When examining these markets, we
see that the uneven distribution of teaching talent across schools and
districts is a function of both supply and demand forces and that distinguishing between the two sets of factors is often difficult. For example,
the faculty teaching in a particular school or district at any given time
is determined by both supply factors (i.e., who applied for a job there
and who accepted an offer) and demand factors (i.e., who was offered).

The Supply of Effective Teachers

The supply of effective teachers who are willing to work in a particular local district depends on local teacher wage level, working conditions, the wages and working conditions available to them in other
professions (i.e., the "opportunity cost" of teaching), and the cost of
local services. More teachers will offer their services if local wages
are high than if they are low, all else being equal. That is, the supply

curve for teachers is upward-sloping. A change in supply-side factors other than teacher wage levels will shift the teacher supply curve. For example, a decline in local neighborhood conditions would shift the supply curve inward, reducing the number of teachers seeking work at any given wage level.

The teacher labor market is in equilibrium when the number of effective teachers who are seeking work equals the number of effective teachers the local schools are willing to hire. The wage at which the quantity of teachers demanded equals the quantity supplied is the equilibrium (i.e., "market clearing") wage. In theory, any wage above the equilibrium level will produce a surplus of teachers, while a wage below the equilibrium level will produce a shortage. As Murnane and Steele (2007) observe, school districts often respond to a shortage of effective teachers not by leaving teaching positions vacant but by filling vacancies with underqualified teachers. Consequently, teacher shortages are often measured not in terms of actual vacancies, but by the share of positions filled by teachers lacking full credentials (e.g., those with "emergency" or otherwise temporary licenses). Of course, in a perfectly competitive teacher labor market, where wage is freely adjustable, shortages may be eliminated by raising the wage, and surpluses eliminated by lowering the wage.

So why do shortages of effective teachers persist in many local markets? First, local teacher markets are subject to shocks, including enrollment volatility (which will impact demand) and changes in opportunity costs (which will impact supply). These shocks will alter the equilibrium wage. Studies of teacher labor markets in the United States, the United Kingdom, and Australia show that college graduates' decisions about whether to enter and remain in teaching depend not only on teacher salary levels but also on salaries in alternative professions (Chevalier, Dolton, and McIntosh 2002; Leigh 2005; Murnane et al. 1991). Ladd (2007), examining teacher labor markets in the 30 industrialized countries of the Organisation for Economic Co-operation and Development (OECD), finds that teacher shortages also arise from policies of uniform salary schedules across academic subject areas and geographic regions. Such salary schedules ignore the reality of differential opportunity costs for teachers who have different subject areas of expertise or who look for work in different local labor markets. Consequently, it is not surprising that teacher shortages are particularly prevalent in math and science and in large cities.

Teacher salaries and teacher supply

Actual teacher salaries adjust only slowly to changes in the equilibrium wage. Teacher salaries are generally negotiated for extended periods. Furthermore, teacher supply is often sticky upward—that is, the great majority of potential entrants into the profession must complete a lengthy preparation program in order to acquire a teaching license. Nevertheless, teacher salaries can be an important policy tool for school systems' efforts to ensure an adequate supply of high-quality teachers. But they can also be quite costly. Because salaries generally make up about two-thirds of education operating budgets in the United States (and other developed countries), across-the-board increases in teacher salaries can require substantial increases in education spending (Ladd 2007). But when a school system does not pay salaries high enough to attract high-quality teachers, it must endure position vacancies or underqualified teachers.

Ladd (2007) notes that teacher salary setting in the U.S. is far more decentralized than in most developed countries, where salaries are negotiated through a national bargaining process between the government and one or more unions. Consequently, any simple comparison of U.S. public-school teacher salaries with those in other countries will fail to recognize the substantial variation in salaries across U.S. school districts. But such comparisons are nonetheless informative, and Ladd provides several approaches, each based on a reasonable but different metric. A comparison of absolute salaries adjusted for differences in purchasing power across countries finds the U.S. in the top third of OECD countries. However, measuring teacher salaries relative to a country's gross domestic product (GDP) per capita places the U.S. in the bottom third of the group. By that measure, the average U.S. teacher salary is 117 percent of GDP per capita, on a par with Italy and Austria but far below Korea (242 percent), Germany (180 percent), and Japan (160 percent). Ladd argues that the latter, relative measure, though imperfect, is a more accurate indicator of teacher salary competitiveness within each country.[3] Furthermore, the fact that average U.S. teacher salaries are low by this measure indicates both that the United

States has the capacity to pay teachers more and that teacher salaries may not be high enough to attract a teaching force of sufficient quality.

Ladd (2007) also ranks national average teacher salaries relative to hours of net teaching time (an important indicator of working conditions) and finds that U.S. teacher salaries rank in the bottom third among OECD nations for high school and in the middle third for elementary school. And again, Germany, Japan, and Korea rank in the top third at both levels.

Teacher Quality and Teacher Pay

Much criticism has been directed at the traditional pay structure for public school teachers. Critics contend that the standard determinants of compensation level—teaching experience and education credentials—are only weakly correlated with student outcomes. They urge policymakers and school leaders to adopt compensation systems that incorporate a performance component (i.e., "merit pay"), typically a value-added measure of student achievement, along with a market-sensitive component that offers a premium for teachers in chronic shortage subjects such as math, science, and special education.

Tying teacher pay to productivity has theoretical appeal, but actual efforts to do so have generally failed to produce positive results.[4] There have been some qualified successes. Dee and Wyckoff (2015) find some evidence that a strategic combination of teacher evaluations and financial incentives can yield marginal improvements in the average rate of student achievement growth for retained teachers. Balch and Springer (2015) find that a pay-for-performance program in the Austin, Texas, school district was associated with student test-score gains in reading and math in its first year. The gains were maintained in the second year, but no further growth was detected. A larger achievement effect is found by Fryer and colleagues from a novel experiment designed to detect "loss aversion." Teachers were paid bonuses in advance and had to return the payment if their students' test scores did not improve sufficiently. They find that math scores rose between 0.2 and 0.4 standard deviations, roughly equivalent to the effect of raising teacher quality by one standard deviation (Fryer et al. 2012, cited in Baker 2016a, p. 6).

Nevertheless, despite these few documented instances of achievement gains with alternative pay schemes, we have no evidence that pay-for-performance schemes are more cost effective than traditional "step-and-lane" teacher compensation systems based on experience and professional credentials. Moreover, as Baker (2016a) notes, any such assertions that pay-for-performance is more cost effective than traditional systems ignore the considerable variability among traditional salary schedules. These differences, which center on salary compression and the relative weights given to experience and credentials, hold different implications for the recruitment and retention of teaching talent. For example, exploiting variability in salary schedules, Hendricks (2015a,b), cited in Baker (2016a, p. 6), finds the following:

> Increasing salaries for teachers with 3 or more years of experience differentially *retains* high-ability teachers, while higher salaries for teachers with 0–2 years of experience differentially *retain* low-ability teachers. This likely occurs because higher early-career salaries disrupt a positive sorting process that exists among novice teachers. (emphasis added)

Hendricks (2015b), cited in Baker (2016a, p. 6), also finds that restructuring traditional salary structures may be an effective way to improve teacher recruitment:

> Pay increases have the largest effect on hire rates among teachers with 2–3 years of experience and the effect diminishes with experience. . . . Higher teacher salaries provide a dual benefit of retaining and attracting a more effective distribution of teachers. Districts may also improve student achievement growth at no cost by reshaping their salary schedules so that they are increasing and concave in teacher experience.

A "concave" salary schedule exhibits two important characteristics: first, as is typical of traditional "step-and-lane" schedules, teacher pay rises with experience; second, pay rises at an accelerating rate in the early years of a teaching career and a declining rate later on. Such a structure would be entirely consistent with a new and growing literature revealing that student achievement gains and other outcomes resulting from teacher experience extend well beyond the first several years in the classroom. Examples from this literature include Papay and Kraft (2015), cited in Baker (2016a), and Ladd and Sorensen (2017), who examine both student test scores and behavior and observe that "once we control statistically for the quality of individual teachers by the use of teacher fixed effects, we find large returns to experience for middle school teachers in the form both of higher test scores and improvements in student behavior, with the clearest behavioral effects emerging for reductions in student absenteeism. Moreover, these returns extend well beyond the first few years of teaching" (Baker 2016a, p. 7).

Teacher pay and teacher supply: Summing up

We have abundant evidence that teacher pay impacts the recruitment and retention of talent into the profession. The evidence in support of "pay-for-performance" systems, however, is much less compelling. Weak or inconsistent findings regarding possible links between alternative pay structures and measured student achievement, combined with evidence of misalignment between teacher productivity and measured performance, call into serious question costly efforts to redesign teacher compensation systems. At the same time, mounting evidence points to substantial returns to experience for teachers, often extending well beyond the first few years in the classroom. *How* teachers are paid appears to be far less important than *how much* they are paid. The levels of teacher pay, particularly in comparison with pay levels offered to comparably educated professionals in other fields, clearly impact the quality of entrants to the teaching profession, the likelihood of their remaining in the classroom, and the outcomes of their students.

The Teacher Wage Gap

Allegretto, Corcoran, and Mishel (2008) and Allegretto and Mishel (2016, 2019, 2020) have carefully documented the erosion of teacher pay relative to the pay of other college graduates. They define the "teacher wage penalty" or "wage gap" as the percentage by which public school teachers' pay falls short of the pay of comparable workers, adjusted for education level, experience, and other factors. They find that this penalty has grown substantially in the long run, as depicted in Figure 2.6.

As a profession, teaching was relatively good for females in 1979, when they made 6.9 percent more than other comparable female college graduates. In the 1980s and early 1990s, female teachers earned wages generally comparable to those of other female college graduates. By 2000, however, they were earning 4.7 percent less than comparable workers, and by 2008, the wage gap had reached 8.0 percent. The gap

Figure 2.6 Teacher Wage Penalty, 1979–2018

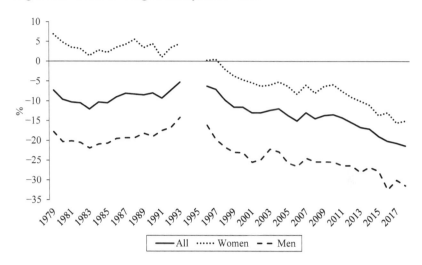

NOTE: Data are for workers aged 18 to 64, excluding self-employed workers. Estimates for 1994 and 1995 are omitted because of data limitations.
SOURCE: Allegretto and Mishel (2019), analysis of Current Population Survey Outgoing Rotation Group data.

narrowed somewhat during the Great Recession but began to widen again in 2011, reaching its largest deficit of 15.6 percent in 2017 before falling slightly in 2018.

The teacher wage gap has always been larger for male teachers, exceeding 20 percent for the majority of the 40 years examined and reaching 31.5 percent in 2018. Allegretto and Mishel (2020) note that this larger male teacher wage gap reflects the fact that teaching is a predominantly female occupation, where wages are depressed by gender discrimination and more limited employment options. Men in predominantly female professions will thus earn substantially less than men in male-dominated professions. The authors observe that "the large wage penalty that men face in the teaching profession goes a long way toward explaining why the gender makeup of the teaching profession has not changed much over the past few decades. Today, roughly three-fourths of teachers are women, which is about what it was in 1960" (pp. 5–6).

The teacher wage penalty declined slightly in 2019 following a number of notable teacher strikes, including teacher walkouts in a half-dozen states in the spring of 2018 and additional strikes in 2019 in Los Angeles, Denver, and Oakland. Whether this single data point marks a turning point in the long downward trend in teacher pay relative to other college-educated workers remains to be seen. In any event, the overall teacher pay penalty remained substantial in 2019, exceeding 30 percent for men, 13 percent for women, and 19 percent overall (Allegretto and Mishel 2020).

Hard-to-Staff Schools and Districts

Hard-to-staff schools and districts are often inhibited by poor working conditions, including large classes, excessive contact hours, poor facilities, poor leadership, low staff morale and a lack of collegiality, and poor parental support (Jacob 2007). And their problems are often compounded by ineffective district hiring practices. Murnane et al. (1991) emphasize the importance of decentralized and flexible procedures that allow principals and teachers, who are now held accountable for outcomes in their respective schools, to select their new colleagues. Highly centralized recruiting, screening, and hiring processes, where decisions are made by the superintendent and central office staff, provide little opportunity for school principals and department heads to meet new teachers before classes begin. Moreover, such centralized procedures are often associated with restrictive collective bargaining rules governing transfers within the district. Incumbent teachers have first opportunity to apply for new job openings, and seniority determines who is hired. The transfer then creates a new vacancy, often at a different school. It may be several months before details of the final vacancy are available. As a result, job openings advertised to external candidates are likely to be in schools where working conditions are particularly difficult.

A more decentralized and flexible hiring process creates two important advantages for schools and districts. First, job offers are more transparent to a prospective teacher, who knows who the department head will be, as well as the school, subject(s) to be taught, and grade level. With the more cumbersome, centralized procedures, the prospective hire generally has only a salary offer to consider. Second, the district is not limited to offering to new candidates only those positions that are unwanted by current staff.

Such schools and districts also enroll high proportions of educationally at-risk children (i.e., low-income, racial minorities, English language learners, and special needs). Teaching at-risk children is particularly difficult, and schools with large concentrations of at-risk children must offer both a compensating wage differential to teachers and additional resources in the schools (e.g., counselors, social workers, attendance officers, smaller classes, a longer school day and year, etc.). Jacob (2007) observes that working conditions appear to be even more important than wages, particularly for teachers in urban schools. For example, Hanushek, Kain, and Rivkin (2004) found the mobility patterns among public school teachers in Texas were more strongly correlated with student characteristics than with salary levels.

Engel, Jacob, and Curran (2014), examining applications for teaching positions in Chicago public schools, find that teachers are less likely to apply to higher-poverty schools and find little aggregate relationship between a school's number of applicants and the school's racial composition or achievement level after controlling for school poverty rate. They also find a school's geographic location to be a powerful predictor of teacher applications, even after controlling for a variety of school demographic characteristics, including student poverty, racial composition, and achievement and neighborhood-level characteristics such as poverty, racial composition, and crime rates. The authors hypothesize that the geographic indicators serve as proxies for a number of hard-to-observe school or neighborhood characteristics, such as perceived safety, community attitudes toward education, and school leadership.

Another reason for shortages of effective teachers in urban schools is the localized nature of teacher labor markets. That is, unlike many other professions in the U.S., the market for public school teachers is localized in that teachers in one geographic region typically do not compete for jobs in another region. Thus, teacher shortages are often specific to particular regions, local districts, or schools. Research finds that teachers prefer teaching close to where they grew up, or in similar districts. For example, Boyd and colleagues found that, in 2000, 90 percent of teachers in New York City had attended high school within 40 miles of their first job, and most of these teachers also had attended nearby colleges (Boyd et al. 2005). The high turnover in low-achieving urban schools, particularly among more highly qualified teachers, may thus reflect a preference for working close to home or in a community *like* home, thereby compounding the challenge of staffing high-need, urban schools with highly qualified teachers. Because economically disadvantaged areas have fewer college graduates than more affluent areas do, they also have more difficulty providing their own educators. In this way, the lack of educational attainment in these localities becomes a self-sustaining cycle. The systematic variation in teacher quality across local communities, or "teacher sorting," is summarized in Box 2.1.

Another characteristic of teacher supply has been the relatively high attrition rate among new teachers, although recent research suggests the rate is lower than previously thought. Using data from nationally representative 1991–1992 Teacher Follow-Up Survey (TFS), Grissmer and Kirby (1997) find that the attrition rate for teachers with one to three years of experience is roughly 8 percent annually, compared with 4.5 percent for teachers with four to nine years of experience. Using TFS data from 1989–1990, 1991–1992, and 1994–1995, Ingersoll estimated that one-third of new teachers leave the profession within three years of entry, and that almost half leave within five years (Ingersoll 2003). Murnane and Steele (2007) note, however, that neither of these estimates considers the number of teachers who return to teaching. This "reserve pool" of licensed teachers who have "stopped out" has been an important source of supply when the demand for teachers has risen (Murnane et al. 1991).

More recently, according to the National Center of Education Statistics, there were 3.6 million pre-K through 12 teachers nationwide in 2009, with annual turnover rates of 16 percent (8 percent switching schools and 8 percent leaving the profession). Turnover rates were particularly high among novice teachers (25 percent), charter-school teachers (24 percent), and teachers in disadvantaged schools. Furthermore, an April 2015 report published by the U.S. Department of Education's Institute for Education Sciences (IES) finds a much lower rate of attrition than had previously been reported in the research literature. Following a cohort of approximately 1,990 public school teachers who began teaching in 2007 or 2008, this Beginning Teacher Longitudinal Study (BTLS) found that after five years of teaching, only 17 percent had exited the profession. More specifically, among all beginning teachers in 2007–2008, 10 percent did not teach in 2008–2009, 12 percent did not teach in 2009–2010, 15 percent did not teach in 2010–2011, and 17 percent did not teach in 2011–2012. Interestingly, in each follow-

Box 2.1 The Problem of "Teacher Sorting"

Pressure for test score improvements, and the associated fear of school sanctions applied in the absence of such improvements, has led, predictably, to a troubling trend in the teaching profession. The problem of "teacher sorting" has escalated since the mid-1980s (the "age of accountability"), as more high-quality teachers have taken jobs in higher socioeconomic communities. Such self-sorting leaves less-qualified teachers disproportionately working in schools with large concentrations of children from poor families or racial and ethnic minorities (Clotfelter, Ladd, and Vigdor 2005, 2006; Corcoran and Evans 2008), exacerbating the achievement gap in terms of both race and class.

In a landmark study of New York state, Lankford, Loeb, and Wyckoff (2002) find that teachers with more experience, high licensure test scores, degrees from selective colleges, and advanced certification from the National Board for Professional Teaching Standards are much more prevalent in schools with fewer low-income and minority students. Similarly, Goldhaber, Lavery, and Theobald (2015), exploiting a rich, statewide administrative database, demonstrate that across elementary school, middle school, and high school classrooms in Washington state, both input measures like teacher experience and output measures like value-added estimates of teacher quality are inequitably distributed across each of a set of indicators of student disadvantage. Specifically, they find that teacher experience, licensure exam scores, and value-added measures of effectiveness are inequitably correlated with student free/reduced-price lunch status, student minority status, and prior academic performance. (The sole exception was licensure exam scores in high school math classrooms.) They generally find that most inequity comes from teacher sorting across classrooms within schools, but that patterns in teacher sorting at all three levels (i.e., across districts, across schools within districts, and across classrooms within schools) contribute to the teacher quality gap between advantaged and disadvantaged students.

This sorting phenomenon, or structural gap in students' exposure to high-quality teachers, will not be easily rectified, however, as many teachers consider the class and racial composition of students when choosing where to work, and more senior teachers are given priority in this process (Bacolod 2007; Corcoran 2009; Hanushek, Kain, and

Box 2.1 (continued)

Rivkin 2004; Moe 2011; Scafidi, Sjoquist, and Stinebricker 2007). Many collective bargaining agreements allow teachers to act on their preferences about assignments by protecting senior teachers from involuntary transfers and allowing senior teachers to voluntarily transfer to more desirable positions within their district. Removing these protections is a daunting political task. Moe (2011), compiling responses from a 2003 national survey of public school teachers, reports that fully 70 percent of union members in districts with collective bargaining believe that seniority-based transfer rights make schools more effective, and 62 percent believe that principals can abuse their discretion and need to be constrained by contract rules. Moe found similar responses from union members in districts without collective bargaining. Unions represent teachers' interests, and favorable working conditions are highly valued by membership.

Given this institutionalization of teacher quality gaps between advantaged and disadvantaged students, what are the possibilities for their amelioration? Clotfelter et al. (2008) find that a small bonus for teachers in high-poverty and low-performing schools in North Carolina lowered the mean teacher turnover rate in these schools by 17 percent. Grissom, Loeb, and Nakashima (2014) find that a policy change in Miami-Dade County Public Schools that allowed principals in low-performing schools to reassign ineffective teachers (who would probably have remained in place) to higher-performing schools improved the equity of teacher distribution in the district and boosted the performance of the transfers.

Both the overall decline in teacher quality and the growing structural gap in teacher quality between poor and middle/upper class communities may be further exacerbated by recent school- and teacher-accountability initiatives, including the public ranking of schools and evaluation of individual teachers on the basis of student scores on standardized assessments. This recent emphasis on accountability and incentives (i.e., pay for performance) in public education, following in the wake of sustained criticism of school performance in the U.S., may well dissuade talented college graduates from considering the profession.

up year, the percentage of beginning teachers who were still teaching was substantially larger among those who had been assigned a first-year mentor than among those who had not (Gray and Taie 2015).[5]

The Demand for Effective Teachers

The number of effective teachers that will be demanded by a local school district depends on student enrollments, class size targets, curriculum requirements, local district wealth and fiscal capacity (most notably, the property tax base), and teacher wage levels. Districts will seek to hire more teachers when wages are low relative to other costs (e.g., educational technology costs) and fewer teachers when wages are relatively high. That is, the demand curve for teachers is downward sloping. But, of course, the number of teachers a school or district seeks to hire depends on more than teacher wages. Changes in labor market conditions other than wages will shift the demand for effective teachers outward or inward. For example, an increase in enrollment would shift demand outward, meaning that more teachers would be demanded *at any given wage*, while improved cost-effectiveness of educational technology would shift demand inward as schools substituted capital for labor and demanded fewer teachers at any given wage.

Some determinants of teacher demand, such as student enrollments, are generally not influenced by education policy. Save for an obvious exception like raising the mandatory attendance age from 16 to 18, as was done in Michigan in 2009, enrollments depend on population changes and mobility. Other elements of teacher demand, such as class sizes, curriculum priorities (e.g., the new emphasis on STEM), and teacher attrition rates, are directly influenced by education policy decisions.

The demand for teachers increased sharply in the 1950s and 1960s in response to the baby boom. Given that most children begin school at age five, it takes about five years for elementary schools to register the effects of changes in the number of births. And, of course, secondary schools would experience these demand changes several years after that. Enrollment declined as baby boomers exited the K–12 system, but the size of the teaching force remained roughly constant, as school districts demonstrated less sensitivity to enrollment loss than gain. The enrollment decline, however, did lead to a weakened demand for new teachers, an aging workforce, and a decline in relative teacher salaries. Between Fall 2000 and Fall 2016, total public K–12 enrollment grew by 7 percent, reaching 50.6 million. Total public-school enrollment is projected to continue growing through Fall 2028, rising a projected 2 percent between Fall 2016 and Fall 2028, to 51.4 million. Over this period, enrollment in pre-K through grade 8 is projected to fall by 1 percent to 35.2 million students between 2016 and 2022 and then grow by 3 percent to 36.1 million by 2028. Enrollment in grades 9 through 12 is projected to rise by 5 percent to 15.9 million students between 2016 and 2023 and then fall by 3 percent to 15.3 million by 2028 (National Center for Education Statistics 2019a).

The proportion of children living in poverty has also generally risen over the past three decades. In 2016, approximately 18 percent of school-age children in the U.S. were in families living in poverty. The comparable proportion was 17 percent in 1990 and 16 percent in 2000 (National Center for Education Statistics 2019a). In addition, the proportion of children of color in public schools has risen from 30.9 percent in 1970 to 41.3 percent in 2009 and 51 percent in 2015, and is projected to rise to 55 percent by 2027 (National Center for Education Statistics 2019b). This increase in the proportions of low-income and minority students in our public schools has significantly increased teacher demand. As Linda Darling-Hammond has observed:

> Regardless of the state, students in high-poverty and high-minority schools typically feel the largest impact of teacher shortages. Historical patterns reveal a long-standing trend that has been a subject of many desegregation and school finance lawsuits: Students in high-poverty, high-minority schools are most likely to be taught by underprepared, inexperienced, and out-of-field teachers. These schools often experience difficulty hiring and high turnover on a regular basis, and they are the most severely affected when teacher shortages become widespread. (Sutcher, Darling-Hammond, and Carver-Thomas 2016, p. 13, citing Darling-Hammond 2010)

The rising numbers of poor students and students of color increase demand for teachers who are effective in raising achievement levels of these students, who often have struggled academically in the past. Using data from the Tennessee class size reduction experiment, which randomly assigned teachers and students to classrooms, Dee (2004) finds that an additional year with a teacher of the same race increases student performance by 2 to 4 percentile points. Another study of teacher effectiveness in a large urban Texas district finds that black students gain roughly 0.1 standard deviation (about 4 percentile points) more when they have a black teacher than when they have a white teacher. Furthermore, while these effects are small, other, unmeasured effects on minority students, such as improved self-image and heightened aspirations, may arise when minority students are taught by a teacher of their own race. The share of teachers of color in public school classrooms has risen in recent years but remains low. Between 1986 and 2011, the proportion of black teachers rose a mere percentage point, from 6 to 7 percent, while the proportion who were Hispanic rose from 2 to 6 percent (Feistritzer 2011). By the 2015–2016 school year, the proportion of black teachers remained at 7 percent, while the proportion of Hispanic teachers had risen to 9 percent (National Center for Education Statistics 2019b). And both figures continue to lag behind the corresponding proportions of black and Hispanic schoolchildren by wide margins.

The changing demographics of American schoolchildren suggest an increasing demand for teachers of color and, more frequently, teachers who are effective with educationally at-risk children (Murnane and Steele 2007). Meeting this demand will be a challenge for local school districts. For example, with the population of Hispanic students rising rapidly, it will take time for the number of Hispanic college graduates— and future teachers—to catch up.

Declining class size

Class sizes also affect the demand for teachers, and average class sizes have trended downward for decades. The most commonly cited proxy for class size, the ratio of pupils to teachers, has fallen steadily since the 1950s. In 1955, the ratio for U.S. public schools was 26.9; by 1985 it was 17.9, and by 2005 it had fallen to 15.6. By 2008, the ratio was down to 15.3, but by 2011, in the aftermath of the Great Recession, it had risen to 16.0. Furthermore, a 2012 survey of school administrators found that 54 percent of respondents had increased class sizes for the 2011–2012 school year, and 57 percent anticipated doing so for the 2012–2013 school year (Ellerson 2012). Accordingly, the ratio rose to 16.1 by 2014. The ratio was projected by NCES to remain at 16.1 through 2018 and then slowly decline to 15.4 by 2026. NCES projects new teacher hires to rise from 259,000 in 2014 (actual) to 266,000 in 2021 and 274,000 in 2025 before falling to 270,000 in 2026 (Snyder, de Brey, and Dillow 2019).

Raising the Bar on Teacher Quality

The demand for teachers is about more than sheer numbers, and a heightened emphasis on teacher effectiveness has been evident since at least the early 1990s. For example, Tennessee has used value-added modeling (VAM, examined more closely in Chapter 5) as part of its school evaluation system since 1992, and in 1996 it began using three years of VAM estimates to gauge the effects of individual teachers on student learning (Baker, Xu, and Detch 1995, cited in Murnane and Steele 2007, p. 25). Although the VAM estimates were not used in their formal evaluations, Tennessee teachers could use these measures to demonstrate compliance with the state's definition of a highly qualified teacher under the NCLB (Selvers 2005, cited in Murnane and Steele 2007). This 2001 reauthorization of the Elementary and Secondary Education Act (ESEA) required that teachers be "highly qualified" by 2006 in schools that received federal Title I funding. Specifically, as noted in Chapter 1, such teachers were required to meet three criteria: 1) be fully certified or licensed by the state, 2) hold at least a bachelor's degree from a four-year institution, and 3) be proficient in the subject matter that the teacher teaches. States were given discretion to set the details of these criteria, particularly regarding certification and subject-matter proficiency. Furthermore, all *new* teachers hired, starting in the 2002–2003 school year, were required to be "highly qualified."

These aspects of NCLB, along with requirements for standardized student testing, reflected policymakers' strong interest in teacher effectiveness as a means of raising student achievement and focused public schools more than ever before on recruiting and retaining talented and effective teachers. Identifying effective teachers, however, remains a challenge for school leaders, particularly with regard to candidates just entering the profession. A teaching license or certificate, while signaling to employers that the candidate has successfully completed a preparation program required for professional practice by the licensing state (generally including completion of a bachelor's degree, specified education courses covering both content and teaching methods, student teaching, and passage of a state examination), has not been shown to be a reliable predictor of teaching effectiveness (Harris and Sass 2011; Kane, Rockoff, and Staiger 2008; Rockoff 2004).

More streamlined alternative preparation programs have been adopted by a number of states in an effort to attract candidates who may find the traditional programs too costly and cumbersome. These alternative programs, developed by states and run by local school districts, nonprofit organizations, or schools of education, are designed to attract potential candidates who have not obtained a degree in education but have an interest in a teaching career. In these alternative licensure programs, candidates usually complete content courses but little or no coursework in methods or student teaching prior to working as full-time teachers. They typically complete methods courses after they begin teaching full-time.

Does "Alternative Certification" Raise Teacher Quality?

Sophisticated panel data studies and randomized experiments have found no significant difference between traditionally certified teachers and teachers certified through alternative preparation programs in raising student achievement (Boyd et al. 2006; Constantine et al. 2009; Harris and Sass 2011; Xu, Hannaway, and Taylor 2008). Because the characteristics of traditional and alternative preparation programs vary greatly and overlap to some extent, the variation in teacher effectiveness *within* each group is much greater than differences *between* the two groups (Boyd et al. 2008; Kane, Rockoff, and Staiger 2008).[6]

So, lacking clear signals as to the superiority of either traditional or alternative programs in consistently preparing effective classroom teachers, can schools and districts make sound choices when hiring novice teachers? Some recent research suggests they can. Much of the research that has found little or no association between standard teaching credentials and teaching effectiveness has been hampered by small samples, scant information on teacher characteristics, and weak measures of teacher performance. The pessimistic message of this literature—that school leaders must simply "roll the dice" when hiring newly minted candidates who lack a teaching track record—is contradicted by Jacob et al. (2016). Analyzing particularly rich data on teacher job applications, employment, and performance in the Washington, D.C.,

Public Schools (DCPS), Jacob and colleagues find that several background characteristics (e.g., undergraduate GPA, SAT/ACT scores, college selectivity, completion of a graduate degree) along with district screening measures (e.g., written assessment, interview, and teaching audition) strongly predict teacher effectiveness.

Significantly, however, these factors did not predict a candidate's likelihood of being hired—strongly suggesting that teacher quality can be improved considerably through improvements in schools' hiring process. To that point, the authors find that teachers whose applications are in the top quartile of predicted effectiveness score roughly 0.65 standard deviations higher on average in actual teaching effectiveness than those whose applications are in the bottom quartile of predicted effectiveness. They compare this measurement to the on-the-job improvement exhibited by DCPS teachers over their early years, when performance has been consistently shown to improve rapidly (e.g., Ost 2014; Papay and Kraft 2015). For those new teachers in the sample who remained in DCPS for three years, their average growth over this period is 0.30 standard deviations, less than half the difference in improvement between the top- and bottom-quartile applicants entering DCPS. These recent findings strongly suggest that the quality of a district's teaching force can be increased substantially through improvements in the workings of the demand side of the labor market.

Finally, a close look at the content of a candidate's preparation program, whether traditional or not, may also reveal clues as to a candidate's future performance. A detailed analysis of 31 elementary teacher preparation programs, both traditional and alternative, that serve New York City public schools found that programs focused on the work of classroom teaching, including close oversight of student-teaching experiences, curricula study, and a capstone project, were most effective in raising student achievement (Boyd et al. 2009). Clearly, research on teacher labor markets is uncovering important signals of teacher quality among new entrants to the profession, signals that should be closely observed by prospective employers on the demand side of the market.

TEACHER PENSIONS: HOW EFFICIENT AND HOW FAIR?

A part of the compensation of a professional employee, whether in the public or private sector, consists of employer contributions for retirement. From the end of World War II until the early 1970s, public- and private-sector professionals had similar types of retirement plans. But increased federal regulation of private-sector plans and growing worker mobility led to a divergence between the structures of plans in the two sectors. Currently, most private-sector employees are in so-called defined contribution (DC) plans, in which employers make contributions to a retirement account owned by employees. Most public-sector employees, including the overwhelming majority of classroom teachers, are enrolled in "defined benefit" (DB) plans, which guarantee employees a specified annual retirement benefit based on a formula and payable until death. The benefit is funded by the assets in a fund consisting of employer and employee contributions.

A Brief History of Teacher Pensions

Retirement benefits for teachers preceded those of other American workers and evolved along a different path.[7] The earliest retirement benefits for state or local employees were offered by some large cities to police officers and firefighters, owing to the hazards of their work, in the mid- to late 1800s. Back then, there were no private retirement plans (Hansen 2010). The first publicly funded teacher pension plans were municipal plans. Previously, any assistance for teachers' old age or illness came from voluntary programs to which teachers contributed. Local school boards typically needed state permission to commit public resources to retirement benefits. In the late nineteenth century, states began granting this authority to some large districts. Clark, Craig, and Wilson (2003) observe that "the United States was quite late in offering universal old-age pensions to its public schoolteachers" (p. 182). By 1911, at least 20 other nations had pension plans for teachers.

Gradually, states began enacting statewide pension plans for teachers. In some cases, the state plan absorbed existing municipal plans, and in others, the city plans continued as separate entities. By the late 1920s, 23 states had teacher pension plans, 4 others allowed individual districts to create plans, and in Missouri teachers organized their own plan (Clark, Craig, and Wilson 2003).

During the early decades of the twentieth century, retirement benefits expanded more rapidly for teachers than for either private workers or other workers in the public sector. Graebner (1980) suggests that policymakers' interest in helping aging teachers was due to the fact that so many were single women (marriage was often grounds for dismissal) and unlikely to be able to support themselves after years in low-paying jobs. During this time, public and private employers were known to deal with the problem of pensionless aging workers by moving them to less demanding jobs. But, as Graebner observes, this tactic was not well suited to schools:

> A corporation might shift an older worker to some less demanding task, or a government agency, existing outside a market framework, could absorb a limited number of older employees who did nothing at all; the result might not be productive, but neither was it particularly difficult to achieve physically[,] nor was it of much negative impact. The teacher's work, on the other hand, was perceived as an indivisible unit—one teacher, before one class, all day. That a teacher of declining skills or energies might teach less than a full day or assist in another's classroom seems not to have been considered. (Graebner 1980, p. 91; cited in Hansen 2010)

While some early pension plans were essentially forced saving programs, others based retiree benefits on earnings and years of service, thus providing a template for the defined benefit (DB) plan that became the standard for both public and private systems in the mid-twentieth century. For teachers (and most public-sector workers), the most prevalent DB plan was based on a "final pay" formula, with benefits based on average earnings during the worker's final (highest) few years of earnings. The benefit equals a percentage of the worker's final average earnings multiplied by years of service: $B = F*YOS*FAS$. In this equation, B represents the annual benefit; F is a benefit factor (or "multiplier"), usually between 1.5 and 2.5 percent; YOS is years of service in the system; and FAS is the teacher's final average salary, often an average of the final three years. Unlike most private pensions, teacher plans include an automatic cost-of-living adjustment (COLA)—sometimes a fixed adjustment (e.g., 3 percent annually); in other cases tied to the Consumer Price Index. In some states, the adjustments are ad hoc decisions made by the state legislature or administrative governing board (Hansen 2010).

Retiring young

The great majority of teacher retirement plans allow teachers to take "normal" retirement and draw full pensions earlier than Social Security and many private-sector programs. Many teacher plans permit normal retirement for long-serving individuals in their fifties (Hansen 2010). In some states, teachers can retire with full benefits when their age and years of service sum to a specified number (e.g., the "rule of 80"). After decades of generally lowering the retirement age, some states have begun raising the age for normal retirement for new hires so as to reduce future liabilities.

Early retirement benefits

Another feature of most teacher DB plans rarely found in the private sector is the availability of pension benefits before the normal retirement date. According to the National Education Association (NEA), "Early retirement benefits are usually computed based on the normal retirement formula, and the benefit is then reduced by either a specified annual percentage or by an actuarial reduction applied according to the number of years that the early retirement age precedes the normal age retirement" (NEA 2008, p. 29, cited in Hansen 2010). As with rules for normal retirement, some states have amended early retirement rules so as to limit future pension costs.

Impacts on Teacher Labor Markets

Teacher pensions have attracted widened attention in recent years, both within the policymaking community and the wider public. Three questions dominate the policy debate: First, are they financially sustainable, particularly in the post–Great Recession period of shrinking K–12 fiscal support? Second, do they treat short-term and mobile teachers fairly? And third, do they exacerbate teacher shortages?

Fiscal sustainability

The rising costs of public pensions have generated growing concern from policymakers in recent years and have provided critics of public schools and teacher unions with an effective issue to hype their case for pension reform.[8] For example, writing in 2005, before the Great Recession, the conservative Reason Foundation estimated then-current unfunded public pension liabilities of more than $350 billion and spoke of "a national, systemic problem" (Passantino and Summers 2005, executive summary, cited in Hansen 2010). However, as Hansen notes, "recent studies by credible, objective organizations (written, it must be stressed, before the major financial market upheavals of 2008) did not find a broad crisis in the public pension arena" (p. 414). For example, the Government Accountability Office (GAO) reported in late 2007 that state and local governments appeared able to fully fund their pension programs with only a small increase (0.3 percent of salaries) in their current contributions (USGAO 2008, cited in Hansen 2010).

When a plan's assets equal its liabilities, the plan is said to be fully funded. If the assets are less than the liabilities, the plan is described as being underfunded. Some plans are overfunded, with assets greater, in actuarial terms, than those needed to meet the present value of current liabilities. According to the Public Fund Survey (2009), data on the 125 plans in its report indicate that public pension systems had $2.585 trillion in actuarial assets and $3.031 trillion in actuarial liabilities, for an aggregate actuarial funding ratio of 85.3 percent. This is close to the aggregate funding ratio of 84.7 percent for the 59 teacher plans, and it is also close to the ratio found by the Pew Center on the States in its 2007 survey of public-sector pensions, which concluded that "from a national perspective, states' pension plans seem to be in reasonable shape." And the GAO has noted that "a funded ratio of 80 percent or more is within the range that many public-sector experts, union officials, and advocates view as a healthy pension system" (USGAO 2007, p. 30).

The Public Fund Survey did find wide variation in funding ratios across the 59 individual teacher plans, with 14 funded at 90 percent or more, 17 funded at between 80 percent and 90 percent, and 28 at below 80 percent (Public Fund Survey 2009, cited in Hansen 2010). And these funding ratios, while useful indicators of fiscal health, must be interpreted in context. As Hansen observes,

They are statements at a particular time about how the assets in a pension plan compare with the present value of the benefits that plan members have accrued. Ratios do not indicate anything about whether a plan is moving in a healthy or unhealthy direction. If a plan is amortizing previous unfunded liabilities, for example, it may appear at a given point to have a large unfunded liability; but in fact its funding ratio might be on target with a planned schedule for achieving financial soundness. Since unfunded liabilities are typically amortized over thirty years, the key question for an underfunded plan is whether it is making progress in reducing its unfunded liabilities. (Hansen 2010, p. 415)

How do pensions get into financial trouble?

One common problem of state and local governments is their failure to make their "actuarially required contribution" (ARC) every year—that is, the amount needed to pay for new liabilities accrued in that year ("normal cost") and to pay off a portion of the unfunded liabilities accrued in previous years. Another problem is the tendency of lawmakers to boost benefits, particularly when the economy is strong and investment portfolio earnings exceed projected levels or immediate system needs. A third pitfall associated with DB pension plans arises from the practice of "spiking"—that is, inflating end-of-career salaries so as to boost the formula-based annuities, although some states have taken steps to prevent this practice.

A major source of pension liability stress comes from unfunded commitments outside the pension system, notably retiree health care. Most public school teachers are covered by health insurance provided by their employer while they are working. In most cases, these health plans are managed at the state level. At retirement, teachers with sufficient years of service may remain in the health plan. These plans are an important part of the compensation for public school teachers in the United States. Many teachers begin their careers in their early twenties, immediately after completing their college degrees. Those who remain in the profession will complete thirty years of service by their mid-fifties and, in most states, will then be eligible for full retirement benefits (Clark 2010). For those retiring before age 65, the age of Medicare eligibility, retaining health coverage in an employer-provided medical plan is an important benefit.

Teacher retiree health plans differ across the states, with some paying the full premium and others requiring full payment by the retiree. Until 2004, the cost of retiree health care was treated as an annual expense for public employers and attracted little attention or scrutiny (Clark 2010). In that year, however, the Governmental Accounting Standards Board (GASB) promulgated new rules mandating that public-sector employees report the accrued liabilities associated with these plans. The actuarial reports issued since then have revealed large and growing unfunded liabilities in some states, along with rapidly growing annual costs (Clark 2008, 2009).[9]

While retiree medical coverage is far more prevalent in the public sector than in the private, relatively few public-sector employers have established trust funds to help finance future retiree medical costs. And these unfunded liabilities continue to grow. In 2006, the annual cost to state and local governments for these plans averaged about 2 percent of employee salaries. If employers continue to fund these benefits on a pay-as-you-go basis, the cost is projected to rise to 5 percent of payroll by 2050 (GAO 2008). In response to these cost pressures, policymakers and public school leaders can increase revenues to support their schools or reduce benefits. Government spending on retiree health care can be lowered by reducing benefits or shifting the cost from the employer to active and retired teachers through higher premiums, copayments, and deductibles. Employers can also increase the years of service required for eligibility. State and local governments could eliminate these plans altogether or shift from DB plans to health savings accounts. Unlike public pensions, retiree health plans are statutory and not constitutionally protected.

But such benefit cuts would come at a cost. As Clark (2010) observes,

> Reducing the generosity of retiree health plans for public teachers will not come without some adverse labor market effects. A decline in total compensation will make public education jobs less attractive relative to teaching in private schools and other private sector jobs. Increases in the number of years of service required for participation in the retiree health plan or increases in the premium the retiree is required to pay will likely delay retirement. School administrators will have to assess the impact of later retirement on teaching quality and the cost of other forms of compensation, such as salaries and pension contributions. (p. 459)

Do Teacher Pension Plans Treat All Teachers Fairly?

Apart from the question of financial sustainability is the matter of teacher equity—that is, do pension plans treat all teachers fairly, and how do these plans affect schools' ability to recruit and retain qualified teachers? The backloaded pension benefits provided by the traditional final-average-salary DB formula are intended to ensure schools a long-term, stable teaching staff and to provide such a dedicated staff with a secure retirement income. But what about teachers who don't remain in the classroom for 20 years or more or change job locations throughout their careers? Pension benefits for teachers who leave the profession after relatively short careers are much less generous, and these short-timers would be better off with a plan (such as a DC plan) that accumulates benefits more evenly throughout a teaching career.

Examining the accrual of pension wealth in six state plans, Costrell and Podgursky (2010) compare the distribution of pension wealth from existing DB teacher pension plans with fiscally equivalent plans that would have distributionally neutral accrual paths (e.g., a DC plan, in which pension wealth grows at a uniform rate throughout one's working career). Compared with such a neutral system, they find that "teacher systems often redistribute about half the net pension wealth of an entering cohort toward those who separate in their mid-fifties from those who leave the system earlier" (Costrell and Podgursky 2010, p. 521). A big reason for this is that teachers who work into their fifties can start collecting their pensions immediately, while teachers who exit earlier must defer their pensions (e.g., until age 60), so they collect fewer payments in retirement. Furthermore, Costrell and Podgursky add, the backloading of benefits in the typical DB plan penalizes teachers who move across state lines: "Compared with a teacher who has worked thirty years in a single state system, a teacher who has put in the same years but split them between two systems will often lose well over one-half her net pension wealth. . . . Rules permitting service purchases do very little to ameliorate these losses. We find it difficult to justify on efficiency grounds this system of rewards and penalties that generates such unequal benefits" (p. 522).[10]

These inefficiencies probably reflect not only a lack of coordination across states but the relative political influence of veteran teachers as compared with their more novice colleagues in setting policy. And they most assuredly discourage teachers from responding to conditions of surplus and shortage in teacher markets.

CROSSING STATE LINES

In many professions, including architecture, engineering, accounting, psychology, and medicine, national standards and state licensing requirements aligned with those standards allow for relatively easy movement of licensed professionals across state lines. But this is not true for classroom teaching. While states do set teacher licensing requirements with the goal of ensuring an adequate supply of qualified professionals across their local districts, the absence of national licensing standards, and the considerable variability across states in both the stringency of their licensure standards and their willingness to enforce them, seriously impede mobility across states (Wise 2016). Some states have created teacher-licensing standards but lack the authority to enforce them. And while all states require that prospective teachers graduate from a four-year college, specific licensure requirements vary from state to state. Moreover, states often relax their standards in an effort to boost supply.

Most states have reciprocity agreements intended to ensure that teaching licenses are accepted across states. Because all public school teachers must be certified in the state where they teach, these agreements purportedly allow out-of-state applicants to secure a license without having to retake the courses or exams required for their initial licensure. In general, the new state issues a provisional license while the candidate completes any additional certification requirements. However, given the differences across states in these licensure requirements and the degree to which states are willing to relax them when faced with looming teacher shortages, interstate reciprocity is often cumbersome and costly for candidates, leading to resignations and exacerbating the very shortages these arrangements are intended to abate. As Arthur Wise, former president of the National Council for Accreditation of Teacher Education and coauthor of *A License to Teach*, observes, "Legislators and other state bodies routinely compromise teacher licensing standards to ensure an adequate supply of teachers. It is no wonder that states do not trust the teaching licenses of other states" (Wise 2016).

To facilitate interstate teacher mobility, Wise calls for creation of a National Board for Teacher Licensing, modeled after comparable bodies in other professions, to develop standards for new teachers and to coordinate with state licensing boards, which enjoy the enforcement powers of state boards that regulate other professions.

LONG-TERM TRENDS

The past 60 years have witnessed dramatic shifts in the quantity and quality of teachers. In response to the baby boom, which increased the *demand* for teachers in the 1950s and 1960s, the number of public school teachers nearly doubled between 1955 and 1970, rising from 1.1 million to 2.1 million. Enrollment declined as baby boomers exited the system, but the size of the teaching force remained roughly constant. This led to a weakened demand for new teachers, an aging of the workforce, and a decline in relative salaries. The size of the teacher workforce has steadily increased since 1990, though the Great Recession of 2008–2009 brought about localized reductions in force.

There is also evidence of a long-term decline in the quality of graduates entering the teaching profession. Corcoran, Evans, and Schwab (2004) document a decline in the quality of new teachers between 1960 and 2000, as measured by math and verbal skills, driven by a sharp drop in the percentage of high-achieving women choosing to teach. This decline corresponded with significant changes in the labor market for women, as high-achieving women gained access to professions traditionally held by men. Specifically, the noted long-run decline in teacher quality has been linked to relative growth in the earnings of college-educated women outside of teaching and the teacher salary schedule, which has not historically rewarded high performers to the same extent as other professions (see, for example, Hoxby and Leigh 2004).

This finding is consistent with human capital theory, whereby individuals choose to invest in education and training in a manner similar to investments in physical capital. Like physical capital, investments in human capital (i.e., education and training) involve costs that are typically incurred by individuals early on, with benefits received later. So investments in education and training lead to an increase in individuals' skills and productivity in the labor market. This in turn leads to higher earnings. Human capital theory predicts that an individual will invest in education and training when the (expected) present value of benefits exceeds the present value of costs.

Evidence is mounting, however, that the long-term decline in average teacher ability has been reversed in recent years as education policymakers at all levels of government have come to recognize the importance of classroom teachers in children's academic success (Figlio and Loeb 2011). Many states have raised licensure requirements, while the federal government, through NCLB, has required that school districts receiving Title I funds ensure that all teachers of core academic subjects meet the "highly qualified teacher" provision by the 2006–2007 academic year, as noted above. Careful research suggests that these policy initiatives have boosted teacher quality. Examining national survey data, Goldhaber and Walch (2013) find that the average SAT percentile ranking of teachers fell from 45 in 1994 to 42 in 2001 but increased to 50 by 2009. Lankford et al. (2014), analyzing a rich 25-year data set on the academic ability of teachers in New York state, find that since 1999 the academic ability of both individuals certified and those entering teaching has steadily increased, with the increase much larger among those actually hired.

This pattern of greater improvement in average academic ability among those hired than those certified suggests that while the supply of candidates has improved in quality, the demand side of the market has exerted an even greater influence on the rising academic quality of the New York state teaching force. Moreover, these improvements were found to be widely distributed, resulting in a substantial narrowing of differences in average teacher academic ability between high- and low-poverty schools and between white and minority teachers (Lankford et al. 2014). Whether these encouraging trends in New York state can be replicated elsewhere remains to be seen.

Supporting teacher markets: The task ahead

Much evidence suggests that schools' challenges in hiring teachers are becoming more severe. At the same time, it is apparent that these challenges are concentrated in high-need subject areas, particularly science, math, and special education, and in hard-to-staff schools—that is, those serving populations of concentrated poverty. Accordingly, policy efforts to support teacher labor markets and better connect the supply of effective teachers with labor market needs must be targeted to areas of local shortage. These challenges have plagued our public schools for decades and call for new measures to ameliorate existing rigidities in teacher labor markets, including targeted financial incentives, improved district hiring practices, more flexibility for entry into the teaching profession, and greater interstate coordination of licensure reciprocity.

Notes

1. This section, in large part, follows Ingersoll et al. (2021). Richard Ingersoll and colleagues at the University of Pennsylvania have closely chronicled the composition of the U.S. K–12 teaching force, including turnover and shortages, for over two decades.
2. Chetty, Friedman, and Rockoff (2014) acknowledge issues surrounding the use of value-added metrics (VAM) for education policy making and formal teacher evaluation (a topic addressed in Chapter 5). Nevertheless, they close their rigorous analysis by reiterating their main point: "Improving the quality of teaching—whether via use of value-added metrics or other policy levers—is likely to have substantial economic and social benefits" (p. 2677).
3. This lack of competitiveness of teacher salaries with salaries offered by other professions has been widely documented. See, for example, Allegretto and Mishel (2016), who show that this "penalty" teachers pay increases the longer they remain in the classroom.
4. For major studies on the topic of merit pay, each of which generally finds no positive effects on student outcomes, see Glazerman and Seifullah (2010), Marsh et al. (2011), and Springer et al. (2010).
5. In the fifth year, fully 86 percent of the original cohort who had been assigned a first-year mentor were still teaching, as opposed to 71 percent of the cohort who had not.
6. Recent research does suggest that highly selective alternative certification programs may be particularly effective. A random assignment study of the Teach for America (TFA) program found that TFA graduates produce significantly greater gains in math for secondary school students (Clark et al. 2013).
7. This section follows Hansen (2010).
8. For a more detailed discussion of pension fiscal sustainability, see Hansen (2010), upon which this summary is based.
9. For a detailed discussion of teachers' retiree health plans, see Clark (2010).

10. Virtually all teacher pension plans provide for "purchase of service credit," but the provisions are limited in scope and vary across plans. A teacher who cashes out of one plan without receiving full credit for all employer and employee contributions and interest may not be able to afford purchasing credit in the new plan. And those entering teaching in mid-career may not be allowed to purchase credits, particularly if they are coming from the private sector (Hansen 2010).

3
Teachers' Unions in the Crosshairs

A man must always live by his work, and his wages must at least be sufficient to maintain him.
                                        —Adam Smith, *The Wealth of Nations*

The harshest criticism and most strident political opposition leveled at public school teaching are reserved for teacher unions, particularly their most prized benefits: tenure and pensions. Political attacks on public employee unions have been characterized by their agents as a crusade on behalf of hard-working nonunion taxpayers in the private sector (Lafer 2017). For example, Wisconsin Governor Scott Walker justified his campaign against union rights by asserting that "we can no longer live in a society where the public employees are the haves and taxpayers who foot the bills are the have-nots."[1]

In sharp contrast to the U.S. private sector, where the decline of manufacturing has been accompanied by a steep drop in union membership (from about 35 percent in 1960 to a mere 7 percent by the turn of the century), the teaching profession remained highly unionized in 2000, with fully 79.1 percent of its members claiming union membership. Soon thereafter, however, the unionized share began drifting downward, to 77.6 percent in 2004 and 76.4 percent in 2008.[2] This downward trend in the unionized share of the teaching profession accelerated following the Great Recession but remains much higher than in the private sector. By 2013, the proportion of unionized teachers had fallen to 50 percent; by 2014, to 49 percent (U.S. Bureau of Labor Statistics 2016).[3]

Despite these recent precipitous declines, however, public school teacher unions still make up the largest single segment of unionized workers in America today and remain both a potent political force and inviting target. The two predominant unions—the National Education Association and the American Federation of Teachers—have active affiliates in every state and nearly every district in the nation and maintain a collective membership of about 4.7 million education professionals. Their critics include members of both professional and working classes, with members of the former viewing unions as economically inefficient and members of the latter resentful of union job protections and benefits now rarely found in the private sector.

Union critics are also prominent in both major political parties. While red-state Republicans have actively battled teacher unions for decades, the Obama administration, led by Education Secretary Arne Duncan, aggressively pursued a corporate-backed, pro–charter school, antiunion agenda. This remarkable development, whereby leaders of the Democratic Party mounted a political assault against a substantial part of its own electoral base, is only now starting to abate.

The Decline of Unions and Workers

The strong and growing antiunion sentiment in the United States is a relatively new phenomenon. Unionization increased rapidly in the U.S. following enactment of the National Labor Relations Act (NLRA, also called the Wagner Act) in 1935. This legislation established the National Labor Relations Board (NLRB) as the governing mechanism for labor relations in all firms engaged in interstate commerce.[4]

The trends in U.S. union membership are presented in Figure 3.1. Although the data for 1980 and later are not entirely comparable with those for 1930 through 1975, they are sufficiently similar to support the conclusion that unionization as a percentage of the labor force peaked during the period from the mid-1940s to around 1960 and has declined steadily since then.[5]

In the 1950s, about one in three wage and salary workers enjoyed union membership (Mayer 2004). But since then the trend has been downward. Despite periods of high unemployment since 1974, unionization has declined rapidly. Why? Increasing foreign competition in the early 1980s raised the cost of higher union wages, increasing employers' resistance to new organization and imposing a cost on already organized plants (Freeman and Kleiner 1990). Furthermore, the mix of workers in the labor force shifted toward people who are less likely to be unionized, including women and white-collar workers (Dickens and Leonard 1985). The passage of state and federal legislation restricting employers' rights to dismiss workers, often arising from union lobbying efforts, may also have contributed to the decline in demand for unions (Farber 1990; Neumann and Rissman 1984).

**Figure 3.1 Union Membership in the U.S., Selected Years, 1930–2016
(number in thousands and as a percentage of labor force)**

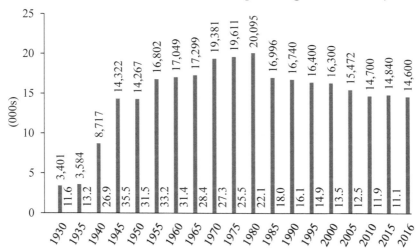

SOURCE: For 1930–1975, from *Handbook of Labor Statistics, 1980,* Table 165; for 1980, from Bureau of Labor Statistics, *Earnings and Other Characteristics of Organized Workers*, Bulletin No. 2105; for 1985, from *Employment and Earnings*, January 1986, p. 213; for 1990, from *Employment and Earnings*, January 1991, p. 228; for 1995 and later, from Bureau of Labor Statistics, https://www.bls.gov/news.release/history.

Moreover, since the late 1970s, unions have been the target of unrelenting criticism by advocates of neoliberalism, a "free market" ideology that espouses freedom of contracts and holds that wages should be set by the unfettered workings of supply and demand and not propped up by collective bargaining agreements or minimum wage rules.[6] A prominent leader of this intellectual and political movement was conservative economist and Nobel laureate Milton Friedman, who argued that unions have "not only harmed the public at large and workers as a whole by distorting the use of labor, they have also made the incomes of the working class more unequal by reducing the opportunities available to the most disadvantaged workers" (Friedman 1962).

One consequence of the union movement's steady decline is unmistakable: since the early 1970s, the wages of the overwhelming majority of U.S. workers, including classroom teachers, have not kept pace with overall economic growth. And the widening of the gap between worker pay and productivity has accelerated since the Great Recession of 2008. From roughly the end of World War II to the early 1970s, workers' real wages grew with the rest of the economy. On average, wage increases in the United States tracked productivity almost perfectly from 1947 to 1973. U.S. production continued to grow after 1973, but wages did not. Somehow, wages became disconnected from economic growth. From 1973 to 2014, productivity increased by 72.2 percent, but worker compensation rose a mere 9.2 percent.[7] This opening of a gap between U.S. productivity and worker pay is depicted in Figure 3.2.

Over this 42-year period, productivity grew 1.33 percent annually, much faster than the mere 0.20 percent annual growth in median hourly compensation. Put another way, only about 15 percent of productivity growth between 1973 and 2014 was converted into higher hourly wages and benefits for the typical worker. Since 2000, the productivity-pay gap has widened at an accelerating rate. The net productivity growth of 21.6 percent from 2000 to 2014 yielded a paltry 1.8 percent increase in

Figure 3.2 The U.S. Pay-Productivity Gap, 1949–2015

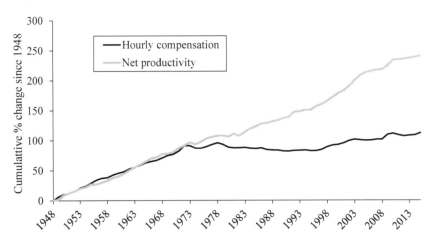

NOTE: Data are for average hourly compensation of production/nonsupervisory workers in the private sector and net productivity of the total economy. "Net productivity" is the growth of output of goods and services minus depreciation per hour worked.
SOURCE: Economic Policy Institute (EPI) analysis of data from the Bureau of Economic Analysis (BEA) and the Bureau of Labor Statistics (BLS), found in Bivens and Mishel (2015).

real compensation for the median worker, or just 8 percent of productivity growth (Bivens and Mishel 2015).

Where do teachers fall in this startling decline in workers' fortunes? Peter Temin, in his notable 2017 book *The Vanishing Middle Class*, argues that this widening disparity between productivity and wages has created a dual economy in the United States, with the upper sector consisting of the 20 percent of the population whose income is growing in real terms, and the lower sector containing the remaining 80 percent, whose incomes are stagnating.[8] Temin distinguishes between the two sectors by the skills and occupations of their workers:

> The first sector consists of skilled workers and managers who have college degrees and command good and even very high salaries in our technological society. I call this the FTE sector to highlight the roles of finance, technology, and electronics in this part of the economy. The other group consists of low-skilled workers who are suffering some of the ills of globalization. I call this the low-wage sector to highlight the role of politics and technology in reducing the demand for semi-skilled workers. (Temin 2017, p. 8)

The FTE sector includes most, but not all, college graduates. These workers earn enough to buy a house in a good school district, drive a new car, and generally enjoy what used to be called a middle-class living. So where does Temin see the dividing line between the FTE and low-income sectors? He notes that the top 10 percent of U.S. wage earners, those with incomes of $100,000 and above, are comfortably in this middle class and that the median U.S. worker, earning about $40,000, finds middle-class security out of reach. The dividing line between sectors lies somewhere "in the gap between these two figures" (Temin 2017, p. 25). And where do public school teachers fall? Temin provides a telling example:

> John-David Bowman, who teaches Advanced Placement history and a class called Theory of Knowledge in the International Baccalaureate program at Westwood High School in Mesa, AZ, has not had a raise since he was hired, in 2008. He has two bachelor's degrees and a master's degree, and was voted Arizona's Teacher of the Year for 2015. The honor allowed him to shake hands with President Obama at the White House. Still, Bowman said, "I could retire in 20 years, under $50,000." This distinguished high school teacher is and will remain in the low-wage sector if he continues teaching in this setting. (Temin 2017, p. 25)

Teachers are thus consigned to the low-wage sector despite their extensive formal education, often including graduate degrees and other postbaccalaureate credentials, and their still substantial union presence.

A BRIEF HISTORY OF TEACHER UNIONS IN THE U.S.

After amassing great power over public education in the 1960s, '70s, and '80s, teacher unions are now under assault. As union leaders seek to preserve job protections and compensation gains bargained for during the time of union ascendancy, while positioning themselves among the staunchest defenders of public schools, they find themselves targeted by school reformers who seek to marginalize, if not eliminate, their role in public education. Reformers from both major political parties, while differing starkly on key policies such as school funding, vouchers, and the incursion of for-profit companies into public education, often find themselves in agreement over the elimination or weakening of job protections negotiated by teacher unions in collective bargaining agreements.

Much of the history of teacher unions has been marked by a steady accumulation of power and influence accompanied by a simultaneous decline in their public regard. A brief look at the history of public-sector unions helps us better understand the teacher unions' current professional and political circumstances and challenges.

The origins of public-sector unions

The early public-sector unions sought an end to the patronage systems that dominated much of American government from the late 1800s through the first several decades of the twentieth century. Under these systems, government jobs were controlled by political parties. As a consequence, these jobs were inherently insecure and often filled by hacks who were beholden to the party in power. The early public-sector unions sought to make these jobs more secure for workers and more supportive of their occupational interests (Moe 2011).

Progress, however, was slow, and it was not until the 1950s that most vestiges of political patronage were cleared away.[9] And even then, unionism in the public sector did not enjoy wide support. Although unions were well established in the private sector, particularly in larger firms and industries, many public employee organizations—often professional associations supportive of civil service protection for their members—did not support collective bargaining or strikes, which many members considered unprofessional. Even George Meany, president of the American Federation of Labor and Congress of Industrial Organizations (AFL-CIO), was prompted to say in 1959, "It is impossible to bargain collectively with government" (Green 1996, p. 162).

Nevertheless, the coalition of Democratic office holders and union activists began to make tangible progress in the late 1950s. In 1957, Richardson Dilworth, the Democratic mayor of Philadelphia, recognized the American Federation of State, County, and Municipal Employees (AFSCME)—the largest public-sector union in the country with nearly 180,000 members—as the exclusive bargaining agent for all nonuniformed public employees in the city. And in 1959, collective bargaining rights were extended to New York City public workers, and Wisconsin passed the first state-level labor law allowing unions and collective bargaining for public workers (Moe 2011).

These developments launched the public-sector union movement, but two events in 1962 ushered the movement onto the national stage. The first was a widely publicized and tumultuous strike by New York City teachers, discussed below, and the second was President John F. Kennedy's Executive Order No. 10988—issued in fulfillment of a 1960 presidential campaign promise—which extended collective bargaining rights to federal government workers. As Moe (2011) observes, "This order proved to be of huge symbolic significance, signaling to public officials, unions, and public employees at *all* levels of government that collective bargaining in the public sector was legitimate and attainable. The notion that government was somehow different, that collective bargaining called for an impermissible delegation of authority, had long been on the ropes. Now it was effectively dead" (Moe 2011, p. 37; emphasis in the original).

For the rest of the 1960s and the following decade, state and local governments across most of the United States, excluding the right-to-work South, began to adopt new labor laws permitting public employees to organize and bargain collectively. Strike activity among public workers, exceedingly rare before 1960, became more prevalent, making "labor peace" a concern for state and local governments. By 1983, union membership had reached 42 percent for local government employees, 28 percent for state workers, and 19 percent for federal workers (excluding postal workers, who are heavily organized). These levels have remained steady, standing at 43 percent for local, 32 percent for state, and 18 percent for federal workers in 2009 (Moe 2011, p. 37).

Why the rather sudden breakthrough for organized labor in the government sector in the 1960s and 1970s? Government workers had long been frustrated with low pay and weak job security. But with the rise of civil service protections during the Progressive Era of the 1950s, government work became secure and professional and largely removed from political patronage. Moe (2011) attributes the breakthrough to the passage of new labor laws starting around 1960 and continuing into the 1970s. In support, he cites Richard Freeman's landmark 1986 paper published in the *Journal of Economic Literature*: "What changes led to the sudden organization of traditionally nonunionizable public sector workers? First and foremost were changes in the laws regulating public sector unions" (Moe 2011, p. 38, quoting Freeman 1986, p. 45).

As union membership rose rapidly among public-sector workers in the 1960s and 1970s, it declined steadily in the private sector, from about 35 percent in the mid-1950s to 17 percent in 1983 and a mere 8 percent by 2009 (Moe 2011, p. 39). Organized labor is now centered in the public sector. Although public employees make up just 17 percent of the U.S. labor force (excluding the Postal Service and the military), they constitute half of all union members, and their major unions—the NEA, AFT, AFSCME, and the Service Employees International Union (SEIU)—are the leading forces of the union movement (Moe 2011).

Moe (2011) cites two primary reasons for the decline of private-sector unions and their ascendency in the public sector. First, competitive pressures in the private sector, which intensified in the 1970s and 1980s because of economic globalization and technological progress, led firms to resist unionization. Competition undermines unions directly, by diminishing their membership and power, and indirectly, by prompting firms to effect structural cost-cutting measures and inducing a shift from manufacturing (highly unionized) to services (weakly unionized). Such competition is generally not found in the public sector. While economic downturns and rising antitax sentiment among voters (as seen, for example, during the Great Recession of 2008 and its aftermath) may lead to pay concessions and layoffs among public union members and the privatization of some services, the consequences of the competition and cost cutting seen in the private sector have not yet been as severe in the public sector. A second reason is that the "employers" in the public sector are elected officials. So to the extent that public-sector unions can influence election outcomes, they can literally handpick the employers whom they will be bargaining with and who will make government policy appropriations.

Of course, government is not always union friendly. Unions may fail to get their candidates—most often Democrats—elected to office. And even if they do so, the elected officials may not serve union interests. As we will see in Chapter 5, for example, the Obama administration pursued policies and programs quite at odds with the interests of teacher unions. But unions, in recent decades, have found less (albeit growing) resistance in the public sphere than in the more competitive and cost-sensitive private sector.

The Rise of Teacher Unions

The National Education Association (NEA), today by far the largest and most powerful teacher union in the U.S., was established in 1857 as a professional association of educators and was initially controlled by school administrators. The NEA's mission was the professionalization of public education, rescuing the public schools from local politics and patronage and placing them under the stewardship of trained educational administrators. With a more centralized and rule-based governance structure, classroom teaching would also become more professional, through more rigorous training, higher licensing standards, better pay and pensions, and tenure. The NEA agenda was part of the progressive reform movement that sought to depoliticize and professionalize public employment. The NEA opposed teacher unionization, which it considered to be unprofessional and antithetical to the interests of school administrators. Indeed, teachers themselves preferred membership in a professional organization rather than a union. With local administrators across the country often encouraging—and sometimes requiring—teacher membership, the ranks of the NEA swelled from about 2,000 in 1900 to 203,000 in 1940 and more than 700,000 in 1960 (Murphy 1990, p. 277, cited in Moe 2011, p. 45).

The early American Federation of Teachers (AFT) and its affiliates, on the other hand, were unions, serving the particular interests of teachers, principally workplace autonomy. But they faced strong opposition from both the NEA and the political parties, who opposed all public unions. Furthermore, with the rise of progressivism, school boards (often controlled by local business leaders) actively opposed teacher unions, sometimes firing teachers who became union activists. And most teachers were women and less inclined than men to join a union. (Indeed, women couldn't vote until 1920.) Finally, conflicts within the teaching profession (e.g., men versus women, elementary versus secondary, etc.) impaired solidarity (Moe 2011).

As a result, progress for the teacher union movement was slow. It began in Chicago with the formation of the Chicago Federation of Teachers in 1897, followed in 1916 by the AFT, a national union chartered by the American Federation of Labor, which joined together big-city locals from around the country. Their memberships consisted largely of activists as opposed to rank-and-file teachers, and were modest in aggregate numbers: 30,000 in 1940 and 59,000 in 1960 (Murphy 1990, p. 277, cited in Moe 2011). And for the first half of the century, members did not have collective bargaining rights or the right to strike. Indeed, strikes were prohibited by union policy.

Policy and practice were to change dramatically, however, in 1960 in New York City, when Mayor Robert Wagner reneged on a promise to authorize an election in which teachers could decide whether they wished to bargain collectively. In protest, the United Federation of Teachers (UFT), the local AFT affiliate, staged a one-day walkout. Although only about 5,000 of the city's 50,000 teachers participated, Mayor Wagner relented and authorized an election, in which New York City teachers adopted collective bargaining, with the UFT as their exclusive representative. The union bargained for "a substantial pay raise, free lunch periods, check-off for union dues, and one hundred and forty-seven other items dealing with workplace conditions" (Murphy 1990, p. 216, cited in Moe 2011, p. 46). When the demands were not met, UFT leader Al Shanker called a strike despite a state law prohibiting such an action. The result was a landmark in the history of American labor relations. Although fewer than half of the city's teachers actually walked off the job, the UFT won a major victory: the first major collective bargaining contract in public education, a large pay increase, a duty-free lunch period, and other workplace concessions. More importantly, the strike and union gains showed teachers across the country that organization and aggressive tactics could pay off.

Teacher Unions Rise in Power and Fall in Public Regard

In 1961, under pressure from the AFT, the NEA reversed itself and reluctantly supported collective bargaining for teachers. In 1967, it approved of teacher strikes in special circumstances, and by 1970, administrators were no longer active within the organization. By the mid-1970s, public school teaching had become the most unionized profession in America, with 90 percent of teachers holding membership in either the NEA or AFT, and more than 70 percent working in districts whose unions had achieved collective bargaining rights. And with collective bargaining came the possibility of strikes. Between 1960 and 1980, there were more than 1,000 teacher strikes across the United States, despite laws in many states prohibiting such action by public employees (Goldstein 2014).

The ascendency of teachers' unions in terms of membership and power, however, was accompanied by a parallel decline in their public popularity, and no event contributed more to this paradox than the 1968 AFT-led teacher walkout in the Ocean Hill–Brownsville community district in New York City. This teacher strike, the largest and most notorious in U.S. history, created fissures between teachers' unions and civil rights activists that persist today and are evident in recent judicial challenges of union rules and practices.

Ocean Hill–Brownsville Community District

By the early 1960s, most white families had fled this economically depressed neighborhood in central Brooklyn for Long Island or the New Jersey suburbs.[10] Remaining parents and community leaders were deeply concerned with conditions in the schools, as were many members of the UFT, the AFT's local affiliate. But local activists disagreed with teacher union leaders as to the remedy. The community activists wanted parents empowered to directly elect board members to set policy for the schools, while the union called for the neighborhood schools to join a program called More Effective Schools (MES), which the UFT had designed and convinced the city to adopt. The MES program provided select schools in poor neighborhoods with extra funding for smaller classes, prekindergarten, and more social workers, reading specialists, and other support staff. Program directors also sought to end tracking by training teachers to work with students of differing backgrounds and abilities in the same classroom (Goldstein 2014). But the MES program never materialized in Ocean Hill–Brownsville. In the spring of 1967, New York City Mayor John Lindsay granted community control to the neighborhood and denied the district MES funding.

This experiment in community control, instituted in the 1967–1968 school year, soon brought conflict between the elected community board and the teachers' union. The board selected Rhody McCoy, a black principal and union critic, to oversee the project. McCoy and the board then hired black and Puerto Rican administrators for each of the district's eight schools, replacing several popular principals in the process (Goldstein 2014). In May of 1968, following a student fight at a junior high school in the district, McCoy and the community board dismissed 19 white teachers and administrators. The teachers were not terminated but were directed to report to city school board headquarters for new assignments. The message was clear: black parents and administrators should have authority to terminate the employment of white teachers. Community control should trump due process. The union, of course, argued that neighborhood boards and school leaders had no such authority to hire and fire teachers and sent several of the dismissed Ocean Hill–Brownsville teachers back to work, where they were met by activists who physically prevented them from entering the schools. Two weeks later, when 350 UFT teachers walked out of the Ocean Hill–Brownsville schools in solidarity with their dismissed colleagues, the community board attempted to terminate all their contracts, too, thereby triggering the most notorious teachers' strike in U.S. history.

On one side of the Ocean Hill–Brownsville confrontation, community control advocates argued that the education of poor minority children was too important to be compromised by labor protections and due process (much the same argument that would be made decades later by plaintiffs in *Vergara v. State of California*, filed in 2014). On the other side, the UFT maintained that allowing parents and noneducators to fire teachers they did not approve of would diminish the profession and return teachers to the very state of job insecurity from which tenure was designed to deliver them. Furthermore, union members feared that a community control movement associated with Afrocentrism could turn neighborhood schools into places of political indoctrination.

On August 26, 1968, a judge ordered the community district to reinstate the dismissed teachers, along with the 350 who had struck in solidarity back in May. However, on the first day of classes, when the UFT teachers reported for work at Junior High School (JHS) 271, a focal point of unrest in the district, the conditions had been changed. Administrators "paired" returning union loyalists with teachers considered supportive of community control. Several union members reported that their classes were disrupted by their teaching partners (Fox 1968, cited in Goldstein 2014). In response, UFT President Al Shanker called for a citywide teacher strike, and the union's delegate assembly voted to walk out. This time, in contrast to the membership's tepid support of the UFT's first walkout in 1960, fully 93 percent of New York City teachers honored the picket line.

The 1968 UFT strikes in New York City—with 60,000 teachers participating, the largest in U.S. history—were particularly disruptive because they were staggered at intervals of several days and weeks between September and November. In all, a fifth of the school year's instructional time was lost, and nearly one million children were affected. Students had to enter JHS 271 (ground zero for the strike) through police barricades erected to separate picketing teachers from community activists, some of them armed Black Panthers (Berube and Gittell 1969, cited in Goldstein 2014). Media attention was unrelenting and national in scope.[11] The walkout ended in late November, when the New York State Board of Regents placed Ocean Hill–Brownsville and the city's two other demonstration districts under state management, essentially ending the experiment in community control. But racial animosity persisted long after the walkout ended. Parents and activists in communities of color remained antagonistic toward white union members. This lingering sentiment has been skillfully exploited by school reformers and union critics, who continue to portray veteran union teachers as both incompetent in the classroom and indifferent toward the academic success of poor children of color. And teacher tenure is often their target.

Tenure: The Profession's Prize and Critics' Target

Teacher tenure predates both the legalization of teacher unions and, by more than 50 years, the institution of teacher collective bargaining. U.S. teachers first won tenure rights in New Jersey in 1909. New York teachers then secured these rights in 1917. During the Progressive Era (the 1890s through the 1920s), teacher tenure was supported by both education reformers and then newly formed teacher unions as protection against political patronage and as a right to challenge dismissals or demotions, then commonplace, based on politics or ideology and not at all on job performance or competence. As a result, long before the advent of collective bargaining, it became difficult for school districts to fire an experienced teacher. As Goldstein observes, "Only in rare cases (or during moral panics, like the Red Scare) would districts undertake the costly and time-consuming task of terminating a tenured teacher. This 'due process' was the bedrock principle of teacher unionism, the protection that could help prevent teachers from being fired because of their political leanings, gender, race, religious beliefs, pregnancy, or opposition to administrative policies" (Goldstein 2014, p. 147).

By the late 1960s, however, many education reformers feared that the pendulum had swung too far in the other direction, keeping incompetent teachers on the payroll, if not always in the classroom. In the public's view, two ignominious developments came to personify the profession's shortcomings. The "Dance of the Lemons" was coined by reformers in the late 1990s to refer to union protections for bad teachers who, instead of being fired, are bounced from school to school, often ending up at schools in poor neighborhoods. The second phenomenon, less widespread but more notorious, was the "Rubber Rooms" of New York City, brought to the public's attention by attorney and author Steven Brill in a 2009 *New Yorker* article (Brill 2009). These rooms, officially termed "temporary reassignment centers," housed teachers deemed so incompetent that they needed to be kept out of the classroom altogether. In 2009, more than 700 New York City teachers were banished to these rooms across the city, where they idled away the normal working hours while receiving full salary and benefits, including vacation days and summers off. This program, although small and local, was an embarrassment to the profession and costly to the city. Annual salary and benefit costs were estimated at between $35 million and $65 million, while additional costs were incurred for substitute teachers to cover the vacated classrooms, rental costs of the Rubber Rooms, and half a million dollars for Rubber Room security guards (Moe 2011, p. 1).

States Take Aim at Teacher Tenure

The steady erosion in recent decades of union membership and job security in America, where a mere 7 percent of workers remain organized, combined with escalating calls for school and teacher accountability and sensational headlines about outrages like the Rubber Rooms, has galvanized critics of teacher unions. And tenure is a particularly prime target. Two states, North Carolina and Colorado, illustrate alternative legislative approaches to eliminating teacher tenure. In both states, teacher unions have filed suit to block legislation intended to abolish tenure. The cases help clarify the limits of legislative discretion in attempts to circumscribe school districts' contractual obligations and teachers' property rights.[12]

North Carolina. In 2013, the North Carolina legislature passed a statute revoking tenure. The new law stated that probationary teachers would be eligible for multiyear contracts, but not tenure. For teachers with tenure, their protections would expire in 2015 and be replaced by the same systems of multiyear contracts. The North Carolina Association of Educators (NCAE) sued the state in *NCAE v. State*, claiming that the law violated both the North Carolina constitution's prohibition on taking property without just compensation and the U.S. Constitution's prohibition on state laws "impairing the Obligation of Contracts." In 2014, a trial court ruled that the new law did violate the property and contractual rights of tenured teachers but not probationary teachers. This decision was upheld by an appellate court.

The state supreme court, in a unanimous decision, also ruled for the tenured teachers. The high court's ruling, however, rested solely on the U.S. Constitution's contract clause and did not address the plaintiffs' property-rights claims under the state constitution. The court held that teachers' right to tenure was "vested" when they signed a contract following their probationary period. The court ruled that while dismissing ineffective tenured teachers was a legitimate state interest, the state had failed to prove that existing employment policies were insufficient for making such dismissals. The state chose not to appeal in federal court, settling for the elimination of tenure for probationary teachers and future hires.

Colorado. In 2010, the Colorado legislature passed the Great Teachers and Leaders Act with bipartisan support. A section of the statute sought to eliminate the so-called Dance of the Lemons, a term of art, mentioned above, that in Colorado was used to refer to guaranteed placement rights of tenured teachers who lost their jobs owing to school circumstances such as declining enrollments or program changes. The new law eliminated the guarantee and required approval ("mutual consent") of the receiving school's administration and teacher representatives. Displaced teachers who could not find a school willing to take them were placed on paid leave for 12 months and on unpaid leave thereafter.

The Denver Classroom Teachers Association sued the Denver Public Schools on the grounds that the "mutual consent" requirement violated the teachers' contract clause and property rights under the Colorado constitution. In 2014, a trial court ruled against the union, reasoning that displacement is not dismissal. That ruling was overturned by an appellate court the following year. However, the appellate court ruling was itself reversed by the Colorado Supreme Court in 2018. The high court held that the "mutual consent" requirement did not impair teachers' right to due process.[13]

Colorado's law, if not abused, provides for the "just cause" dismissal of poorly performing teachers, and not the wholesale elimination of tenure called for by the North Carolina statute. As such, the Colorado statute is not a fundamental departure from tenure law and rules in other states. These cases serve as a caution for other states not to attempt a universal "taking" of tenure from teachers who have earned it. But state legislatures may well have the authority to eliminate tenure for probationary teachers and new hires.

Vergara v. State of California

On June 10, 2014, a Los Angeles County Superior Court judge struck down California's teacher-tenure system, ruling that laws protecting teachers from dismissal violated the state's constitutional responsibility to provide "a basically equal opportunity to achieve a quality education." The court maintained that by giving tenure to teachers after less than two years of teaching and then making it expensive and time-consuming to dismiss them, the California law permitted ineffective teachers to remain in the classroom, with particularly damaging consequences for low-income students in high-need schools. *Vergara* also addressed the "last in, first out" (LIFO) statutes governing reductions in force. Under California law, it was illegal to consider teacher effectiveness in deciding on layoffs before *Vergara*; layoffs had to be determined solely on the basis of seniority.

Plaintiffs in *Vergara* consisted of a well-funded coalition intent on weakening job protections for teachers. As such, they are part of a large movement of reformers who view teacher unions as major obstacles to school improvement. The plaintiffs' case and the Superior Court's ruling rested on the presumption that tenure and other job protections contribute significantly to the prevalence of ineffective teachers and that these protected poor performers have no incentive to improve their classroom performance. The ruling further presumed that by weakening teachers' job protections, school administrators can weed out the poor performers, however identified, and replace them with better-qualified and more effective teachers. Such latitude for school leaders, it was argued, would be particularly beneficial for students in high-poverty schools.

Plaintiffs' victory in *Vergara* was momentous but short-lived. The Superior Court's ruling was reversed in 2016 by the California Court of Appeals, and this reversal was upheld by the California Supreme Court later that year by a four-to-three vote. In reversing the decision of the Superior Court, a three-judge Appellate Court panel did not dispute the argument that poor and minority students were often saddled with poorly qualified teachers, but disagreed that tenure and teacher retention statutes were to blame. The problem, the panel asserted, was "deplorable staffing decisions made by some local administrators" (Fensterwald 2016).

Nevertheless, despite the reversal of the Superior Court ruling, the issues raised in *Vergara* remain salient. The plaintiffs and their broader coalition of reformers succeeded in framing the issue of teacher quality as one of civil rights for poor and minority children, not the rights of teachers. Interestingly, this renewed emphasis on schoolchildren's civil rights comes just as the public has apparently lost interest in school desegregation as a means of educational improvement, despite considerable evidence of the educational benefits of racially and socioeconomically integrated schools.[14] This dual emphasis on the racial and socioeconomic achievement gaps in K–12 education and the importance of teacher quality as a means of narrowing them has resonated with political leaders and policymakers and focused their attention on teacher labor law and human resource policies, to the exclusion of school integration, community redevelopment, or other policy approaches.

Critics of the original *Vergara* decision, while recognizing the problems of current school personnel laws and practices, including short probationary periods and perfunctory tenure approvals, view the elimination of tenure and other job protections (e.g., due process rights) as counterproductive. Rather than improving the quality of the teaching force, these actions would merely make classroom teaching a riskier career choice and less attractive to potential entrants, unless accompanied by compensating wage differentials. And critics see these adverse consequences as being even more pronounced in high-needs schools, where the work of classroom teachers is already exceptionally challenging and problems of teacher recruitment and retention particularly difficult. *Vergara* triggered copycat lawsuits in Minnesota and New York.

Ultimately, the effects of any litigation that succeeds in eliminating tenure or substantially weakening its protections will depend on the implementation of the new laws in the states involved. How would the loss or weakening of tenure protection alter teacher contracts? For example, would such a change result in more short-term teacher contracts? If so, on what basis would such contracts be renewed? Presumably, renewal would depend on performance evaluation. What criteria would be used in these evaluations? As mentioned earlier and discussed at length in Chapter 5, researchers have identified serious limitations in value-added measures of individual teacher performance and recommend the use of multiple performance measures, including classroom observation by both administrators and peers.

Teacher Unions and School Productivity

Antipathy toward teacher unions, evident in recent years among leadership of both major political parties, is motivated by multiple factors, including union positions on public and educational policy matters and the vigorous and well-funded political activity undertaken in union members' support. But much of the union criticism, fueled by recent research that reveals the importance of classroom teaching in the educational process, stems from long-standing concerns about school productivity and costs (e.g., Hanushek 1994) and strongly held beliefs that teacher collective bargaining agreements impede efforts to recruit and retain effective teachers, hinder the matching of teachers with students based on educational abilities and needs, and stifle creative problem solving with rigid work rules.

Comparing the quality and productivity of education in unionized and nonunionized districts and states, however, is not straightforward because unionization is not a random phenomenon. Any valid comparison of unionized and nonunionized school systems must account for unobserved characteristics of school systems that make teachers more likely to organize. Failure to do so could create a "selection bias" and lead to invalid conclusions about the productivity consequences of unionization. For example, if urban schools are more likely to unionize and to enroll large concentrations of low-income and educationally disadvantaged children than suburban and rural districts, then unionized schools will have lower average student achievement. The relationship, however, should not be interpreted as causal. Similarly, a district struggling with such problems as enrollment loss and declining resources, ineffective leadership, or teacher flight may experience both falling achievement and a rising desire of the remaining faculty to organize. Such adverse selection into unionization is not evidence of union effects on school productivity.

A small but sophisticated research literature has tried to address the selection bias inherent in estimating a causal relationship between teacher unions and school productivity, with mixed results. Eberts and Stone (1987), analyzing national cross-sectional survey data to compare teacher effectiveness in raising student achievement in districts with and without collective bargaining agreements, find a positive association between unionization and productivity. A more recent cross-sectional study finds negative relationships between union strength (proxied by a union's ability to influence local school board elections) and student achievement among organized school districts in California (Rose and Sonstelie 2010). Other studies have utilized panel data.

Using changes in districts' unionization status instrumented by changes in states' teacher collective bargaining laws between 1972 and 1992, Hoxby (1996) estimates that teacher collective bargaining increases school spending by 12 percent and dropout rates by 2.3 percent. But Lovenheim (2009), using a similar research design to examine a panel of school districts in three states over the same period, finds that unionization has no effect on dropout rates.

More recently, Lovenheim and Willen (2019) find that exposure as students to collective bargaining laws worsens the future labor market outcomes (earnings and employment rates) of men. Using American Community Survey data on educational attainment and labor market outcomes linked to individuals' state of birth, and exploiting the timing of passage of duty-to-bargain laws across cohorts within states and across states over time, the researchers find that in the first 10 years after passage of a duty-to-bargain law, male earnings fall by nearly 4 percent, and hours worked fall by 0.42 hours per week. They also find evidence of lower male employment rates, driven by lower labor force participation. These effects were largest among black and Hispanic men.

This article, published in 2019, is arguably the most comprehensive analysis to date of the effects of teacher collective bargaining on student outcomes. However, recognizing the changing landscape of public education law and policy across the states and over time, the authors offer a couple of caveats to generalizing their findings to today's students. First, the individuals examined in the study attended public school during the 1960s, '70s, and '80s, when school laws and policies differed substantially from those of the present time. For example, as the authors note, school choice as well as teacher and school accountability policies and programs, so prevalent today, were virtually nonexistent when the study's subjects attended school. Thus, some of the effects of teacher collective bargaining estimated in the study may have been motivated by teacher unions' interactions with aspects of educational systems that no longer exist. Second, collective bargaining laws not only differ across states but are often amended over time, and the study was unable to account for these differences. As the authors note, it is possible that lawmakers across the states could amend collective bargaining laws to reduce the negative impacts on student outcomes while still providing teachers with the bargaining benefits they value (Lovenheim and Willen 2019).

A particularly thorough study by Hart and Sojourner (2014) finds little effect of unionization among charter schools in California. Using a generalized difference-in-difference approach combining California union certification data with student achievement data from 2002 through 2012, the authors present some evidence of a dip in student performance around the time the union is formed but find that achievement rebounds to previous levels within a few years. Their findings are robust to estimation using different specifications, samples, and achievement measures. The authors provide several possible explanations for their findings. First, the unionization process itself may temporarily distract teachers, administrators, or students from achievement. Second, a decline in leadership quality may drive down achievement and compel teachers to organize. With a union, teachers may be able to increase control over the school, circumvent leadership mistakes, and get achievement back on track. Third, teachers may feel a need to organize because of some temporary disruption in the school that also temporarily impairs student learning (e.g., student or staff confusion over a new policy, or influx of new students or staff). This disruption may be resolved (or resolve itself), leaving teachers unionized and achievement back on track.

Beyond their effects on student achievement, unions may positively impact schools in other ways. Exploiting an exceptionally rich set of nationally representative panel data matching classroom teachers with school districts, Han (2016) finds that districts with strong unions dismiss more underperforming teachers and have lower teacher attrition than districts with weak unions. (See the accompanying Box 3.1, "Assessing Union Strength.") She finds that districts with strong unions have more teachers with stronger qualifications and lower high school dropout rates than districts with weak unions. She also finds that legal challenges weakening unions in four states negatively affect teacher turnover patterns and teacher quality.[15] More generally, Han finds significant empirical support for her stated hypothesis: "Through the dynamics of teacher turnover, unions ultimately raise teacher quality, as unionized districts can better retain good teachers and dismiss more underperforming teachers" (pp. 48–49).

Box 3.1 Assessing Union Strength

The impact of a teacher union on resource allocation and student achievement in a district can be expected to depend on the strength of the union. Accordingly, researchers have developed measures of union strength along several dimensions. Two dimensions, utilized by Moe (2011) and Han (2016), are the legal status of collective bargaining (CB) and the existence of agency shop, a union agreement stipulating that nonunion employees must pay union dues ("agency fees"), as their wage contracts are covered by CB regardless of their union status. Agency fees, however, were struck down by the U.S. Supreme Court in its June 2018 decision in *Janus v. AFSCME, Council 31*. This five-to-four ruling is discussed later in this chapter.

In 2016, 23 states had compulsory CB laws ("duty to bargain") mandating districts to bargain with a representative union in good faith when the union so requests. These states allowed mandatory agency fees for nonunion members. Eleven states had compulsory CB laws but prohibited mandatory agency fees. Nine states allowed local school districts to sign CB agreements, but bargaining was not mandatory. Finally, seven states banned CB for teachers.

State classification across these four groups was as follows prior to *Janus*:

Compulsory CB and mandatory agency fees allowed: Alaska, California, Connecticut, Delaware, Hawaii, Illinois, Maine, Maryland, Massachusetts, Michigan, Minnesota, Montana, New Hampshire, New Jersey, New Mexico, New York, Ohio, Oregon, Pennsylvania, Rhode Island, Vermont, Washington, and Wisconsin. *Janus* nullified the laws of these states permitting agency fees.

Compulsory CB but agency fees prohibited: Florida, Idaho, Indiana, Iowa, Kansas, Nebraska, Nevada, North Dakota, Oklahoma, South Dakota, and Tennessee.

CB allowed but not mandatory: Alabama, Arkansas, Colorado, Kentucky, Louisiana, Missouri, Utah, West Virginia, and Wyoming.

CB banned: Arizona, Georgia, Mississippi, North Carolina, South Carolina, Texas, and Virginia.

> **Box 3.1 (continued)**
>
> Even among unionized districts within a state, union power can vary substantially. Brown and Medoff (1988) find that wages paid by unionized local government employers are substantially higher in larger districts than in smaller districts, suggesting that unions in larger districts have greater bargaining power. Similarly, Rose and Sonstelie (2010) find that beginning teacher salaries and the salary premium paid to experienced teachers in California both increase with district size. Brunner and Squires (2013) find that in states that mandate collective bargaining, base salaries and the salary premium for experienced teachers increase with district size, while the teacher-pupil ratio declines with district size.
>
> Teacher unions can also flex their muscles at the ballot box. Moe (2005), Rose and Sonstelie (2010), and Strunk and Grissom (2010) observe that the primary source of union bargaining power comes from a union's ability to influence local school board elections ("Help elect your own bosses," in words attributed to one labor leader). A sophisticated research literature provides both theoretical and empirical support for the notion that larger districts are more successful than smaller ones at influencing school board elections (see, for example, Hoyt 1999; Moe 2005; Rose and Sonstelie 2010).

Teacher Unions and School Performance: Summing Up

We are still trying to better understand the impact of teacher unions on important educational outcomes. This line of research is complicated by the wide variety of topics addressed in different ways by teachers' collective bargaining agreements (CBAs) within and across states. These topics include not just teacher compensation, evaluations, class sizes, and school schedules, but also professional development, noninstructional duties, student discipline, transfer and vacancy policies, teacher and school safety, leaves of absence, and more. Empirical studies of the effects of CBAs on educational outcomes, however rigorous, will be hard-pressed to account for the great diversity among these agreements. In the meantime, educators, policymakers, and parents alike should understand that classroom teaching is difficult work, and those who do it need job protections. And the more challenging the school and district prove to be for achieving effective teaching, the more such protections are needed.

Janus v. AFSCME, Council 31

On June 27, 2018, a divided U.S. Supreme Court dealt a major blow to the nation's public employee unions. In *Janus v. AFSCME, Council 31*, the court's conservative majority resulted in a five-to-four ruling that unions cannot collect fees from nonmembers to defray the costs of negotiating and enforcing collective bargaining agreements. These "agency" or "fair share" fees for nonpolitical activities usually constitute about 80 percent of the full membership cost. The majority opinion by Justice Samuel Alito held that "the First Amendment is violated when money is taken from nonconsenting employees for a public-sector union." With this ruling, which overturned a 41-year-old precedent—that being the court's 1977 decision in *Abood v. Detroit Board of Education*—the court nullified the laws of 23 states and the District of Columbia that permitted these fees to be collected from nonmembers covered by these agreements.[16]

What Janus might portend

This decision caps nearly two decades of antiunion policies, starting with President George W. Bush's denial of bargaining rights for federal airport screeners on the grounds that collective bargaining could compromise national security. As of this writing, 28 states have passed right-to-work laws prohibiting agency fees. Union leaders fear that elimination of these fees will reduce membership by allowing "free riding," in which the benefits of collective bargaining become available to all workers, whether they are union members or not.

To gauge the likely impact of *Janus* on union membership, we can look at the 28 states that currently ban agency fees. These states employ about 1.9 million workers represented by unions, with about 1.6 million of them paying dues. This gap represents a "free-riding" rate of just over 17 percent, substantially higher than the equivalent 6.5 percent rate found in the 22 states that allowed agency fees prior to *Janus*. So while the proportion of nonmembers required to pay agency fees is much smaller than the number of dues-paying union members (the

American Federation of Teachers reports having about 94,000 agency payers versus nearly 1.6 million dues payers), the economic incentive for free riding will undoubtedly erode union membership, as antiunion groups aggressively lobby workers to stop paying dues.

This decision comes, however, at a time when 61 percent of Americans approve of labor unions, the highest rating in Gallup polls since 2003. And while organized labor has seen a 70-year decline in union membership, with union members now comprising less than 11 percent of the nation's workforce (down from 35 percent during World War II), and the percentage of public school teachers who are organized has fallen steadily for the past two decades, union membership in the public sector as a whole has remained steady for decades at a little more than one-third of the workforce. More recently, public support for teachers and their unions was strikingly evident in the #RedForEd movement, which began in February 2018 with a statewide teacher walkout in West Virginia. That helped ignite walkouts in Oklahoma and Arizona, as well as in Los Angeles, where the union *added* membership during its post-*Janus* strike vote of January 2019. (The #RedForEd movement, as it came to be called, most likely for a Facebook group with the name "Wear Red for Public Ed," which formed in Florida in 2011, is examined in more detail in Chapter 7.)

Nevertheless, the threat posed by the *Janus* decision is substantial. The decision not only frees nonmembers from agency fees, but dues-paying members may now "ride free" as well, saving the full cost of membership as opposed to the roughly 20 percent associated with political activities, while continuing to enjoy the benefits of representation. In particular, while most members may choose to stay in the union, new membership may suffer. Union leaders, faced with this new and substantial threat to their membership, must strengthen their ties to workers and members by reinforcing their message of economic justice, opportunity, and security, and by delivering on that message.

Well before *Janus* and its judicial precursors, many reformers expressed hope that new entrants into the profession would mute its strong union identification. And there has been some movement in this direction. In a 2012 survey of 10,000 U.S. teachers, respondents said tenure should be granted after 5.4 years on the job, much increased from the then current national average of 3.1 years. Other polls show that nearly half of teachers under 35 support charter schools, in which teachers and staff are generally not unionized. In contrast, less than a third of teachers over 50 favor charter schools. Nevertheless, educators remain committed to their unions, with more than 80 percent supporting collective bargaining and the majority claiming the right to strike.[17] Higher teacher salaries, more transparent pay scales, and greater control over working conditions may succeed in attracting more talented and qualified candidates to the classroom. And teachers having an increased voice would likely reduce teacher turnover, which disrupts student learning and raises school operating costs.

Shanker's Legacy: Reform or Intransigence?

Between 1960 and 1980, school districts across the United States endured more than 1,000 teacher strikes. By the mid-1970s, public school teaching had become the most unionized profession in America, with 90 percent of teachers claiming membership in either the AFT or the NEA, and more than 70 percent working in districts whose unions had secured collective bargaining rights.

In 1964, Al Shanker was elected president of the United Federation of Teachers (UFT) in New York City, the first major teachers' union to gain collective bargaining rights. By leading a series of illegal strikes (and being jailed twice for doing so), Shanker succeeded in raising teachers' pay, improving their working conditions through such reforms as smaller classes and more support staff (e.g., reading specialists, social workers, etc.), and generally empowering teachers in school reform debates. In 1974, Shanker was elected president of the national AFT, and in that visible position he came to be widely viewed as a progressive, even visionary, labor leader.[18] Shanker's progressive ideas influenced union leadership well beyond his presidential tenure at the AFT. For example, in a remarkable 1997 speech at the National Press Club in Washington, D.C., Bob Chase, president of the rival (and much larger) NEA, conceded that "in some instances, we have used our power to block uncomfortable changes, to protect the narrow interests of our members, and not advance the interests of students and schools. . . . There are indeed some bad teachers in America's schools. And it is our job to improve those teachers or—that failing—*to get them out of the classroom.* . . . We must revitalize the public schools from within or they will be dismantled from without" (emphasis added; Chase 1997, cited in Moe 2011).

In numerous writings, including a regular column in the *New York Times*, and in many speeches and interviews, Shanker called for greater teacher accountability, including tests of teachers' subject matter knowledge, differential compensation, early childhood education, and national standards for student achievement. And while not the originator of the charter school idea, he worked, albeit unsuccessfully, to extend and popularize the concept as a workable alternative to vouchers, both as a means of providing school choice and as a way to enhance the professionalism of public school teaching through autonomous ("empowered") schools led by teachers. His vision of such an accountable and autonomous teaching profession, however, remains more aspirational than real.

Notes

1. Text of Governor Walker's budget address, State of Wisconsin, Department of Administration, March 1, 2011.
2. National Center for Education Statistics, Schools and Staffing Survey (SASS), https://nces.ed.gov/surveys/sass/tables/sass0708_043_t1s.asp.
3. The Bureau of Labor Statistics reports two figures for each period: 1) the proportion of teachers who are members of a union and 2) the proportion who are either union members or those who report no union affiliation but whose jobs are covered by a union contract.
4. This federal law governs private-sector interstate commerce. All states have laws governing private-sector labor relations in firms not subject to the National Labor Relations Act (NLRA). Significantly, as there is no federal law covering public-sector employment, states have passed laws regulating collective bargaining by state and local government employees.
5. Since 1983, the data on union membership are collected as part of the Current Population Survey (CPS), a monthly sample survey of about 60,000 eligible households that gathers information on employment and unemployment among the nation's civilian population aged 16 and over.
6. For an eloquent critique of this ideology, see James Kwak (2017), pp. 74–75.
7. Bivens and Mishel (2015), p. 4. The authors measure worker compensation as real hourly compensation of production for nonsupervisory workers, who comprise 80 percent of the workforce.
8. Temin's (2017) model of a "dual economy" in the U.S. draws from a theory of economic development conceived by W. Arthur Lewis, a professor at the University of Manchester and the only person of African descent to be awarded a Nobel Prize in economics.

9. For a detailed account of this history, see Moe (2011).
10. This section draws upon Goldstein (2014).
11. As a result of his aggressive leadership in the Ocean Hill–Brownsville teacher strike, UFT president Shanker was "immortalized" in Woody Allen's 1973 movie *Sleeper*, in which the protagonist is cryogenically unfrozen 200 years in the future and learns that civilization had been destroyed because "a man by the name of Al Shanker got hold of a nuclear warhead."
12. This summary of the litigation in North Carolina and Colorado follows Dunn (2017).
13. Supreme Court Case No. 15SC1062, published March 12, 2018.
14. See, for example, Johnson (2015) and Century Foundation (2019).
15. The four states are Indiana, Idaho, Tennessee, and Wisconsin.
16. Antiunion forces had been working to overturn agency fees for decades. More recently, plaintiffs mounted unsuccessful efforts to overturn *Abood* in 2012, 2014, and 2016. Following the last of these failed attempts, when the court deadlocked four to four, letting stand a lower-court ruling allowing unions to continue collecting the fees, plaintiffs' attorneys, noting that the deadlock was not unexpected following the passing of Justice Antonin Scalia, declared their intention to ask the court for a rehearing, to be conducted after the court vacancy was filled. The rehearing was denied, but *Janus* provided union foes with a new opportunity to overturn *Abood* following the confirmation of Justice Neil Gorsuch to the court.
17. American Teachers on the Teaching Profession (poll from Scholastic and the Bill and Melinda Gates Foundation, 2012), and Moe (2011), pp. 404–405, cited in Goldstein (2014), p. 220.
18. For the definitive, and sympathetic, biography, see Kahlenberg (2007). For a brief but critical account of his leadership, see Moe (2011), especially pp. 241–274.

4

Charter School Teachers

Empowered or Expendable?

*Capitalism is the extraordinary belief that the nastiest of men, for
the nastiest of reasons, will somehow work for the benefit of us all.*

—John Maynard Keynes

On March 15, 2017, Kentucky became the forty-third state to pass
legislation for charter schools. While the Bluegrass State was late to
the charter school movement, its new law is expansive, placing no limit
on the number of schools and permitting charter operators to outsource
school management to for-profit firms. Since passage of Kentucky's
law, Alabama and West Virginia have also joined the charter ranks.[1] In
its nearly three decades of existence, the charter school movement has
had a marked influence on the profession of public school teaching in
the United States, and one quite unlike the impact envisioned by the
movement's founders and early advocates.

The term "charter school" was coined by Ray Budde, a retired
professor of educational administration at the University of Massachusetts, in a 1974 conference paper he titled "Education by Charter."
Budde, who had also been a classroom teacher and then a junior high
principal, envisioned these new public schools as teacher-run laboratories for instructional innovations, created with permission from the
local school district board (Kolderie 2005; Vergari 2007). This new
concept of a public school was not popularized, however, until more
than a decade later, when education reformer and AFT President Albert
Shanker expanded on the charter concept in a heralded March 31, 1988,
address to the National Press Club in Washington, D.C. Consistent with
Budde's vision, Shanker's charter schools would be a new type of public school: small, autonomous, innovative, and teacher-led, and would
be open to all district residents.

In his address to the National Press Club, Shanker introduced to the
public a new type of school he later referred to as "charter schools."
Proposals for these new public schools, each designed by a small group

of 6 to 12 teachers in consultation with parents, would be evaluated and approved or rejected by panels that included teacher union representatives and school board members. Charters would be innovative schools of choice and would be given ample time to prove themselves—between 5 and 10 years. Shorter time periods, Shanker argued, would simply encourage "play it safe" schools unlikely to produce breakthroughs in curriculum or pedagogy. And in order to make these new schools successful centers of educational innovation, Shanker called for two critical requirements: 1) that the schools provide their teachers with a strong voice, and 2) that the schools educate a racially and economically diverse student body.

The strong teacher voice would come from union membership. Not only would union representatives sit on charter school authorizing boards, but charter school teachers would be represented by unions and charter school proposals would include "a plan for faculty decision making" (Shanker 1988). Shanker argued that, while particular work rules like class size limits or individual teaching schedules could be relaxed to accommodate educational practices (e.g., team teaching, teaching mentoring initiatives, and so forth), basic teacher protections such as tenure and due process would remain in place. Such protections, Shanker maintained, were essential for classroom teachers' willingness to take risks associated with educational innovations. Teachers would work in teams, with the more accomplished faculty members assisting those who struggled and recommending the termination of those who failed to improve (Kahlenberg 2007).

Conservatives were generally not supportive of Shanker's vision of innovative, teacher-led public schools. For example, Chester Finn, then assistant secretary of education in the Reagan administration, attacked the proposal for, as he said, failing to recognize that we already know what works in education (Kahlenberg 2007, p. 312). Some influential and progressive educators and policymakers, however, were more receptive. In October 1988, Shanker spoke at the Minneapolis Foundation's Itasca Seminar about the charter school idea. In attendance was Democratic-Farmer-Labor state senator Ember Reichgott (later Reichgott Junge), a member of the Education Committee. Intrigued by Shanker's idea to create new and innovative schools led by teachers, Senator Junge went on to draft the nation's first charter school statute. She recalls: "For me, chartering was all about empowering teachers—giving them the authority to take leadership as professionals by spearheading and forming new chartered schools. I felt it was an option for entrepreneurial teachers to break away from the system—the status quo—and try something new" (Junge 2012, p. 113; cited in Kahlenberg and Potter 2014).

Minnesota's nascent charter school movement received another key endorsement in November 1988 when the Citizens League, a community policy organization, published *Charter Schools = Choices for Educators + Quality for All Students*, an influential report that called for empowered teachers and "cooperative management of schools." The report also envisioned these new schools enrolling students of all races and achievement levels: "The committee's vision for chartered public schools is that they must, like any public school, serve all children" (Citizens League 1988, p. 14).

In 1990, the idea of charter schools gained further currency among education reformers as an alternative to (or firewall against) vouchers, after the legislature in neighboring Wisconsin passed the nation's first private-school voucher law. Introduced by black Democratic legislator Polly Williams, the legislation provided public support for low-income Milwaukee students to attend private and parochial schools. Charter supporters, most notably Ted Kolderie, former director of the Citizens League and member of the committee that authored that group's heralded report, boosted charters as a way to strengthen public schools, not undermine them, as vouchers would. This argument has come to resonate with much of the public. In contrast to the general unpopularity of vouchers, the public's view of charter schools has been largely favorable, with support growing over time. A 2014 PDK/Gallup Poll found that fully 70 percent of respondents favored the idea of charter schools, twice the proportion from a 2002 survey. At the same time, however, much of the public remained confused about core aspects of charters, with 48 percent believing that charter schools are free to teach religion, 57 percent believing that charter schools can charge tuition, 68 percent believing that charter schools can select students on the basis of ability, and only 50 percent understanding that charter schools are public schools (Epple, Romano, and Zimmer 2015).

Kahlenberg and Potter (2014) characterize the charter vision of Shanker and the Minnesota progressives in terms of three foundational principles:

1) Charter schools should be free to experiment with new approaches to teaching and learning, including curriculum, pedagogy, school and classroom organization, and personnel matters.

2) Charter schools should provide teachers with a level of responsibility and discretion in school matters that clearly exceeds levels accorded teachers in traditional public schools.

3) Charters should be schools of choice, not tied to a particular neighborhood or other geographic locality. In this way, children of different races, ethnicities, and socioeconomic backgrounds would learn together and benefit from such student diversity.

Shanker's embrace of parental choice, along with such traditionally antilabor programs as merit pay and teacher peer review, was surprising for a union leader and marked him in the eyes of some as a visionary labor leader. The primacy of teacher unions in this vision, however, has not been overlooked by union critics. For example, Moe (2011) characterizes Shanker's conception as something of a Trojan horse:

> Shanker's vision of freeing schools and teachers to be innovative, however, was really a vision of freeing them from *district* control. They were *not* to be freed from union control. Quite the contrary, Shanker's charter schools would be run by teachers, who in turn would be unionized and covered by collective bargaining contracts, making the schools subject to the power and control of local unions. By offering his dramatic proposal for charter schools, then, Shanker was "embracing" choice and innovation—but in a distinctive, highly selective way that reflected his interests as a union president. (Moe 2011, p. 331; emphasis in original)

Thus, while this small group of education policy leaders may have shared consensus on these broad principles, the first-in-the-nation charter school law that emerged from the Minnesota legislature diverged from Shanker's fundamental conception of the teaching profession. Specifically, the new law required neither universal teacher certification requirements nor collective bargaining rights for teachers in the charter schools. For these reasons, the Minnesota Federation of Teachers opposed the legislation (Junge 2012, cited in Kahlenberg and Potter 2014). Ironically, as the charter school debate spread across the states, many Republican school reformers who initially viewed the charter concept as a union power play and an attempt to sidestep state school rules came to look upon charter laws as something quite different: an opportunity to open nonunion public schools and even allow private, for-profit management companies to run public schools. Indeed, just one year after the first charter school opened in Minnesota in 1992, Shanker was calling charter schools an antiunion "gimmick" and expressing concern that "hucksters" would use the charter movement to divert public funding away from public school classrooms and toward private profit (Kahlenberg 2007, pp. 308–316).

Since Shanker's 1988 address, the U.S. charter school movement has grown dramatically, but in a direction entirely contrary to the founders' vision. Instead of autonomous, local, teacher-led laboratories of instructional innovation, charter schools have been transformed by many state legislatures into vehicles for privatizing public education, where teachers are employees of for-profit education management companies (EMOs). In general, the teachers are poorly compensated, enjoy little autonomy, and are expected to deliver scripted curriculum within programs designed largely around preparation for standardized testing in reading and math. By 2015, EMOs operated an estimated 40 percent of all charter schools in the U.S. and accounted for about 45 percent of all charter school students, enrolling more than 1.2 million students (Baker and Miron 2015).

Such has been the stunning reversal of Shanker's charter concept as a means of empowering public school teachers. In state after state, critics of teacher unions, who view those organizations as defenders of unjustifiable privileges like tenure and their members as incompetents insufficiently committed to closing race- and class-based gaps in student achievement, have refused to provide automatic collective bargaining rights to charter school teachers, in contrast to their traditional public school counterparts. At the time of this writing, a mere 5 of the 43 states with charter school statutes require charter school teachers to be covered by district collective bargaining agreements (National Alliance for Public Charter Schools 2014, cited in Kahlenberg and Potter 2014). In contrast, fully 60 percent of public school districts have an agreement with a union, and more than three-quarters of public school teachers nationwide are union members (National Center for Education Statistics 2012, cited in Kahlenberg and Potter 2014).

This evolution of the charter school movement from a union-friendly model of teacher-led, innovative schools to nonunion schools generally run by private management companies, often for profit, and staffed with relatively inexperienced teachers, many of whom have entered the profession in nontraditional ways, has impacted teacher labor markets dramatically, particularly in urban areas. More specifically, the movement has divided the public school teaching profession into two market sectors, one still highly unionized and subject to collective bargaining, and a second much smaller but growing sector, almost completely nonunionized at the time of this writing. And while the main focus of charter school effects on U.S. public education has been on student achievement (for a brief summary of that literature, see Box 4.1, "Are Charter Schools More Effective than Traditional Public Schools?"), the movement's impact on the rights of teachers and other workers has been substantial, if often overlooked.

CHARTER SCHOOLS AND THE SCHOOL WORKPLACE TRANSFORMATION

As the U.S. charter school movement has proceeded, marked by the growing presence of both for-profit and nonprofit "educational management companies" (EMOs), it has acquired some characteristics of the contemporary private workplace, not only in the absence of unions but more generally in the way work is organized and the way the relationship between employer and worker is defined. In his notable 2014 book *The Fissured Workplace*, economist David Weil observes that, in the private sector, employment is no longer a clear relationship between a well-defined employer and a worker. The basic terms of employment—hiring, evaluation, pay, supervision, training—now involve multiple organizations. A lead business, usually one enjoying a national or international reputation or "brand," no longer employs legions of workers to supply goods or services. Rather, the central enterprise actively sheds workers and transfers this work to a complicated network of smaller business units. These lower-level firms operate in more highly competitive markets than those of the lead companies that shift jobs to them.

Box 4.1 Are Charter Schools More Effective than Traditional Public Schools?

Although charter schools have been operating in the U.S. for more than 25 years, their impact on student achievement remains a highly contentious issue among researchers and educators nationwide. A central question in this debate is whether charter schools are more effective than traditional public schools in improving student achievement. A rapidly growing research literature has addressed the educational effects of charter schools. A full discussion of these findings and the issues involved in this line of research is beyond the scope of this book. This section summarizes the challenges facing researchers of this topic and their findings to date.

Methodological issues. The biggest challenge facing researchers is addressing the problem of "selection bias." The problem arises from the self-selection of charter school students. That is, students are not randomly assigned to charter schools; they choose to attend. Consequently, any observed differences in achievement levels or growth between students in charter and traditional public schools may not be attributable to differences in school quality. Rather, they may result from different unobserved characteristics of students. Failure to account for these unobserved characteristics could lead to invalid conclusions about the relative quality of charter and traditional public schools.

The most effective way to avoid selection bias is to conduct an experiment: randomly assign students to charter and traditional public schools from a common pool. Because of random assignment, any differences in average student performance across the two student groups can be attributed to differences between the two groups of schools. Such an experiment, however, requiring as it would either voluntary or coerced participation, has never been conducted; nor is one likely, given current laws and norms of public education emphasizing access and choice.

In lieu of a pure randomized experiment, researchers have used alternative approaches to address the problem of selection bias. Two such methods are *fixed-effects modeling* and a matching strategy known as *virtual control records* (VCR). The fixed-effects approach assumes that

Box 4.1 (continued)

there are no time-varying unobserved changes for students that would lead to differences in student achievement over time. A second limitation of fixed effects is that it relies on students switching between charter and traditional public schools. That is, the fixed-effects approach estimates charter school effectiveness by comparing the performance of students while attending charter schools with their performance while attending a traditional school. As such, the findings do not generalize to students who attend only charter schools throughout their school careers.

The VCR approach, employed in a set of notable studies by the Center for Research on Education Outcomes (CREDO) at Stanford University, is a matching procedure where a "virtual" match for each charter student is found in a traditional public school. The student matching is based on demographic characteristics, grade in school, eligibility for support services such as free or reduced lunch, special education, or English language learner programs, and a baseline test score. Compared to the fixed-effect approach, the VCR method has the advantage of including a large student sample, not just students moving between charter and traditional public schools. VCR includes all students who have a baseline achievement test score in a charter school. As such, the analysis cannot assess the total accumulated charter school impact for students who attend a charter school prior to their baseline assessment.

Achievement effects. Several fixed-effect studies represent the earliest and most notable explorations of charter school effects on student achievement (Bifulco and Ladd 2006; Booker et al. 2007; Hanushek et al. 2007; Imberman 2011; Zimmer et al. 2003). These studies, which examined schools in various geographic locations, generally found no charter school effects on student achievement or small effects in either direction. However, the years of charter school operation and students' duration of charter school attendance *were* found to matter. A number of studies have found that student achievement effects for charter schools are often negative in their early years but improve as the schools mature (Bifulco and Ladd 2006; Booker et al. 2007; Hanushek et al. 2007; Ni and Rorrer 2012; Sass 2006; Zimmer et al. 2012). More

Box 4.1 (continued)

recently, several fixed-effect studies have found positive charter school effects (Curto and Fryer 2011; Hoxby, Murarka, and Kang 2009; Tuttle et al. 2013), while a study of middle schools found no general charter effects, although it did find positive effects for urban charter middle schools (Gleason et al. 2010).

Two widely reported studies by CREDO applied the VCR matching procedure to exceptionally large, longitudinal data sets involving multiple states (CREDO 2009, 2013). These studies reported the proportion of charter schools that outperformed their locally matched traditional school district. The 2009 study, which included 15 states and the District of Columbia, found that 17 percent of charter schools outperformed their TPS counterparts in math, while 31 percent of charters underperformed their TPS matches. Charter schools fared better in the broader 2013 study, covering 25 states plus the District of Columbia and New York City. Here, 29 percent of charters outperformed their TPS counterparts in math, while only 19 percent underperformed their TPS matches.

Epple, Romano, and Zimmer (2015) offer an essentially neutral interpretation of these comprehensive CREDO studies:

> While this suggests some improvement between the timeframes of the studies, the 2013 study's overall national estimate of charter schools suggests little average impact with no statistically significant difference in math and a slight positive effect in reading of 0.01 of standard deviation. In general, these results have been interpreted in two ways. The more optimistic view is that overall performance of charter schools is improving over time. The more negative view is that many students' performance in many charter schools [is] still lagging behind students in TPSs and, overall, the results across the two studies do not show a pattern of systematic improvement. (p. 27)

Achievement in virtual charter schools. As noted in Chapter I, student achievement in fully online charters ("cyber schools") has generally been abysmal. A 2015 literature review published by the National Association of Charter School Authorizers that looked at proficiency, growth, performance on state accountability measures, and graduation

> **Box 4.1 (continued)**
>
> and dropout rates found cyber school performance "lackluster" and failed to identify any virtual school consistently producing strong academic results (National Association of Charter School Authorizers and Public Impact 2015, p. 17). A 2015 CREDO study of 17 states and the District of Columbia using the VCR matching procedure described above concluded that "online charter students have much weaker growth overall" than their traditional school counterparts, with deficits of -0.25 standard deviations in math and -0.10 standard deviations in reading (Woodworth et al. 2015). The generally poor performance of online charters is confirmed by Zimmer et al. (2019) in an up-to-date survey of charter school research.

As those central enterprises have invested in building their brands and customer base, they have shed their role as direct employer of the people who supply their goods and services. And as Weil (2014) demonstrates with numerous examples, this fissuring generates downward pressure on wages and benefits, blurs lines of responsibility for work conditions, and increases the likelihood that basic labor standards will be violated. Employers competing for contracts with lead businesses face significant pressures on wages and conditions they can offer their workers, particularly in industries where labor supply is elastic, skill requirements are relatively low, and labor costs account for a significant share of total costs.

These labor markets are characterized by falling real wages, declining benefits, reduced employment security, and diminished opportunity to complain about, much less improve, the work environment. Employers in these markets replace jobs that were once full time and permanent with a different type of employment contract, one with reduced commitment to employee longevity or even stable hours. Most of the cases Weil examines involve the impact of fissured workplaces on workers in low-wage occupations and industries. But the author also finds that fissuring alters jobs and restructures companies for highly skilled and educated workers, including those in law, journalism, and finance (Weil 2014).

Evidence reveals that fissuring not only tends to increase the profitability of lead companies and degrade compensation and working conditions for employees at lower-level firms, but also contributes to the widely recognized redistribution of wealth from labor to capital (see, for example, Piketty 2014). Real wages for median workers in the U.S. (those at the 50th percentile of the wage distribution) grew by only 0.5 percent between 2000 and 2012. Median hourly compensation (wages plus benefits) grew by only 4 percent. Yet productivity (measured as output of goods and services per hour worked) rose by 23 percent over this same period (Weil 2014, p. 16). (The divergence between worker productivity and real wages is depicted in Figure 3.2.)

While this model of fissured, or contingent, employment is essentially a private-sector phenomenon, we do see growing evidence of its pursuit and presence in public education by charter school entrepreneurs and their allies in state legislatures (e.g., Baker 2016b; Baker and Miron 2015). Diane Ravitch, in her acclaimed 2013 book *Reign of Error*, characterizes the growth of the charter sector in terms remarkably similar to those used by Weil to describe the fissuring phenomenon of the private sector:

> The rapid proliferation of charter legislation and the growth of the charter sector produced a new phenomenon in American education: national charter school chains. These are described either as educational management organizations (EMOs) or as charter management organizations (CMOs). The terms are used interchangeably. The development of chain schools is akin to the development of retail chain stores, like Walmart or Target or McDonald's, which provide a central management structure and an economy of scale in some aspects of the operation. The CMO or EMO provides a "brand" and a certain uniformity of administration, curriculum, and policies, as well as financial oversight, back-office operations, human resources, marketing, and public relations. (Ravitch 2013, p. 165)

By 2012, there were about 300 different EMOs or CMOs (hereafter referred to as *EMOs* or *private management organizations*). About 36 percent of all charter schools in the U.S. were part of an EMO. Collectively, these charter chain schools enrolled more than 900,000 students, about 44 percent of the total charter school enrollment nationwide (Miron and Gulosino 2013). These private management organizations consist of both for-profit and nonprofit companies, with for-profit EMOs operating in 35 states and nonprofits in 29. Some of them work with charter schools, some with traditional district schools, and some with both. For-profit EMOs are businesses that seek to return a profit to the company owners or shareholders, while many of the nonprofits pursue educational and social objectives or seek to expand the charter school movement. Historically, only a small fraction of EMOs have been nonprofits, but Miron and Gulosino say their share has grown rapidly in recent years.

The distinction between for-profit and nonprofit EMOs matters little, however, in terms of their capacity to lessen government control of public schools, shift assets from the public to the private sector, and curb teacher and other employee compensation and job protections. All EMOs, both for-profit and nonprofit, contract with "vendors"—private companies that provide for a fee specific services such as accounting, payroll and benefits administration, transportation, financial and legal advice, personnel recruitment, professional development, substitute teachers, and special education (Miron and Gulosino 2013). Just as the fissuring phenomenon has blurred the relationship between employer and employee in the private sector, distancing the worker from the lead enterprises and rendering her employment less well compensated and less secure, so too has the charter school movement and associated rise of the EMO served to weaken the relationship between the public school teacher and the public, with parallel adverse consequences for teacher compensation and job security. Charter school legislation adopted in state after state is designed to distance teachers and other workers in the school from the public sector and its traditional worker protections, while at the same time preserving the school's access to public funds.

This privatization agenda, while enacted by individual state legislatures, has been coordinated nationally across the states by the American Legislative Exchange Council (ALEC), an Arlington, Virginia, based organization committed to advancing conservative "free market" principles and antilabor efforts in state legislatures across the United States. Founded in 1973 with funding from conservative philanthropist Richard Mellon Scaife and businessmen Charles and David Koch and now consisting of some 2,000 state legislators and business leaders, ALEC disseminates model legislation promoting business interests and privatization.[2] Established as a tax-exempt 501(c)(3) "educational" organization but referred to derisively by critics as a corporate "bill mill," ALEC has drafted model charter school legislation. Dubbed the Next Generation Charter Schools Act, the model statute emphasizes that charter schools are public schools for purposes of public funding but controllable by private boards, managed by private companies, and exempt from many rules and regulations that apply to traditional public schools, including worker protections such as due process and the ability to organize.

This conception of public K–12 education as a public-private hybrid, with public funding and private employees, has been challenged before courts and regulatory tribunals. In 2010, the Ninth Circuit Court of Appeals ruled that a charter school operator in Arizona was a private, nonprofit corporation, not an agency of the state, when a teacher who was discharged sued the school. While Arizona law defines charters as public schools, the federal court rejected the plaintiff's claim that charters are state actors.[3] As legal scholars and public school advocates have noted, this decision and others that have held that charter schools are not government agencies limit public oversight of these schools and circumscribe the rights and prerogatives of students and teachers.[4] Such decisions have been issued by administrative agencies as well as courts.

The Chicago Mathematics and Science Charter School Inc.

In 2011, two-thirds of the teachers at the Chicago Math and Science Academy (CMSA) sought to form a union. The charter operator fought the action by claiming that the school was not subject to state law because it was a "private entity." In 2012, the National Labor Relations Board (NLRB) agreed that the charter school was not a public agency but a private, nonprofit corporation whose board is selected not by government but by the board itself. In ruling that the charter school is not a public entity, the majority opinion had to contend with the plain language of the Illinois Charter School Law, which states in part,

> In authorizing charter schools, it is the intent of the General Assembly to create a legitimate avenue for parents, teachers, and community members to take responsible risks and create new, innovative, and more flexible ways of educating children *within the public school system*. The General Assembly seeks to create opportunities *within the public school system of Illinois* for development of innovative and accountable teaching techniques. (emphasis added; Illinois General Assembly 2022, p. 1)

The statute goes on to state that a charter school must be sponsored and authorized by a local public school board and certified by the Illinois State Board of Education. Furthermore, CMSA's charter agreement may be revoked by the Board of Chicago Public Schools if its terms, including the student accountability plan and achievement goals and standards of fiscal management, are not met. (CMSA received about 80 percent of its operating revenue from Chicago Public Schools, with the remainder coming from state and federal sources.) CMSA was also required to contribute to the Chicago Teachers' Pension Fund on behalf of its teachers.

Nevertheless, despite these and other statutory provisions that bind Illinois charter schools to the public school system generally and to Chicago Public Schools particularly, the NLRB, by majority vote, overturned the decision of the acting regional director and ruled that charter schools in Illinois are private entities. This majority opinion rested upon two findings: first, that "[CMSA] was created by private individuals, and not by a government entity, special legislative act, or public official" (p. 6); second, that "we find it dispositive that none of CMSA's governing board members are appointed by or subject to removal by any public official. No further inquiry is required" (p. 8). Consequently, as private entities operating under contract to the government, Illinois charter schools, although publicly funded, are subject to federal laws governing the private sector.[5]

Public School Profiteers: The Case of Michigan

Among the states, Michigan stands out as an anomaly, as fully 79 percent of its charter schools are operated by for-profit EMOs and another 10 percent are operated by nonprofits. (The state with the next highest percentages of charter schools operated by for-profit EMOs is Missouri with 37 percent, followed by Florida with 34 percent.) Of the 35 states with for-profit EMOs operating charter or traditional district public schools (or both), Michigan has the largest number, with a total of 33 EMOs operating one or more public schools, mostly charters. Arizona ranks second with 27 for-profit EMOs, while Ohio (4) and Pennsylvania (4) are the only remaining states with more than two for-profit EMOs operating within their borders (Miron and Gulosino 2013, p. 18). Michigan accounts for nearly 20 percent (90,263 students) of all students in for-profit EMO-operated schools in the U.S. Florida is second with 75,407 students, and Ohio is third with 63,225. No other state had more than 20,565, and only nine exceeded 7,000 (p. 19).

In Michigan, where charter schools enrolled nearly 10 percent of all public elementary and secondary school students in 2014–2015, charter-friendly Republican lawmakers sought to create a new teaching certificate that would recast public school teaching in much the same mold as the contingent private-sector workers profiled by Weil (2014, p. 5). Called "adjunct instructor," this new teacher classification would "provide instruction to pupils on an hourly, daily, or other periodic basis."[6] The bill goes on to describe a condition of worker vulnerability remarkably consistent with Weil's depiction of the fissured workplace. Under the proposed legislation, the new category of public school teacher "shall be a part-time contractor serving at the public school and shall not be an employee of the public school. An adjunct instructor is not eligible for continuing service status or to participate in the retirement system. . . . Service as an adjunct instructor is not creditable for purposes of obtaining a teaching certificate under this act."[7] This bill died in committee when Republican lawmakers succeeded in passing a more far-reaching "right to work" law and then adjourned in December 2012. It was a transparent attempt to reduce labor costs in Michigan public schools by permitting school leaders, including executives of Michigan's many for-profit EMOs, to shed direct employees and shift their labor-intensive instructional work to less costly and more expendable contractors. This was done in a fashion closely paralleling the fissuring phenomenon observed in the private sector. In effect, the bill would have relegated public school teachers to what has become known as the "gig economy," where workers are technically self-employed, responsible for their own expenses and tax witholdings, and lack access to employer-subsidized health care, union protections, and federal statutory antidiscrimination protections.

A core objective of the fissuring strategy in the private sector and the privatization movement in the public sector is to lower labor costs. Central to this strategy is the elimination of unions, which raise wages, increase benefits, reduce management authority to unilaterally dismiss workers, and increase scrutiny of compliance with workplace regulations.[8] Much of this is accomplished indirectly. The National Labor Relations Act precludes employers from closing workplaces solely because of the presence of unions, or from threatening to do so if a union is elected, although case law reveals this to be a gray area of labor law (Weil 2014). However, the fissuring process can provide companies with more subtle ways to shift away from a highly unionized workforce or move work to forms of employment (e.g., contractors or franchises) that are both legally and strategically difficult for unions to organize (Weil 2014).

Who Teaches in Charter Schools

Charter school teachers differ from traditional public school (TPS) teachers in a number of important ways. These differences are summarized in Table 4.1.

All data are taken from the 2011–2012 Schools and Staffing Survey, a nationally representative sample drawn by the National Center for

Table 4.1 Teacher Characteristics in Traditional and Charter Public Schools, 2011–2012

	Traditional	Charter
Percent white, non-Hispanic	82.3	69.9
Percent black, non-Hispanic	6.6	11.8[a]
Percent Hispanic	7.6	13.1
Percent male	23.6	25.1
Average age	42.6	37.4
Percent younger than 30	14.7	31.0
Average teaching experience (years)	14.0	8.7
Average years at current school	8.1	3.6
Percent less than 4 years' teaching experience	10.7	26.3
Percent highest degree = bachelor's	39.4	52.3
Percent regular full-time	92.8	91.0
Required hours (typical week)	30.7	32.0
Total hours per week	52.2	53.5
Average school year earnings	$55,400	$46,300
Percent teachers receiving "merit pay" for student performance/average amount	4.0/$1,400	15.8/$1,300

[a] Coefficient of variation between 30 and 50 percent; interpret with caution.
SOURCE: All values from Goldring, Gray, and Bitterman (2013). Adapted from Epple, Romano, and Zimmer (2015), Table 4, p. 59.

Education Statistics, and are reported in Epple, Romano, and Zimmer (2015).

Minority teachers make up a substantially larger proportion of teachers in charter schools than in traditional schools. Charter school teachers are also much younger and less experienced than their TPS counterparts: the average tenure of teachers in charter schools is just 3.6 years, as compared to 8.1 years for TPS teachers. Charter school teachers have less formal, academic training, with 52.3 percent having no credentials beyond a bachelor's degree, while 56.8 percent of TPS teachers hold an advanced degree. Charter school teachers earn substantially less than TPS teachers, and a higher (though still small) proportion of their earnings are linked to student performance.

While states require certification of all TPS teachers, charter school teachers are often not certified or teach out of their area of certification. In 2011, of the then 41 states that maintained charter school programs, only 23 of them held charter school teachers to the same certification requirements as TPS teachers. And of the latter group, 14 did not require that all charter teachers be certified, with the minimum percentage ranging from 30 to 90 (Exstrom 2012).[9] These findings are generally consistent with Addonizio, Kearney, and Gawlik (2015), who found that only 57 percent of charter school teachers in Michigan were certified in 2005–2006, as compared with 66 percent for TPS teachers. The Michigan study also found that the percentage of teachers with substitute teacher permits was substantially higher in charter schools (47.22) than in traditional public schools (10.40).

College selectivity

Findings on the selectivity of colleges attended by charter school teachers and TPS teachers are mixed. Addonizio, Kearney, and Gawlik (2015) found that charter school teachers in the tricounty Detroit metropolitan region were more likely, on average, to have graduated from a competitive college, as defined in *Barron's Profile of American Colleges* (Barron's Educational Series 1998). Baker and Dickerson (2006), analyzing 1999 SASS data from 18 states and the District of Columbia, find that 12.1 percent of charter teachers graduated from the top two selectivity groups, as compared with 8.1 percent in traditional public schools. In contrast, Stuit and Smith (2009), examining a larger geographic area, find virtually no difference between the two groups, while Cannata and Penaloza (2012), in a study of eight states, find that charter school teachers attend somewhat less competitive colleges than their TPS counterparts.

Teacher Turnover in Charter Schools

Much published research has confirmed that turnover rates—both school changes (mobility) and exits from the profession (attrition)— are significantly higher in charter schools than in traditional public schools (Addonizio, Kearney, and Gawlik 2015; Miron and Applegate 2007; Smith and Ingersoll 2004). Certainly, teacher turnover is not an unqualified impediment to educational achievement. The exit of ineffective teachers and their replacement by more skilled educators clearly benefits students and teachers alike. Nevertheless, high rates of teacher turnover generally indicate a school's inability to establish a stable and effective teaching faculty and signal a poor environment for teaching and learning (Clotfelter, Ladd, and Vigdor 2007; Lankford, Loeb, and Wyckoff 2002). High attrition rates are costly for schools and districts in both fiscal and educational terms. Attrition rates are highest among new teachers (Ingersoll and Smith 2003). In light of the compelling evidence that teachers generally improve dramatically during the early years of their careers (Clotfelter, Ladd, and Vigdor 2007; Goldhaber 2008), it is clear that many teachers are leaving the classroom before reaching, or even approaching, their full potential. Furthermore, high turnover rates may be disruptive to organizational attributes of schools that enhance classroom instruction, such as collegiality and curricular and pedagogical coherence (Bryk and Schneider 2002). The financial costs of teacher turnover can also be substantial. Nationally, the cost of replacing all teachers who leave the profession or transfer to new schools has been estimated at $4.9 billion annually (Alliance for Excellent Education 2005).[10]

Explaining the "turnover gap"

Using national survey data from the Schools and Staffing Survey, Stuit and Smith (2012) found that the turnover rate of charter schools was twice as high as for traditional public schools in 2003–2004. The authors postulate that this "turnover gap" is attributable to four sets of factors: 1) teacher characteristics, 2) school structure and context (principally location), 3) working conditions, and 4) school personnel policies. Each set of factors has been found to help differentiate charter schools from traditional schools. With regard to teacher characteristics, charter schools are more likely to employ uncertified teachers than their traditional public school counterparts (Addonizio, Kearney, and Gawlik 2015; Burian-Fitzgerald and Harris 2004). As for school structural and contextual factors, it is well established that teachers are more likely to leave schools in high-poverty and high-minority communities (Hanushek, Kain, and Rivkin 2004; Ingersoll 2003; Scafidi, Sjoquist, and Stinebrickner 2007). Working conditions may also contribute to the turnover gap. Survey research suggests that teachers exit schools because of heavy workloads and inadequate instructional support and resources (Malloy and Wohlstetter 2003; Miron and Applegate 2007).

Stuit and Smith (2012) estimate the marginal effects of an extensive list of explanatory variables associated with these factors, measured as the change in the probability of turnover for a one-unit change in the independent variable, holding all other regressors at their means. The baseline turnover rates for charter and TPS teachers were 24.2 percent and 11.9 percent, respectively, indicating a turnover gap of 12.3 percentage points, or more than 103 percent. They find that this gap derives more from higher attrition rates among charter teachers than from higher mobility. That is, charter teachers are leaving the profession at a much greater rate than TPS teachers.

What are the factors driving this turnover gap? Teacher characteristics collectively explain 41.9 percent of the gap. The higher proportion of inexperienced teachers in the charter schools was a major contributor, as was the higher percentage of teachers under age 30 in the charter schools. Another contributor was the difference in the proportion of charter and TPS teachers who were certified, as uncertified teachers were more likely to leave than their certified colleagues. The higher proportion of part-time teachers in the charter schools also contributed to the turnover gap.

The set of school structural and contextual variables was not a statistically significant contributor to the turnover gap. The charters enrolled significantly higher proportions of minority and low-income students and were more heavily concentrated in urban areas. They also had proportionally fewer high school teachers and slightly higher student absentee rates. None of these factors, however, contributed to the charter-TPS turnover gap, implying that the turnover gap is not attributable to differences in school locations or student characteristics after controlling for differences in teacher characteristics between the two sectors. Likewise, a set of working condition variables, including class size and workload, did not make a statistically significant contribution to the turnover gap.

While working conditions did not weigh significantly on teachers' decisions to leave their school or their profession, union membership weighed heavily. Indeed, of the 23 school and teacher characteristics included in the model, union membership was found to be the greatest contributor to the turnover gap. The lower membership rate among charter teachers (24 percent versus 82 percent for TPS teachers) explained fully 18.7 percent of the turnover gap. The authors reason that this may indicate that charter school managers, unencumbered by collectively bargained tenure and seniority rules, are more able to dismiss ineffective teachers. But they note that the finding may also indicate that teachers are voluntarily leaving charter schools and seeking unionized jobs in traditional schools for higher pay and greater job protections.

Why Teachers Leave

Stuit and Smith (2012) examine data from the 2004–2005 Teacher Follow-Up Survey to understand why charter school and TPS teachers change schools or leave the profession. The data show that involuntary exits are more common in charter schools, where leavers were more than twice as likely as TPS teachers to cite "school staffing actions" as the primary reason for attrition. Charter teachers' precise reasons for leaving, however, are unclear, as the question fails to distinguish between termination for poor performance and school closures or reductions in force. Charter teachers may be leaving the profession involuntarily because their school's charter was revoked or was not renewed by its authorizer or because the school was forced to close because of low enrollment or for another reason.

Does the substantially higher rate of involuntary exits in charter schools, where job protections generally associated with union membership are absent, enhance charter schools' ability to upgrade the average quality of their faculties by retaining high performers and helping or dismissing low performers? Available research evidence suggests not. Barrett et al. (2020) compared New Orleans public schools, a unique district in that nearly all schools are charter schools, with neighboring traditional districts from 2010 to 2015, using test score growth as a proxy for teacher performance. They found that teacher retention is more closely related to measured teacher performance in the New Orleans charter schools than in the traditional neighbors. Specifically, lower-performing teachers in New Orleans were 2.5 times more likely to leave their schools than high performers, as compared with 1.9 times in comparable neighboring districts. The researchers also found, however, that this stronger link between performance and retention in charters did not succeed in raising teacher quality faster than in their TPS counterparts. The difference in average teacher performance between New Orleans and comparison districts remained essentially unchanged between 2010 and 2015. The researchers attribute this finding to the larger share of new teachers in New Orleans, whose lower quality offsets the city's advantages in retaining higher-performing teachers.

Compensation and Working Conditions

Compensation matters. Stuit and Smith (2012) found that charter school teachers were more than twice as likely as their TSP counterparts to report that salaries and benefits were the most important reason for their departure. Given the lower compensation in the charter schools and the presence of more nontraditional teachers in the sector (uncertified, noneducation degree), charter teachers may be more inclined to leave the profession for other career options.

General dissatisfaction with the school and working conditions was more prevalent among charter teachers and accounted for more of their turnover than it did for TPS turnover. The authors report that one in five charter school teachers cited being "dissatisfied with previous school or teaching assignment" as the primary reason for leaving the profession, making it the most frequently cited of the 12 reasons listed in the survey. In contrast, only 6.7 percent of the TPS teachers listed this reason as the most important in their decision to leave classroom teaching. Similarly, fully 22.5 percent of charter teachers who changed schools (but remained in the profession) did so because they were dissatisfied with workplace conditions in their former school, compared with 7 percent of TPS teachers. Nearly half of charter school teachers cited dissatisfaction with either working conditions or administrative support as most important to their decision to switch schools.

Finally, attrition in the two teacher groups due to changes in life circumstances varied substantially. Fully 56 percent of TPS teachers who left the profession did so because of changes in residence, pregnancy/child rearing, health, retirement, or for other personal reasons, as compared with only 29.3 percent of charter school teachers, reinforcing the contention that working conditions in charter schools are generally worse for teachers than in traditional public schools.

Charter School Teachers: Empowered or Expendable?

It is clear that the U.S. charter school movement, now completing its third decade, is far from monolithic. Charter laws and rules vary widely across the states, and school policies and practices differ within them, even in the same communities. Many are run by large management chains, including for-profit companies, while others are self-managed. Some schools enforce rigid rules of student behavior and adhere to scripted curricula, while others are progressive in matters of curriculum and pedagogy, giving wide professional berth to their classroom teachers. Many charters exclude children with severe disabilities, while some are dedicated to their needs.

Nevertheless, despite these divergent goals, structures, and practices, research to date does allow for some generalizations about charter school teaching and teachers. From their comprehensive survey on charter school characteristics, Epple, Romano, and Zimmer (2015) conclude,

> On the whole, teachers in charter schools are less experienced, are less credentialed, are less white, and have fewer advanced degrees. They are paid less, their jobs are less secure, and they turn over with higher frequency. Value-added estimation of teacher effectiveness shows charter school teachers to be weaker in increasing test scores. Research explaining differences in teachers is in an early stage, and the relevance of differences in teachers to educational outcomes in charter schools is an open question. (p. 55)

This unflattering profile of the charter school teachers' plight is the product of an educational movement that is clearly at odds with the original visions of educational leaders like Ray Budde and Al Shanker from an earlier era, who called for autonomous and innovative schools where teachers took charge of decisions about curriculum, pedagogy, and even school management. And for Shanker, who was then president of the AFT, teacher union members and district leaders would collaborate closely in this reform movement, jointly evaluating all proposals for these new public schools. As we have seen, however, the charter school movement has proceeded along a very different path, one that challenges traditional districts and especially teacher unions. This path is succinctly described by Frumkin, Manno, and Edgington (2011):

> A fundamental aim of the charter school movement is to break the LEA-level monopoly on public education. Under the current system, states organize public schools into districts, usually with a superintendent; an elected or appointed school board; a unionized, state board–certified workforce of teachers and staff; and a captive student body. The culture is highly politicized, but firmly regulated and entrenched. . . . Charter schools in states with strong charter laws are free to hire nonunionized, noncertified teachers, and are not bound by collective bargaining agreements, thereby weakening union influence within the district. (p. 11)

The contrast between the original concept of LEA-approved and teacher-led schools of innovation and experimentation and the emergent, market-based, and largely privatized structure with teachers serving as relatively low-paid, at-will employees is striking.[11] Whereas the original conception held great promise for elevating the profession of classroom teaching by providing new leadership opportunities for teachers in schools and classrooms, the systems emerging in many states have served as vehicles for privatizing public education, in the process lowering teachers' compensation, degrading working conditions, diminishing their job security, and greatly circumscribing their professional prerogatives. And while the charter movement has attracted many talented college graduates to classroom teaching, few make it a career. Rather, for many, the charter school teaching experience is merely a stepping stone to other professional pursuits.

Notes

1. As this is written, 45 states and the District of Columbia have charter school laws. Only Vermont, Nebraska, South Dakota, North Dakota, and Montana remain without charter school programs. See Education Commission of the States (2020).
2. For a good discussion of ALEC origins, agenda, and operations, see Temin (2017), particularly Chapter 2.
3. Ninth Circuit, *Caviness v. Horizon Community Learning Center Inc.*; Lawrence Pieratt, January 4, 2010, cited in Ravitch (2013), p. 163.
4. For a fuller discussion, see Ravitch (2013), Chapter 16.
5. National Labor Relations Board, Chicago Mathematics and Science Academy Charter School Inc., Employer, and Chicago Alliance of Charter Teachers and Staff, AFT, AFL-CIO, Petitioner, Case 13-RM-001768, December 14, 2012; cited in Ravitch (2013), p. 164.
6. Section 1233c(4) of the House Bill 5923/2011–2012.
7. Ibid.
8. For evidence that teachers generally earn higher compensation in districts where unions are strong, see Brunner and Squires (2013); Rose and Sonstelie (2010).
9. The remaining states do not require teacher certification, although individual charter authorizers may impose requirements.
10. Estimating the costs of teacher turnover is hardly straightforward, involving multiple functions, some of which are difficult to quantify—for example, the disruption to the work of administrators and other teachers. For an analysis that accounts for the separation costs of a departing teacher, hiring and training costs of a new teacher, and the costs associated with replacing experienced teachers with less effective novices, see Synar and Maiden (2012).
11. "LEA" stands for "local education agency," the federal government's term for a traditional (i.e., noncharter) school district.

5

New Approaches to Teacher Accountability

Science or Scapegoating?

The more any quantitative social indicator is used for social decision-making, the more subject it will be to corruption pressures, and the more apt it will be to distort and corrupt the social processes it is intended to monitor.

—Donald T. Campbell (1976)

A growing body of empirical evidence confirms the view of countless educators, parents, and students that the classroom teacher is the most important school-based determinant of student success. Knowing that teachers can make a substantial difference in children's life chances is both intuitive and reassuring. Most of us can remember teachers who have inspired us and left lasting imprints on our lives. The importance of their work is not only verified by researchers but emphasized by policymakers who claim that effective teachers can raise student learning and narrow the "achievement gap"—that is, disparities in student outcomes, most commonly test scores, between different groups of students. Most research has focused on test score gaps between different racial and ethnic groups. Following is a brief summary and analysis of the most closely scrutinized achievement gap in U.S. education: black versus white (Box 5.1).

Recent research has emphasized the importance of high-quality teachers in raising student achievement and reducing achievement gaps related to race-ethnicity, class, and gender. Improving teacher effectiveness and narrowing achievement gaps are at the heart of much contemporary education reform. And the current distribution of teaching talent both within and across our public schools appears to exacerbate existing achievement gaps (e.g., Goldhaber, Lavery, and Theobald 2015; Lankford, Loeb, and Wyckoff 2002). The challenge for researchers, policymakers, and educators, however, is to find a way to assess teacher effectiveness in a valid and reliable way.

Box 5.1 The U.S. Black-White Achievement Gap

Social scientists define achievement gaps as stable and statistically significant (i.e., not due to mere chance) differences in the average performance on standardized tests of students at the same grade level but coming from different racial or socioeconomic groups. Interest in the U.S. black-white achievement gap dates from World War I, when test scores of U.S. Army recruits first revealed its existence (Jencks and Phillips 1998, p. viii). The black-white achievement gap is generally depicted by results from the National Assessment of Educational Progress (NAEP). NAEP reading and math scores for seventeen-year-olds across the U.S. indicate that the racial achievement gap was nearly cut in half between the early 1970s and 1990, but then rose to levels that have remained substantially unchanged since 2000 (Panels A and B).

This rewidening of the racial achievement gap was unexpected and alarming—symptomatic of new problems afflicting black children and signaling a renewed divergence in human capital and economic prospects across the races. The economist Derek Neal observes that the skills and knowledge ("human capital") of blacks and whites should steadily converge as long as society maintains its adequate investment in black children: "Most models of the intergenerational transmission of human capital imply that the black-white human capital gap should become smaller in each successive generation," he writes. "Viewed through the lens of standard economic models of families, the fact that black-white skill gaps shrank during much of the twentieth century is not a surprise" (Neal 2005, p. 42).

When the data are disaggregated by gender and socioeconomic status, the black-white gaps are narrowed but remain large and significant. The gap is particularly acute in areas with large concentrations of poor black and other minority students. And data beyond NAEP scores reveal other troubling disparities in educational opportunities and performance across racial groups. For example, the Civil Rights Project at UCLA found that in 2012, black secondary students were three times more likely than whites to be suspended from school (23 percent of blacks versus 7 percent of whites) (Losen et al. 2015).

Box 5.1 (continued)

Panel A: Black-White Achievement Gap, Grade 12 Reading

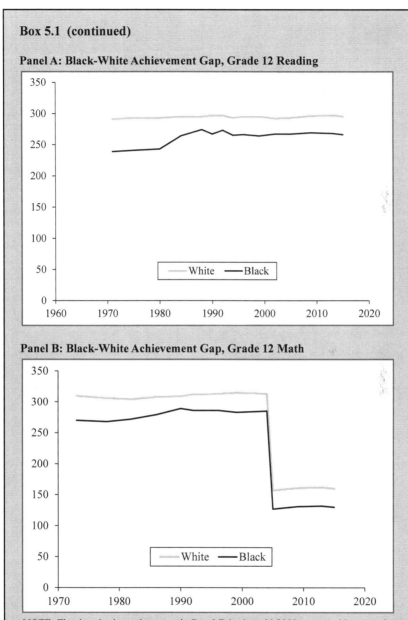

Panel B: Black-White Achievement Gap, Grade 12 Math

NOTE: The drop in the scale scores in Panel B in the mid-2000s occurred because the scoring scale was changed for the exam.
SOURCE: National Assessment of Educational Progress.

Box 5.1 (continued)

Why the Black-White Gap Shrank between 1970 and 1990 and Then Widened

A complete discussion of plausible reasons for the narrowing and subsequent widening of the black-white test score gap is beyond the scope of this brief note. But even a brief review of the research on the origins of the gap makes clear its complexity and intractable nature, with deep roots in racial discrimination and economic inequality.

First, why did the gap narrow in the 1970s and 1980s? One reason identified by social scientists is school desegregation. Darby and Rury (2018) observe that a series of decisions by the U.S. Supreme Court eroded Southern resistance to integration. Particular among these was *Green v. New Kent County*, a 1968 decision in which the Court held that the county's "freedom of choice" plan did not constitute adequate compliance with the mandate of *Brown v. Topeka Board of Education*, which held that state-sanctioned segregation of public schools was unconstitutional. Despite pockets of resistance and the exodus of many white students to private segregated academies, most public schools across the South were desegregated within five years of *Green*.

By 1973, a majority of the region's black high school students attended integrated schools. Furthermore, African American secondary attainment began to reach levels comparable to whites. Shortly after, the black-white test score gap, measured by NAEP, began to shrink dramatically. Test score differences were cut nearly in half between 1970 and 1988, due almost entirely to improvements in African American performance. In many instances, it was children of educated, middle-class parents who exhibited the greatest achievement gains. These children of a growing black middle class added to the rapid gains in black educational attainment of the 1960s and 1970s, evident in rising secondary and postsecondary graduation rates (Berends, Lucas, and Penaloza 2008, cited in Darby and Rury 2018, p. 90).

This dramatic progress by black students came to an abrupt halt around 1990. Why? Darby and Rury (2018) offer the following synopsis:

Box 5.1 (continued)

While some successful African Americans were able to leave their historic ghetto communities by the latter half of the 1970s, millions remained, constrained by a lack of options in segregated housing markets. At the same time, the low-skill jobs that had drawn their families out of the rural South began to disappear, moving elsewhere or being eliminated by technology. The result was rising levels of unemployment and a host of related social problems. As documented by William Julius Williams and other social scientists, growing joblessness contributed to greater instability in black families, higher levels of poverty, and increased crime and drug use. Heightened law enforcement, "zero-tolerance" discipline policies in the schools, and stricter sentencing guidelines in the latter years of the decade contributed to a rising number of incarcerated young black males. . . . Dropout rates in inner-city high schools increased, and achievement scores stagnated. (pp. 94–95)

CAN WE MEASURE TEACHING QUALITY?

Most of us at some level can distinguish between very good and very poor teaching. Teachers vary in their depth of content knowledge, communication skills, creativity in engaging students with different learning styles and levels of interest, and so forth. Trained and experienced educators can discern these and other differences with more acuity than the rest of us. But can these differences be reduced to quantification? And for what purposes? For identifying teachers who need additional training and support? For decisions regarding tenure or compensation levels? Frustrated with near universal granting of tenure, standardized "step and lane" salary schedules (i.e., pay based mostly on experience and education), and the general failure of school systems to distinguish between effective and ineffective teaching when staffing their classrooms, many policymakers and educational leaders have sought a means of measuring teacher quality and incorporating those measures into performance-based promotion and compensation systems.

Such an agenda leads to a question: Does the nature of teaching lend itself to the valid and reliable measurement of *quality*? David Cohen, in his book *Teaching and Its Predicaments*, observes that the success of teachers, along with other practitioners of human improvement, including social workers, pastors, and psychotherapists, depends crucially on the behavior of their clients. To what degree are these practitioners responsible for results? The conventional answers appear to vary across fields in this broadly defined profession. For example, whereas classical psychotherapy places much responsibility on the patient ("patients must recognize problems and work hard to solve them," [Cohen 2011, p. 14]), schoolteachers are assigned substantial responsibility for results:

> State and federal policies have made teachers "accountable" for students' learning; state and local school systems have adopted testing programs that specify minimum levels of student performance, identify rates of success and failure for schools or school systems, and require schools to produce the stipulated learning. If they do not, teachers can be reassigned or removed, and schools can be "reconstituted" or closed. Students have no direct incentives to perform in such schemes, apart from whatever pressure their teachers can create. The assumption is that students' poor performance is due chiefly to teachers' weak effort, and that if teachers are made to take more responsibility for students' learning and work harder, students will do better. (Cohen 2011, p. 74)

The assumption that poor teaching is the root cause of low student achievement has come to dominate state and federal K–12 policymaking, despite the mountain of evidence that has accumulated since the 1968 Coleman Report by Congress attesting to the substantial effects of poverty and other related nonschool factors on student performance. Cohen (2011) anticipates problems stemming from this flawed assumption:

> Human improvement is not like occupations in which objects or ideas are fashioned. A carpenter's specialized knowledge and skills are his distinctive resources; given decent materials and working conditions, he can create decent results. Holding carpenters responsible for results can make sense, other things being equal. But teachers need much more than their own knowledge and skills to do good work; they also require students' skills, knowledge, and commitment, as well as an environment that supports their

work. These things are never under teachers' exclusive control and often are quite far outside it; because teachers' knowledge, skill, and commitment are only a few of the resources required for good results, increasing only their responsibility for results is likely to be counterproductive. (p. 77)

So, while recognizing the importance of factors beyond teachers' control, we seek the illusory precision of a "value-added" calculation that purports to measure the marginal contribution of the teacher's effort to the student's learning. And we turn to standardized student testing for the data to perform these calculations. Assuming that students' scores on standardized achievement tests measure desired educational outcomes, how might we use these scores to assess teacher effectiveness? Students vary widely in the skills, knowledge, and commitment they bring to a teacher's classroom, and teachers enjoy widely disparate levels of support from their schools, districts, parents, and communities. A skilled and conscientious teacher may see low or falling test scores with a class of particularly disadvantaged children, while a mediocre teacher could enjoy high or rising scores with a class of gifted or otherwise motivated students. And the same teacher may well experience quite different outcomes in different years with different students, school leadership, or other circumstances.

So how might student test scores be used to measure teacher performance in a valid and reliable way? Current efforts to solve this puzzle are but the latest round of reformers' long-standing pursuit of "efficiency" in public schools (Box 5.2).

The "Value-Added" Movement

By most accounts, the contemporary "value-added" solution to the teacher quality measurement puzzle was offered in 1982 by statistician William Sanders, who at the time was studying the effects of radiation on farm animals for the Oak Ridge National Laboratory in Tennessee. At that time, Tennessee's governor, Lamar Alexander, who would later serve as U.S. Secretary of Education for President George H. W. Bush, and more recently served as chairman of the U.S. Senate Education Committee before his retirement in 2020, wanted to identify and recognize the state's best classroom teachers. Sanders and a colleague wrote to the governor with an offer to help.[1]

Box 5.2 A Brief History of School Efficiency Metrics

School efficiency metrics in the U.S. date back more than a century. In 1911, Simon Patten, an economics professor at the University of Pennsylvania's Wharton School of Business, writing in the influential *Educational Review*, argued that public schools should demonstrate results that could be "readily seen and measured." He demanded that schools provide evidence of their contribution to society or have their budgets cut: "The advocate of pure water or clean streets shows by how much the death rate will be altered by each proposed addition to his share of the budget. . . . Only the teacher is without such figures" (Patten 1911, quoted in Callahan 1962, p. 48).

School reformers were also influenced by industry's "scientific management" movement, launched by American engineer Frederick Winslow Taylor in 1911. Taylor analyzed the production of pig iron in factories by decomposing the process into its component parts and determining output standards for each job. Each worker's compensation would depend upon his rate of production, which would be closely monitored by management. Taylor aimed "to increase efficiency by standardizing and speeding up work on the factory floor to create mass production" (Muller 2018, p. 32).

"Taylorism," or the specialization and standardization of tasks and the reporting of these activities at the worker level to set compensation, sought to replace worker knowledge and judgment with simplified mass production methods planned, monitored, and controlled by managers. In Taylor's words:

> Under scientific management, the managers assume . . . the burden of gathering together all of the traditional knowledge which in the past has been possessed by the workmen and then of classifying, tabulating, and reducing this knowledge to rules, laws, formulae. . . . Thus all of the planning which under the old system was done by the workmen, must of necessity under the new system be done by management in accordance with the law of science. (Taylor 1911, quoted in Scott 1998, p. 336)

Taylor dismisses worker expertise and judgment and declares management's supremacy: "It is only through *enforced* adoption of the best

Box 5.2 (continued)

implements and working conditions, and *enforced* cooperation that this faster work can be assured. And the duty of enforcing the adoption of standards and enforcing this cooperation rests with *management* alone" (emphasis in the original). Taylor's prescription for greater efficiency through standardization and monitoring was soon adopted by educational leaders. Ellwood Cubberly, dean of Stanford University's School of Education, promoted Taylor's vision in his influential 1916 textbook *Public School Administration*:

> Every manufacturing establishment that turns out a standard product or series of products of any kind maintains a force of efficiency experts to study methods of procedure and to measure and test the output of its works. Such men ultimately bring the manufacturing establishment large returns, by introducing improvements in processes and procedure, and in training the workmen to produce a larger and a better output. *Our schools are, in a sense, factories in which the raw products (children) are to be shaped and fashioned into products to meet the various demands of life.* The specifications for manufacturing come from the demands of twentieth-century civilization, and it is the business of the school to build its students according to the specifications laid down. (emphasis added) (Cubberley 1916, pp. 337–338)

A major part of this efficiency movement in public education was a call to evaluate teachers. For example, Joseph S. Taylor, a district superintendent of schools in New York City, tried to adapt F. W. Taylor's management model to schools, drawing parallels between industry and public education and, more particularly, between factory workers and classroom teachers:

> One may easily trace an analogy between these fundamentals of the science of industrial management and the organization of a public school system. For example: (1) The state as employer must cooperate with the teacher as employee, for the latter does not always understand the science of education; (2) the state provides experts who supervise the teacher, and suggest the processes that are most efficacious and economical; (3) the task system obtains in the school as well as in the shop, each grade being a measured

Box 5.2 (continued)

> quantity of work to be accomplished in a given term; (4) every
> teacher who accomplishes the task receives a bonus, not in money,
> but in the form of a rating which may have money value; (5) those
> who are unable to do the work are eliminated, either through the
> device of a temporary license or of a temporary employment.
> (Taylor 1912, pp. 350–351)

Another prominent advocate of scientific management in public schools at this time was Franklin Bobbitt, an instructor in educational administration at the University of Chicago, who in 1913 called for a measurement and evaluation scheme that presaged today's value-added modeling (VAM) movement. Applying his approach to the teaching of penmanship, in which schools use different schedules for instruction, Bobbitt instructed school managers ("supervisors," not teachers) as follows:

> Now suppose each of these groups of schools to be measured in the
> first week of the school year by the Thorndike or the Ayres writing
> scale as to quality, and tested by the stop-watch as to speed. If they
> are then measured again at the end of the year in the same way, it is
> possible to determine which of the modes of distributing the sixty
> minutes of time for teaching the writing is the superior. (Bobbitt
> 1913, pp. 54–55)

By mid-twentieth century, metrics had moved well beyond manufacturing into the service sector, including public education and teacher evaluation. Education professor A. S. Barr published a comprehensive summary of studies examining the measurement of "teaching efficiency" in the June 1, 1948, issue of the *Journal of Experimental Education*. A substantial subset of these studies employed measures of pupil growth and achievement as a "major criterion of (teacher) success," presaging the value-added movement so integral to NCLB and RTT. Barr, however, cautioned against too narrow a focus when using these metrics:

> A growing number of persons have attempted to define teacher
> efficiency in terms of pupil growth and achievement. If this is
> done, pupil growth and achievement must be broadly viewed to
> include all around pupil growth, the so-called intangibles as well

Box 5.2 (continued)

> as the tangibles, and remote outcomes as well as immediate effects. Then, too, while all of the teacher's activities as directors of learning, as friends and counselors of pupils, as professional workers, and citizens will ultimately have important implications for pupil growth and achievement, some persons may wish to appraise the teacher in these separate roles as well as in terms of overall pupil growth and achievement. When the teacher's influence upon pupil growth and achievement is under investigation, due consideration must also be given to factors other than teaching upon pupil change. (Barr 1948, pp. 205–206)

After observing that many of these studies failed to consider the varying circumstances and working conditions in which teachers may be placed, Barr cautions readers not to be misled by the seeming rigor and precision of inappropriate quantification in social research:

> We need a careful rethinking of our statistical procedures as applied to teacher personnel. . . . Persons not well acquainted with mathematical lore fail to note that most procedures can be used only under a very restricted set of conditions. Probably even more important is the fact that historically in its development mathematics was developed to study physical phenomena; it may not apply in many important respects to human behavior. At least some of its procedures seem to run contrary to reasonably well established facts in human psychology. The difficulty may not be, however, with our mathematics but with those who use it. (p. 226)

Tennessee administered annual tests in five subjects. Sanders reasoned that individual teacher performance could be accurately measured by calculating an expected growth trajectory for each student in each subject based on past test performance and then comparing predicted and actual growth. This method, Sanders argued, would validly gauge each teacher's contribution ("value-added") to student achievement because the influences of all nonschool factors (e.g., talent, wealth, support at home) would be captured in each student's achievement history and projected growth. Teachers whose students consistently exceeded their projected test scores would be deemed the most effective.

Early findings from Tennessee revealed a normal distribution of value-added scores, with small numbers of teachers compiling markedly high or low scores and most landing in the broad middle. And the distribution of scores was wide, with large differences between the highest and lowest scores. Such a distribution of teacher scores provided little rationale, either for existing teacher evaluation systems, which found the great majority of teachers to be "satisfactory" or "outstanding," or for traditional compensation systems that paid teachers according to experience and educational credentials. Value-added scores have since been found to correlate somewhat with classroom experience (e.g., Baker 2016a), but the notion of "pay for performance" held great appeal for critics of the status quo. Educators and students had long known that some teachers are better than others. Now a system had been created that purported to measure those differences. But serious problems with the validity and reliability of these measurements soon became apparent.

One general limitation of value-added measures of teacher performance arises from the effects of unmeasured student characteristics. To control fully for such characteristics that might influence teacher performance, value-added studies sometimes compare teachers within the same school. For example, economists have conducted experiments that randomly assigned students within a school to various teachers and then measured differences in test score growth, thus eliminating selection bias created when principals cluster the most challenging or most able students in particular classrooms. While constituting a strong research design, such an experimental approach can hardly form the basis of ongoing district- or statewide personnel evaluation systems. Researchers and policymakers, including staunch advocates of test-based teacher accountability, prefer value-added models that encompass multiple schools, comparing each teacher's performance with broad groups of teachers across schools, thereby avoiding within-school comparisons and competition that would undermine teamwork and collegiality (Harris and Sass 2009).

In nonexperimental settings, researchers have identified strong statistical controls for factors that influence student test scores but are unrelated to teacher performance, including income, English proficiency, race, gender, disability status, class attendance, summer school participation, and whether the child has recently moved, been sus-pended, or repeated a grade. Nevertheless, while the current practice of annual student testing may make it possible to estimate individual teachers' contributions to student achievement in tested subjects, the state of the art in value-added modeling remains problematic. First, unobserved differences among students have not been fully accounted for, and the statistical properties of the effectiveness measures are cause for concern. To what degree do value-added measures correctly gauge real differences in teacher effectiveness? Some value-added models can replicate teacher performance when teachers and students are randomly assigned (Kane and Staiger 2008), and some models are consistent with principals' confidential teacher assessments (Jacob and Lefgren 2005). At the same time, however, teacher value-added measures are noto-riously unreliable, providing clear distinctions between only the very lowest- and very highest-scoring teachers (Jacob and Lefgren 2008).

Bias, Noise, and Absurd Results

Some demonstrations of value-added modeling's shortcomings have been particularly stark. In a widely cited 2010 article, economist Jesse Rothstein shows how VAM estimates of teacher effects on stu-dent test scores are likely to be highly misleading (Rothstein 2010). Exploiting the fact that a *future* teacher cannot possibly influence a student's *past* achievement, Rothstein performs "falsification tests" for three widely used VAMs. Any apparent evidence of such counterfactual "teacher effects" is, rather, evidence that VAM assumptions of the ran-dom assignment of students to teachers are violated in practice. Exam-ples of such violations are widespread, including student assignments based on teachers' particular strengths or specialties, intentional sepa-ration of incompatible students, principals' efforts to reward favored teachers with "good" students, and concessions to parental requests.

Examining a rich data set from North Carolina, Rothstein does indeed find large "effects" of fifth-grade teachers on fourth-grade test score gains—that is, evidence of nonrandom sorting of students across teachers in ways that bias VAM estimates of teacher effects. He then demonstrates that, to the extent that any of the VAMs examined do identify immediate causal effects (i.e., a teacher's effect in the year of exposure), these effects fade quickly and fail to register a teacher's (arguably more important) longer-run effects, such as turning students into avid readers.

More recently, a 2019 NBER working paper provides more falsification evidence challenging the validity of VAM estimates. Using administrative student data from New York City, Bitler and colleagues apply commonly used VAMs to another outcome teachers cannot plausibly affect: student height (Bitler et al. 2019). They find estimated teacher "effects" on height that are comparable in magnitude to actual teacher effects on math and reading achievement—0.22 standard deviation compared to 0.29 and 0.26, respectively (p. 24). Their subsequent analysis attributes this nonsensical finding primarily to statistical noise arising from sampling error, rather than bias due to student sorting on unobserved factors. This further analysis, which effectively "shrinks" the nonsensical effect to zero, requires multiple years of classroom data for each teacher and, the authors note, is unlikely to be done in practice. And even if it were, such VAMs, while likely permitting the identification of persistently poor performers, would be of little value to the great majority of teachers who seek to improve their craft. The authors conclude, "Taken together, our results provide a cautionary tale for the naive application of VAMs to teacher evaluation and other settings. They point to the possibility of the misidentification of sizable teacher 'effects' where none exist" (p. 24). Given these serious shortcomings with VAM, how else may teacher performance be reliably gauged, and how may such findings be used to improve teaching and learning in our schools?

Teacher Experience and Teacher Effectiveness

Utilizing a rich statewide administrative data set from Florida that linked students' performance to the identity of their classroom teachers at all grade levels and teachers' performance to their preservice and inservice training, Harris and Sass (2011) find that elementary and middle-school teacher effectiveness increases with experience in the teacher's early years. This finding is both intuitive and consistent with a large body of prior research (e.g., Betts, Rueben, and Danenberg 2000; Murnane and Phillips 1981; Rivkin, Hanushek, and Kain 2005). But in contrast to much of the prior research, they also find continuing improvement in teacher productivity beyond the teachers' first five years in the classroom. Using both experimental and econometric methods, labor economists have produced a substantial body of research on teacher effectiveness as a function of classroom teaching experience.

Furthermore, it appears that a teacher's path to the classroom—whether through a traditional teachers college, a graduate program in teaching, or a newer alternative like Teach for America or an urban residency program—matters little in terms of impact on student test scores (Boyd et al. 2009). Another robust finding concerns the typical teacher "learning curve": First-year teachers often struggle mightily but show much greater effectiveness in their second year and continue to improve steadily over the next 5 to 10 years (see, for example, Harris and Sass 2011). Oddly, and unfortunately, teacher effectiveness generally levels off after that. The reasons for this flatlining should be the subject of further research. Possibilities might include the exodus of more talented teachers because of boredom or the absence of a career ladder, poor in-service support for those who have mastered basic teaching skills, and the increasing marginal cost of skill development.

Certainly these research findings are important and should prove useful in devising policies and programs for teacher induction and mentoring, creating new professional opportunities for veteran teachers (e.g., teacher mentors), and designing more authentic in-service programs. But whether value-added measurement should be used to manage, compensate, promote, and terminate individual classroom teachers is an entirely different matter. As Rivkin (2009) observes, "The myriad factors that influence cognitive growth over extended periods, the purposeful sorting of families and teachers into schools and classrooms, and the imperfections of tests as measures of knowledge complicate efforts to estimate teacher fixed effects and rank teachers according to quality of instruction" (p. 189).

Rivkin allows that, despite these shortcomings, value-added analysis can be helpful in evaluating and compensating teachers. But research strongly suggests that policymakers moved too aggressively toward value-added personnel systems. When value-added is calculated for a teacher using just a single year of test-score data, the error rate is 35 percent (Schochet and Chiang 2010). This means that about one in three teachers who are average will be misclassified as either excellent or ineffective, while one in three who are either excellent or ineffec-

tive will be mistaken for average. And even with three years of student test scores, one in four teachers will be erroneously categorized. Furthermore, the value-added model is incompatible with team teaching and with the many teachers whose grades or classes are not subject to standardized testing (ibid.). More generally, the pitfalls of strictly quantitative performance measures and management's slavish adherence to them have not gone unnoticed.

Finally, there is another, more pernicious aspect of policymakers' preoccupation with value-added analysis. If legislators and other leaders become convinced that "good" teachers can by themselves dramatically reduce, if not eliminate entirely, achievement gaps across student groups, they may absolve themselves of responsibility to address other causes of children's poor achievement in school, such as substandard health care and nutrition, inadequate housing, poor parenting, unsafe neighborhoods, and other problems rooted in poverty and racial segregation.

VAM and the Fable of "Five Good Teachers"

Despite researchers' cautions about value-added modeling, particularly in connection with high-stakes school accountability and personnel decisions, VAM has come to enjoy considerable political appeal. Politicians and pundits all along the political spectrum have responded to remarkable claims by some researchers that VAM holds the key to closing race- and class-based achievement gaps in as short a period as three to five years. The broad appeal of such a claim is easy to see: Progressives want to see our chronic and widening achievement gaps closed and economic opportunities spread more evenly across racial and class divides. Conservatives, meanwhile, are particularly attracted to the notion that teachers can close these gaps, thus obviating any need to address other root causes of poor achievement, such as poverty, inadequate nutrition and health care, homelessness, and other social ills.

The idea that value-added assessment could close the achievement gap likely originated with a 2004 paper by Eric Hanushek and Steven Rivkin.[2] Reviewing a number of studies, they note that traditional proxies for teacher quality—education major, graduate degrees, certification, and salary—have little effect on student performance. A teacher's experience in the classroom and her own achievement test scores were found to positively impact student performance in some studies. In view of the apparent irrelevance of traditional ("paper") credentials and the consequent difficulty in identifying good teachers ex ante, Hanushek and Rivkin concluded that the best way to raise teacher quality was to cast a wider net for teaching talent and then focus on teachers' success in raising student achievement test scores. They recommended that states "loosen up" certification requirements for entering the profession and then closely observe their effectiveness in raising test scores. Then school leaders should retain the high VAM performers and dismiss the rest. Veteran teachers with tenure protections would be replaced as they retired or otherwise left voluntarily.

Hanushek and Rivkin (2004) projected that

> having five years of good teachers in a row [that is, teachers at the 85th percentile of the VAM rankings] could overcome the average seventh-grade mathematics achievement gap between lower-income kids (those on the free or reduced-price lunch program) and those from higher-income families. In other words, high-quality teachers can make up for the typical deficits seen in the preparation of kids from disadvantaged backgrounds. (p. 21)

Their claim was remarkably similar to one made by Sanders (2000), who asserted that students with teachers in the top quintile of effectiveness for three consecutive years would gain 50 percentile points as compared to those who were assigned to the lowest-quintile teachers. And their general policy recommendations were reiterated in an influential paper by Gordon, Kane, and Staiger (2006), who noted the irrelevance of traditional teacher credentials (i.e., degrees, licenses, certification) in predicting who would be effective in the classroom. They, too, urged schools to recruit nontraditional candidates and evaluate them using student gain scores. These policy prescriptions acquired substantial weight several years later, when Gordon was recruited by the Obama administration to serve as deputy director for education in the Office of Management and Budget.

The potential economic benefits of a VAM-based teacher personnel policy were elevated to the reassuring realm of quantification by Hanushek in his 2006 article "Alternative School Policies and the Benefits of General Cognitive Skills." His emphasis on teacher effectiveness is stated at the outset:

> The central messages are: first, the economic impact of reforms that enhance student achievement will be very large; second, reform must be thought of in terms of both the *magnitude* of changes and the *speed* with which any changes occur. Third, based on current knowledge, the most productive reforms are almost certainly ones that improve the quality of the teacher force. Fourth, such policies are likely to be ones that improve the hiring, retention, and pay of high quality teachers, i.e., selective policies aimed at the desired outcome. (p. 448, emphasis in the original)

He begins by summarizing several prominent studies estimating the impact of school quality (as proxied by students' performance on standardized tests) on individuals' earnings. These studies suggest that a one-standard-deviation increase in mathematics performance at the end of high school (i.e., improvement from the 50th to the 84th percentile) yields 12 percent higher annual earnings. Using median earnings in 2001 (about $30,000), this improvement in math performance would raise one's annual income by $3,600. This annual return to enhanced math skills would then be summed over one's working life to obtain the total benefit.[3] Hanushek then argues convincingly that the impact of improved achievement on economic growth may be more substantial than its effect on individual incomes, as a more skilled workforce accelerates invention, technological progress, and productivity growth. He quantifies this "quality effect," estimating a growth dividend from a one-half standard deviation improvement in achievement test scores accomplished over 30 years of more than $700 billion in that final year (Hanushek 2006, p. 454).

Hanushek next addresses teacher quality. Summarizing the findings of several notable studies of teacher effectiveness in boosting annual student test scores (Hanushek et al. 2005; Hanushek, Kain, and Rivkin

2004; Rivkin, Hanushek, and Kain 2005), he concludes, "While a bit speculative, if these annual gains accumulate in a linear fashion, disadvantaged students assigned to a good teacher (as opposed to an average teacher) for four to five years in a row could, by these estimates, *entirely close the income gap*" (p. 456, emphasis added). To illustrate the power of his theoretical construct, Hanushek simulates "a simple quality upgrade policy" designed to yield a one-half standard deviation improvement in student achievement. The simulation encompasses varying teacher replacement rates (i.e., rate of exiting the profession or exits plus school changes) and time horizons (10, 20, or 30 years). So, for example, school leaders, blessed with perfect information about teachers' effectiveness, are able to raise student achievement by one-half standard deviation in 10 years by replacing average teachers (i.e., those at the 50th percentile in the achievement-gain rankings) who exit annually with teachers at the 61st percentile. Of course, the target hiring percentile would fall with either a faster annual replacement rate or a longer time horizon.

These and other scenarios (e.g., achieving a full standard-deviation achievement gain) are laid out with mathematical precision. The analysis, however, *assumes the universal availability of perfectly valid and reliable value-added measures of teacher performance.* Nonetheless, despite the author's caution as to the speculative nature of his results, policymakers have been persuaded by this line of research and the policy prescriptions emerging from it to do the following: relax (if not eliminate) traditional teacher certification standards and expand the recruiting pool, evaluate teachers on the basis of their students' achievement-gain scores, retain (and sufficiently compensate) the high performers, and dismiss the rest. Previously tenured teachers would leave through normal attrition. The researchers' models demonstrated how schools, armed with perfect knowledge of the effectiveness of every teacher and teaching candidate, could hire and fire their way to the most exclusive enclaves of the mythical Lake Wobegon, where all teachers are not only above average but approach the top quintile of their profession, and where student achievement gaps disappear.

The problem lies not in the research, but in its misapplication by policymakers who fail to understand or acknowledge the current shortcomings in the state of the art of VAM. As Hanushek has recently observed,

"Without a workable evaluation system, none of the policy proposals built on teacher effectiveness are possible" (Hanushek 2020, p. 13).

VAM Goes to Washington

The vision of an omnipotent teaching force that could eventually close the achievement gap, effectively neutralizing all of the educational obstacles enumerated in a vast research literature dating back to the 1966 Coleman Report, held great appeal for policymakers all along the political spectrum and became a cornerstone of the Obama administration's education policy agenda. When President Obama took office in 2009, his administration quickly focused on teacher evaluation as a key policy issue. This interest was motivated by the emerging line of academic research confirming that teacher quality is the most important school-based determinant of student achievement, and by widespread evidence that teacher effectiveness was given little or no weight in the personnel policies of most school districts. Dubbed the "widget effect" (i.e., teachers being treated as interchangeable parts) in a 2009 report by The New Teacher Project (now known as TNTP), this failure by school leaders to recognize differences in teacher performance led to an outcome that was unacceptable to many observers and policymakers: school districts rated 99 percent of teachers "satisfactory" and overlooked performance entirely when making decisions about compensation, promotion, professional development, or dismissal (Aldeman 2017; Weisberg et al. 2009).

Race to the Top

Despite cautions from testing and measurement experts about the use of value-added measurement (VAM) for individual teacher evaluation and accountability, the Obama administration and Education Secretary Arne Duncan made VAM a cornerstone of their Race to the Top (RTT) education initiative. Approved by Congress as part of the American Recovery and Reinvestment Act of 2009 (ARRA), RTT provided $4.35 billion to states and school districts that adopted a set of reforms focused on improving the quality of teaching through human resource policies, including individual teacher accountability and teacher tenure reform. Specifically, to be eligible for a grant, states had to commit to evaluating, compensating, and making tenure decisions about teachers on the basis of teacher VAM scores. Furthermore, states had to require principals to evaluate every teacher annually and devise a way to remove teachers, even those with tenure, who had chronically low VAM scores.

RTT incentives explicitly encouraged states to measure individual student achievement growth and fashion evaluation systems for teachers and principals that factored in these measures. The evaluations were to occur annually and the results used for virtually all important personnel decisions, including compensation and tenure, teacher and principal dismissals, and the identification and distribution of highly effective teachers. States were also pushed to create alternative routes to teacher certification.

Although total RTT funding (to be spent over four years) represented less than 1 percent of annual K–12 spending across the U.S., leaders of the cash-strapped states generally leaped into the competitive fray. Fully 40 states and the District of Columbia submitted applications to Phase 1 of the competition, but only two winners were announced in March 2010. Tennessee (again, VAM's birthplace) and Delaware were awarded about $500 million and $120 million, respectively, which amounted to 10.0 percent and 5.7 percent of their annual budgets (Howell 2015). A few months later, 35 states and the District of Columbia submitted applications for Phase 2. Ten winners were each awarded between $75 million and $700 million, with Florida and New York landing the largest grants. In the spring of 2011, with the ARRA funds exhausted, Congress allotted funds for a third phase, in which only losing Phase 2 finalists could participate. In December 2011, the Department of Education announced seven Phase 3 winners, but the awards were small, ranging from $17 million to $43 million. In all, the RTT competition yielded 19 winning states and the District of Columbia, 28 losers, and four states that declined to participate. But more importantly, the competition spurred a substantial number of reforms, many designed to free schools from "restrictive" policies (e.g., excluding teacher evaluations in tenure or compensation decisions) found in teacher union contracts across both winning and losing states.[4]

NCLB waivers

Both the Bush and Obama administrations used waivers to address states' demands for relief from NCLB mandates, thereby avoiding a confrontation with Congress over renewal of the increasingly unpopular law. But while the Bush administration used waiver authority gingerly so as to preserve this statutory cornerstone of the Bush domestic agenda, President Obama had no such motivation. His legislative proposal to reform NCLB, the Blueprint for Reform, was announced just weeks before the Affordable Care Act passed without a single Republican vote. When it made little headway in Congress, the president changed strategy. In September 2011, his administration announced its Elementary and Secondary Education Act (ESEA) flexibility waiver program.

Like RTT, the Obama waiver program involved states making reforms in several areas, including teacher evaluation systems. But, unlike RTT, no new money was offered to the states for reform. And local districts were often unsupportive of the evaluation system reforms (which often stress VAM) imposed by their states. Among other problems, teachers' VAM scores were often difficult to interpret and offered teachers no advice on how to improve. Moreover, evidence suggests that the VAM systems often failed in their basic purpose: to differentiate teachers according to their effectiveness in boosting measured achievement. The proportion of teachers receiving a less-than-satisfactory rating barely changed in most states (Kraft and Gilmour 2017).

VAM and Teacher Job Protections

The weakening of teacher tenure protections following the RTT and NCLB waiver programs constituted a sea change for the traditional public school teaching profession. Until recently, teacher tenure laws had been relatively stable over time and similar from state to state. These laws predate equal employment statutes and contemporary hiring practices. New Jersey passed the first teacher tenure statute in 1909, in an era when schools routinely fired teachers for being pregnant, failing to conform to weight charts, or holding particular political views. Considered by proponents as a needed protection against teacher dismissal for political purposes or arbitrary decisions of school boards or administrators, state teacher tenure laws have three main components: 1) tenure requirements, 2) reasons for dismissal, and 3) process for appeals. The first specifies the length of the probationary period after which teachers are eligible for tenure. In most of the 48 states in which teachers are granted tenure, the probationary period is three years. The second holds that while employers may dismiss a nontenured teacher at any time for any reason as long as the decision is not arbitrary, capricious, or discriminatory, tenured teachers can only be dismissed for reasons provided in the law. The third component of tenure laws specifies the appeals process available to dismissed teachers who seek reinstatement (National Council on Teacher Quality 2012).

The RTT incentive grant program succeeded in persuading states to amend their laws regarding teacher evaluation and teacher tenure protections. Although only 19 states and the District of Columbia were awarded RTT grants over the two-year period, fully two-thirds of the states amended their public school personnel statutes, with half mandating that student test scores be incorporated into teacher evaluations and 18 states weakening tenure protections (Goldstein 2014, p. 214). And of course, the teacher evaluation and tenure processes are closely linked, with reform in one having consequences in the other. For example, in 2009 only four states considered student test scores as a criterion for tenure; by 2014, 16 states did (Education Commission of the States 2014).

VAM Reconsidered: The Every Student Succeeds Act

On January 1, 2016, President Obama signed the Every Student Succeeds Act (ESSA), which loosened federal mandates regarding states' assessment and teacher evaluation systems. Whereas NCLB imposed statewide accountability systems and RTT gave states incentives to track students' achievement longitudinally and evaluate teachers by means of measured student gains or VAMs, ESSA allows states to use alternative student growth measures, including portfolios and other nontest evidence. And while VAMs are still prevalent across many local school districts, their influence may now be slowly receding, as only 15 states are using them statewide, down from 21 in 2014. Perhaps more importantly, their role in teacher evaluation appears to be slowly changing, with more states allowing and èven encouraging local districts to use evaluation results to drive teacher professional development, as opposed to tenure or compensation decisions (Close, Amrein-Beardsley, and Collins 2018).

Teacher Evaluation: The Challenge Ahead

The effectiveness of any new evaluation systems in shaping labor market outcomes and improving teaching practice depends crucially on not only their validity and reliability but teachers' perceptions of these matters as well. If the new systems are viewed as unfair or arbitrary, incapable of accurately gauging teacher skill and effectiveness, high-quality teachers can be expected to exit localities where tenure protections have been weakened or eliminated. On the other hand, if teachers believe that the evaluation system will correctly identify the worst performers and either trigger support for their improvement or prompt their departure, then any exodus of high-quality teachers would be less likely and the entry of more such high performers encouraged.

Until teacher leaders are fully engaged in teacher evaluation reforms, progress will remain halting at best. Efforts in Washington, D.C., are illustrative. Dee and Wyckoff (2015) found that the teacher evaluation system (IMPACT) introduced in the Washington, D.C., public schools in the 2009–2010 school year, which linked substantial economic incentives to multiple measures of teacher performance (i.e., several structured observational measures as well as student test scores), did succeed in prompting the voluntary exit of low-performing teachers while boosting the performance of those who stayed. But administrators have repeatedly modified the program since its inception, first employing "master educators" to evaluate teachers, then eliminating them in favor of principals, an approach often opposed by teachers, union leadership, and researchers alike. The district also suspended and then reintroduced VAM as part of the evaluation process, despite mounting research evidence discrediting the practice. Such a pattern of failure, revision, and more failure, all the while ignoring the considered advice of experienced classroom teachers, can only exacerbate teachers' feelings of frustration, alienation, and professional disenfranchisement. Standard setting, enforcement, and in-service training and support are hallmarks of a true profession. Teachers must be full participants in the design and implementation of their evaluation programs.

Progress on teacher evaluation may also help to deescalate conflicts and clarify policymaking regarding teacher job protections and other complementary teacher labor policies (e.g., new career ladders, mentoring programs and other supports for new teachers, compensation levels, and so forth). If accompanied by the adoption of valid and reliable teacher evaluation and human resource systems and an improved capacity of local districts to administer these systems, particularly in high-needs schools, the elimination or relaxation of tenure and related job protections may serve to enhance the perceived professional status of public school teaching and thereby raise the overall quality of teacher supply. In the absence of such complementary systems, however, the elimination or weakening of tenure protections could simply trigger the return of the unfair and discriminatory personnel practices that teacher tenure and due process were intended to deter.

A Final Word of Caution

Today's analysis of student test scores as a means of gauging teacher performance is a marked departure from the notable education research of the 1950s and 1960s by psychologists and sociologists such as Kenneth Clark and James Coleman, who looked at a broad range of factors that influenced children's overall school performance and well-being: how many books their parents owned, what toys they played with, whether their schools had libraries and science labs (Goldstein 2014). Like today's educational researchers, these social scientists of an earlier generation understood the importance of good teaching, but they looked to particular personality traits like warmth, extroversion, and conscientiousness as sources of their classroom effectiveness. Their findings were undoubtedly helpful both for young aspiring professionals who were considering a teaching career and for school administrators seeking to fill teaching positions. But no efforts were made to use these findings to fashion new systems for evaluating and compensating teachers on a broad scale.

In contrast, contemporary statisticians and economists interrogate massive administrative, student-level data sets, compiled by states largely in response to the mandates of the federal No Child Left Behind Act, in an attempt to identify which teachers raise or lower student test scores in reading and math. At the same time, widespread concern over the performance of U.S. public schools—stemming from relatively poor performance on international assessments of student achievement, large and persistent achievement gaps along lines of race and class, and the proliferation of remedial courses at the postsecondary level—have led policymakers to insist that value-added research findings be used to fashion new systems of teacher evaluation and compensation. However, while the validity of the research findings has improved with stronger experimental designs, the challenges inherent in creating value-added personnel evaluation systems based on school district administrative data remain daunting.

Until value-added estimates become a more valid and reliable measure of teacher quality and their use in personnel systems is perceived as fair by educators, resistance will remain strong, and many talented college graduates and other career changers may be dissuaded from entering the teaching profession. In the meantime, policymakers would do well to heed the advice of Donald T. Campbell (1976), one of the twentieth century's most distinguished social scientists, and consider the law that bears his name and appears as the epigram opening this chapter.

Notes

1. Governor Alexander did not take Sanders up on his offer, but eight years later, then-governor Ned McWherter enlisted Sanders's help (Carey 2017).
2. This brief summary is based, in part, on a longer discussion by Diane Ravitch in her notable book *The Death and Life of the Great American School System* (2010), pp. 181–183.
3. Hanushek offers several reasons these estimates are probably conservative and should be considered a lower bound. For example, the impact of cognitive skills grows with worker experience, and the value of skills rises as work becomes more skill intensive. Additional benefits arise as enhanced skills lead to higher high school and college graduation rates.
4. The Obama administration also used the Teacher Incentive Fund (TIF) to promote teacher evaluation and compensation reforms. The TIF program, created in 2006, awards grants to high-needs districts to fund performance-based compensation systems. The administration greatly expanded the program and introduced a new requirement: proposals had to differentiate between teacher and principal effectiveness, based largely on student growth, and create compensation systems reflecting these results. In the Obama administration's first year, 62 districts and schools across the U.S. shared $437 million in TIF grants (Aldeman 2017, p. 63).

6

A Tale of Two States

Massachusetts Soars while Michigan Stumbles

Laws for the liberal education of youth, especially of the lower class of people, are so extremely wise and useful, that, to a humane and generous mind, no expense for this purpose would be thought extravagant.

—John Adams

Government really sucks.

—Betsy DeVos

Massachusetts and Michigan embarked on dramatic education and school finance reform movements almost simultaneously in the early 1990s. At that time, their situations were not dissimilar. Financial support for public schools was roughly equal on average, and while Massachusetts outperformed Michigan on several metrics of the National Assessment of Educational Progress (NAEP), the differences were not glaring. Since the advent of their respective reform movements, however, the two states have experienced far different educational outcomes. While the Bay State is now widely regarded as among the finest, if not *the* foremost, public school systems in the United States, Michigan is now among the worst, ranking dead last among the states in student proficiency gains and school funding growth (Jacob 2017).

It's no surprise, then, that the teacher labor market and workforce in Massachusetts appear, by available metrics, stronger and more stable than their Michigan counterparts. Whether a cause or an effect of these contrasting educational outcomes, these teacher workforces have been shaped in large part by divergent state policies emerging from the interplay of multiple state-level actors: the governor, the State Board of Education, state legislators, business leaders, and state officials in the Department of Education. The quality of public schools depends crucially on the ability of these actors to set aside narrow, self-serving agendas and coalesce around a set of evidence-based policies and actions designed to support students' academic achievement. Massachusetts appears to have largely mastered this, while Michigan has largely failed at it (Box 6.1).

THE BAY STATE'S PATH TO REFORM

In the early 1990s, as the education standards movement was sweeping the country, public schools in Massachusetts were being squeezed by the effects of a voter-approved tax limitation law and an economic downturn. Indeed, fiscal pressures on local schools had been mounting for nearly a decade following voter approval in November 1980 of Proposition 2½, which capped local property tax rates at 2.5 percent of assessed value and restricted growth in the levy limit to 2.5 percent annually plus an allowance for new growth.[1] In the years immediately following adoption of the tax limitation initiative, budgets in the state's poorest districts were largely protected by increases in state aid. But when the Massachusetts economy faltered in the late 1980s, state aid plunged and local school budgets suffered.

One such distressed school district was Brockton, a once-thriving blue-collar shoe manufacturing city that had been economically decimated in the 1970s and 1980s by globalization. In 1990, Jami McDuffy, a 13-year-old Brockton middle schooler, became the lead plaintiff in *McDuffy v. Robertson*, a class action lawsuit filed by 20 school districts against the Commonwealth seeking adequate school funding. In that same year, several business leaders, led by Jack Rennie, the founder of Pacer Systems, a military contractor based in Burlington, formed the Massachusetts Business Alliance for Education (MBAE). The alliance raised private funds for a thorough analysis of the needs of Massachusetts public schools. Such an analysis, termed an *adequacy study*, was a novel endeavor at the time. The concept of *adequacy* originated in the late 1980s as researchers and policymakers began to look beyond funding equity—that is, ensuring that school districts had roughly equal revenue per pupil regardless of local property wealth—to a more complex question: how much money does a school or district need to ensure that all students can meet state educational standards? This question

Box 6.1 Academic Performance in MA and MI: A Study in Contrasts

The National Assessment of Educational Progress (NAEP) is a congressionally mandated program of subject-matter tests administered regularly by the U.S. Department of Education's National Center for Education Statistics to a nationally representative sample of students. The NAEP tests were first administered in 1969 and are most frequently given in math, reading, science, and writing. The subject areas assessed by NAEP have since expanded to include civics, economics, U.S. history, and other topics.

Beginning in 1990, states were given the option of participating in trial assessments that would allow the release of state-level measures of student performance. This is now a permanent feature of NAEP, and nearly all states voluntarily participate in state-level assessments. Commonly referred to as "the nation's report card," these state assessments are used to compare student performance across the states. They are generally considered well-suited for such comparisons because they are not high stakes and thus are not subject to "teaching to the test." NAEP also collects information on students' educational experiences and educational practices in their schools.

Researchers have used NAEP scores along with student demographic data to compare state school systems. For example, at the state level, Jacob (2017) has calculated the proficiency rate one would expect to see in a state, given such factors as state size, population density, median household income, and unemployment rates. Measuring proficiency by a composite of fourth- and eighth-grade reading and math scores, Jacob found that Massachusetts "is not only a high-achieving state, but is scoring substantially higher than what one would expect even after accounting for the relative affluence of the state. . . . In contrast, Maryland, Michigan, and West Virginia all score significantly lower than expected based on the social and economic conditions in these states" (Jacob 2017, p. 3). The analysis reveals that, while the Bay State led the nation with nearly 50 percent of students meeting the rigorous NAEP proficiency standards in 2015, Michigan ranked 41st in the percentage of students meeting those standards, and the state was dead last in terms of proficiency growth (i.e., improvement in the percentage of students meeting the standards) since 2003.

Box 6.1 (continued)

A comparison of student scoring trends in Massachusetts and Michigan on an NAEP scale is presented below. As the data indicate, students in the Bay State's public schools substantially outperform their Michigan peers in fourth- and eighth-grade math and reading, and the performance gap has generally widened over time:

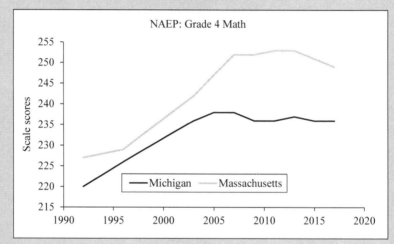

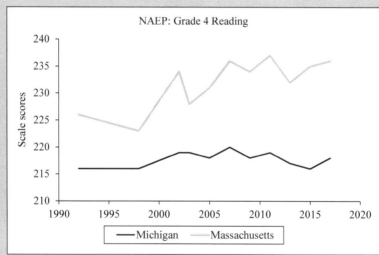

SOURCE: National Assessment of Educational Progress.

Box 6.1 (continued)

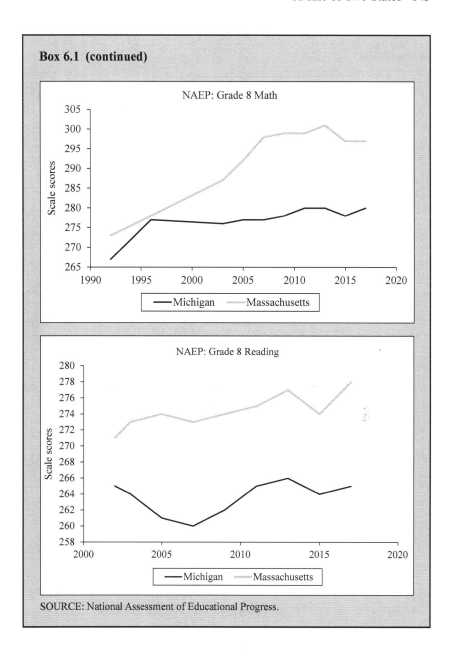

SOURCE: National Assessment of Educational Progress.

assumed growing importance with the rise of the educational standards in the 1990s.[2]

At this time, school finance adequacy studies were viewed skeptically by fiscal conservatives and public school critics, who considered them to be more partisan weaponry than objective analysis. Leaders in the Bay State, however, were fully open to this new line of inquiry that integrated education research and economic analysis. Rennie's leadership was particularly critical in giving educators a seat at the table. Unlike many aspiring education reformers from the business community, who may harbor suspicions, if not contempt, for public school teachers and organized labor more generally, Rennie insisted that the teacher union participate as a full partner in the reform effort. He also opposed charter schools and school choice, two reform strategies generally favored by business reformers.

In 1991, MBAE issued *Every Child a Winner! A Proposal for a Legislative Action Plan for Systemic Reform of Massachusetts's Public Primary and Secondary Education System*. The report addressed three basic issues: 1) accountability through state standards, 2) reforms to improve teacher quality and school management, and 3) a recommendation for a "foundation" budget sufficient to provide funding for students in every community in the state at the same school tax rate (MBAE 1991). The report's emphasis on finance adequacy was unmistakable and provided a framework for legislative action: "The strength of the Commonwealth will be a direct function of the capability of public schools to provide an adequate education to all children, regardless of race, ethnic background, social or economic status or location" (p. 7).

In 1993, Chief Justice Paul Liacos of the Commonwealth's Supreme Judicial Court ruled in *McDuffy* that Massachusetts had failed in its constitutional obligation to provide poor children with an adequate education. Unlike in other states, where a supreme court ruling invalidating a school finance system triggered a round of contentious legislative battles, the *McDuffy* ruling actually *followed* by one week the passage of the Bay State's landmark Education Reform Act of 1993. Signed into law days after the *McDuffy* ruling, the Reform Act followed closely the elements of the MBAE proposal, presenting a school funding formula, curriculum frameworks, and an accountability system.[3]

School funding

The legislation allocated an additional $350 million annually to poor districts. Another $100 million was provided for remediation. The new law, Chapter 70 of the state code, established a "foundation budget" for every district, calculating "adequate" expenditures in 11 categories (e.g., teachers, administration, pupil services, professional development), adjusted for wage costs and for the higher costs of educating children in poverty, English language learners, and special education students. The annual budget also calculated a local district contribution and provided state aid to cover the difference between local revenue and the full foundation budget. To ensure that the foundation budget of each district would keep pace with inflation, Chapter 70 indexed the basic elements of the budget with a price deflator calculated by the U.S. Department of Commerce. As a result of the new funding law and the state's robust economy, state aid per pupil for high-poverty districts rose dramatically through 2000. As the economy slowed after that, per pupil aid for those districts grew more slowly, but it accelerated again in 2005 following another SJC ruling, *Hancock v. Commissioner of Education*, which upheld *McDuffy* and revalidated the Commonwealth's efforts to meet its constitutional responsibilities to educate all children to a high standard. As expected, financial support for schools suffered during the Great Recession, but it resumed its robust growth trajectory in the 2011–2012 fiscal year.

Curriculum frameworks

The frameworks were constructed to support the teaching of core knowledge, including history and classical literature, and were shaped through a highly inclusive, democratic process.[4] Beginning in 1993, the Massachusetts Department of Elementary and Secondary Education convened thousands of educators and citizens to develop both the curriculum frameworks and a high-stakes state test that would assess student mastery of the new academic standards. The level of participation in this process and subsequent buy-in was extraordinary.

School accountability. The broad-based group convened by the state to develop the curriculum frameworks was also tasked with creating the corresponding accountability system, the Massachusetts Comprehensive Assessment System (MCAS). A key component of MCAS was a new tenth-grade test required for high school graduation. The test, called a competency determination, or CD, was created as an addition to each district's local graduation requirements.[5] The state also instituted a requirement that teachers pass both a basic skills test in communication and literacy and a subject matter test. The Massachusetts Tests for Educator Licensure (MTEL) were launched by the Department of Elementary and Secondary Education in 1998. The basic communications and literacy skills test was required for all types of licenses, including support personnel and administrators, while the subject matter test was required for teacher licenses.

The 1993 Education Reform Act authorized the creation of charter schools. However, unlike Michigan's charter statute, also passed in 1993, the Bay State's law carefully modulated the introduction and growth of these schools. The act originally authorized the awarding of no more than 25 charters statewide to boards operating independently of local school committees. Furthermore, the act limited the number of such charters—now termed *Commonwealth charters*—granted in Boston and Springfield to five each, and up to two in any other city or town. The original legislation also delayed the opening of any new charters until 1995 and imposed a statewide enrollment cap of 6,000 students.[6] These statutory limits on charter schools and enrollments were gradually raised by the legislature beginning in 1997.

Massachusetts is one of the few states where the state board of education is the sole authorizer of charter schools. And the Massachusetts board has set a high bar for both entry and continuation. During the first 20 years of the charter school program, 431 prospectuses and 246 full applications for charters were submitted, and 104 charters were awarded. Over this period, 23 charters have been surrendered, revoked, or denied renewal. By 2013–2014, there were 80 operating charters in the Bay State (70 of them Commonwealth charters), enrolling approximately 35,000 students. Of the 70 Commonwealth charters, 19 were in Boston and enrolled about 7,000 students, or 13 percent of the district's enrollment, with another 1 percent attending Commonwealth charters outside the city (Chester 2014, p. 13) (Box 6.2).

Box 6.2   The Bay State Battle over Charter Expansion

The 2010 Achievement Gap Act expanded the limits on charter school enrollments in communities with particularly low-achieving school districts. The impetus for this charter expansion was twofold: first, the federal RTT grant criteria included the lifting of charter caps; and second, an initiative petition then circulating in the Bay State to raise the cap appeared to many as likely to be approved.

The Achievement Gap Act limited cap expansions to those communities where district performance was in the lowest 10 percent of districts statewide. The new law also required charter operators to adopt recruitment and retention plans designed to ensure that the charters serve representative populations within their low-performing districts. Furthermore, the new charters and expansions of existing charters were limited to "proven providers"—that is, charter operators with records of demonstrated success in closing persistent achievement gaps. Finally, the 2010 law created a new category of Horace Mann charters: up to 14 "Horace Mann III" charters would be permitted statewide. These new "in-district" charters would allow districts to directly contract with not-for-profit management companies of proven effectiveness within the Commonwealth, while allowing more flexibility than would be available under district collective bargaining.

The 2010 charter expansion, however, did not quiet the steady drumbeat for charter expansion in the Commonwealth. In 2011, a group backed by the Bill and Melinda Gates Foundation and the Walton Family Foundation established the Boston Compact in order to promote a "portfolio" approach to schooling among public schools, charters, and parochial schools. Such an approach is often justifiably viewed as a procharter strategy intended to pull resources from traditional public schools. Such was the case here: the compact lobbied for legislation creating an electronic enrollment system that would automatically distribute school applications among both charters and traditional public schools, unifying the currently separate systems. Another compact document surfaced that referenced a "trisector facilities plan," interpreted by concerned public school supporters as a charter-backed grab for space in public schools (Gabor 2018).

> **Box 6.2 (continued)**
>
> During the 2016 election, Massachusetts became ground zero in the charter expansion wars. In the most expensive ballot campaign in Bay State history, charter advocates spent $20.5 million in support of Question 2, which called for raising the state's charter cap by 12 schools annually in perpetuity. However, despite being outspent by about two to one, the anticharter side prevailed, with 62 percent of voters opposing the expansion.
>
> Almost a year after the election, the Massachusetts Office of Campaign and Political Finance levied a $426,466 fine on a New York–based organization, Families for Excellent Schools–Advocacy (FESA), for violating campaign finance laws. This "astroturf" group had poured $15.6 million in dark money into the procharter campaign (Gabor 2018, p. 161). Nevertheless, charter advocates from both within and without the state will likely continue their efforts to lift the charter cap in the Bay State.

REVOLUTION, EVOLUTION, AND EDUCATIONAL DECLINE IN MICHIGAN

In the early 1970s, Michigan distributed general aid to local school districts through a foundation formula that guaranteed all districts a minimum amount for each pupil. However, by 1973 this guarantee meant little, as Michigan's highest-spending district tripled the per-pupil expenditures of the districts at the bottom of the spending order. Facing such enormous disparities, along with a court challenge of the school funding system, the Michigan legislature scrapped the foundation formula in favor of a guaranteed tax base (GTB) system, effective with the 1973–1974 fiscal year.

In the first year of the GTB regime, more than 90 percent of Michigan's school districts received formula aid, assuring all of them of equal revenue per pupil for equal tax effort. However, by 1993–1994, this proportion had fallen to about two-thirds, as state aid failed to keep pace with local property-tax growth, property-rich districts outspent their less wealthy peers, and interdistrict disparities returned to early 1970s levels. Moreover, local school property-tax rates had risen to unprecedented levels, with fully 122 school districts within four mills of the state's constitutional limit (Citizens Research Council of Michigan 1992). Voter discontent with local property taxes was expressed most dramatically in rural Kalkaska School District, where the repeated rejection of a millage request led to the closing of schools on March 15, 1993, capping a mere 135-day school year. With this abrupt and unexpected school shutdown, it became clear to policymakers that the local property tax, long a bulwark of school funding in Michigan, was no longer reliable.

Michigan Legislators Blow up School Funding

While political, business, and education leaders in Massachusetts confronted issues of educational adequacy raised by *McDuffy*, Michigan policymakers, unburdened by an adverse court ruling and uninformed by an adequacy study, focused largely on the much narrower issue of property tax relief. In Michigan's 1990 gubernatorial campaign, Republican candidate John Engler promised voters a sizable property tax cut if elected. After upsetting two-term incumbent James Blanchard, Engler launched a petition drive to place on the November 1992 ballot an initiative for a constitutional amendment—known as Proposal C—cutting property taxes and capping future assessment hikes. The legislature placed its own tax relief plan—Proposal A—on the ballot. Both plans were soundly trounced by Michigan voters, extending a string of failed attempts at property-tax and school-finance reform that dated back to the 1970s.[7]

The voters' rejection of Proposals A and C was followed by one more ill-fated attempt at property-tax and school-finance reform. Following marathon negotiations between lawmakers and Governor Engler, both houses of the legislature garnered the two-thirds supermajorities needed to place yet another constitutional ballot proposal before Michigan voters. And, yet again, the voters drubbed the proposal (Proposal A of 1993), this time by a 55 percent to 45 percent margin.

Despite these setbacks at the polls, Governor Engler and Senate Republicans remained committed to delivering some measure of property tax relief in the governor's first term. So, in mid-July 1993, they introduced Senate Bill 1, a relatively modest proposal to lower property assessments over several years. This triggered a surprising and historic event. During debate on the bill, U.S. Senator and declared Democratic gubernatorial candidate Debbie Stabenow stepped to the microphone and challenged the Republican majority with a radical amendment to their modest bill: the total elimination of local property tax as a revenue source for school operations.

Whether a bold effort to break a decades-long string of failed attempts at school finance reform or a bluff aimed at forcing Republicans to rethink their position, the result was stunning: following an immediate recess to confer with the governor, Senate Republicans announced their support for the amendment and, in a quick 29-to-5 postmidnight vote on July 21, 1993, the Senate adopted the radical proposal. The next day, the Michigan House, on a 69-to-35 vote, quickly followed suit, and in mid-August Governor Engler signed Senate Bill 1 into law as Public Act 145 of 1993, eliminating local property taxes for school operations, thereby wiping out two-thirds of schools' operating budgets.

Full replacement of this revenue by state taxes was prohibited by the Michigan constitution, so the governor and legislative leaders crafted a reform package that offered two alternative revenue plans, each calling for a partial restoration of the revenue lost from the elimination of local property taxes. One plan proposed a constitutional amendment to hike Michigan's sales tax cap from 4.0 percent to 6.0 percent, while the alternative statutory plan, which would take effect if voters rejected the constitutional amendment, would hike the state personal income tax rate from 4.6 percent to 6.0 percent.[8] Both plans included a new state property tax. On March 15, 1994, Michigan voters approved the constitutional amendment, Proposal A, by a resounding 69 percent to 31 percent margin.

The State Takes Control

A formula crafted by a bipartisan 14-member House task force became the basis of Michigan's new school funding program. The new law shifted the state from the GTB structure back to a foundation plan but, unlike the pre-1974 regime, Proposal A imposed strict limits on local district options to supplement state funding levels. The state was now in tight control of school spending.

Detailed explanations of Michigan's Proposal A funding program are available elsewhere (e.g., Addonizio and Drake 2005; Addonizio, Kearney, and Prince 1995; Kearney and Addonizio 2002). Our interest in teacher compensation and working conditions, particularly class sizes, teaching loads, and availability of support staff, requires a close look at the arc of financial support for Massachusetts and Michigan schools since their respective 1993–1994 reforms. Unlike in Massachusetts, the Michigan reforms were not motivated by a legal challenge to the school funding system or a shared concern by educational, political, and business leaders over student achievement in the schools. Rather, the basic driver of the reform effort was demand for property tax relief and greater reliance on state revenue for school funding. No school finance adequacy study and no educator-led review of curriculum standards were undertaken or even seriously considered. At the same time, however, the governor and legislative leaders understood that the promise of a generous school aid proposal was needed to secure the required supermajority support in each legislative chamber to place the proposed constitutional amendment before the Michigan voters.

Accordingly, Michigan's new school aid law was generous in its first year. In addition to setting a minimum foundation allowance of $4,200 per pupil (assuring an increase of at least 20 percent for some local schools), the law set a "basic" foundation allowance of $5,000 for 1994–1995, along with a maximum level of $6,500. Districts spending less than $3,950 per pupil were boosted to $4,200 for 1994–1995, while districts spending between $3,950 and $6,500 in 1993–1994 received increases ranging from $160 to $250 on a sliding scale. The 52 districts spending more than $6,500 in 1993–1994 were allowed by the statute to levy a new "hold harmless" millage to boost spending by up to $160. So all districts in Michigan could share in the first-year funding gains.

However, unlike the Massachusetts funding reforms, which were one part of a "grand political bargain" that integrated finance, curriculum standards, and school accountability into a cohesive, evidence-based reform program supported by what became an enduring coalition of political, education, and business leaders, Michigan's Proposal A was essentially a tax shift that, while generously funding the schools for nearly a decade, was not tied to any concept or measure of educational need emanating from the school community. Lacking such a foundational consensus that linked school funding to specific educational standards, the Proposal A reforms eventually fell far short of adequately funding the schools, as the legislature increased the basic foundation allowance a mere $26 annually from 2003 to 2018, well below the rate of inflation (Arsen, Delpier, and Nagel 2019, p. 26).

While the new statute provided for the annual recalculation of foundation allowances according to indices of earmarked revenue and enrollment growth, these promised increases required that funds earmarked for K–12 schools through Michigan's School Aid Fund (SAF) be supplemented by funds from the state's General Fund (GF) budget. But nothing in the Proposal A reforms mandated GF transfers to the SAF. Legislators maintained complete discretion over this annual decision, eventually jettisoning the foundation calculation mandate and abandoning school funding promises made by the Proposal A authors.

The change in policy has been striking. In the early years of the Proposal A program, GF transfers to the SAF were relatively generous, averaging about $560 million annually between 1995 and 2003 (Arsen, Delpier, and Nagel 2019). At that point, however, the GF contributions were sharply curtailed, as legislated cuts in state business and personal income taxes in 2000 and 2001 contributed to a structural deficit in the 2004 GF budget (Citizens Research Council of Michigan 2003).

Further cuts in business taxes and other state policy changes, combined with effects of the Great Recession, not only brought an end to GF support for schools, but actually reversed the direction of these transfers, as portions of Michigan's postsecondary education budget formerly supported by the General Fund were now financed with SAF revenue (Arsen, Delpier, and Nagel 2019).[9] Indeed, in light of additional business tax breaks paid with SAF revenue, along with the 2018 transfer of $500 million from the fund to pay income tax refunds, it is clear that the SAF, long dedicated to K–12 education, has come to be used by the Michigan legislature as a slush fund for other priorities, including tax relief.

Diverging Priorities, Policies, and Educational Outcomes

For more than a quarter century now, political leaders in Massachusetts and Michigan have been making starkly different choices about their public schools, including resources, standards, and accountability. The differences in the financing of K–12 education are particularly

acute and reflective of differing priorities. Michigan's declining support for public schools is not the unavoidable consequence of economic
decline. Rather, it is a deliberate policy choice to facilitate cutting taxes.
A 2019 Education Policy Report from Michigan State University notes
that while Michigan's tax effort (i.e., "effective tax rate," or state and
local taxes as a percentage of personal income) surpassed the national
average in most years prior to 2002, it has since fallen well below the
(simultaneously declining) effective national rate, with the sharpest
drop occurring since 2010. As a result, between 1995 and 2015 (essentially the Proposal A era), Michigan was dead last among the 50 states
in K–12 revenue growth, with inflation-adjusted 2015 revenue amounting to a mere 82 percent of the 1995 level. And Michigan was quite
alone at the bottom: West Virginia, the next lowest, was at 97 percent
of its 1995 level.[10]

Massachusetts, in contrast, enjoyed real 2015 K–12 revenue
amounting to 126 percent of its 1995 level. The Bay State's relative
advantage began in the early 1990s, as leaders in both states tackled
education and tax reforms. Figure 6.1 compares K–12 spending per
pupil in the two states beginning in 1992–1993, when both were nearly
equal by this metric.

Figure 6.1 Total Current Spending per Pupil

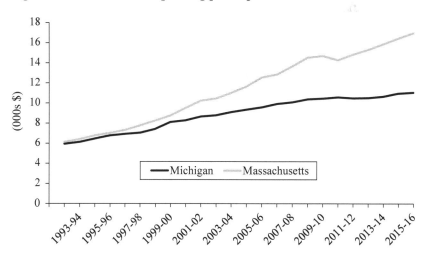

SOURCE: U.S. Department of Education, National Center for Education Statistics,
Common Core of Data, State Fiscal Reports.

Figure 6.2 Average Teacher Salary

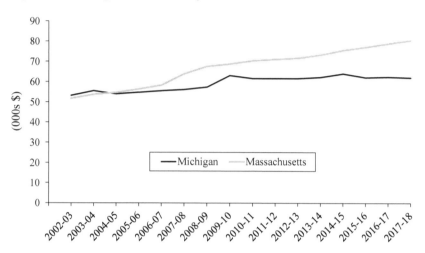

SOURCE: National Education Association.

As Figure 6.1 shows, over this period, the Bay State has consistently chosen to finance its public schools at a higher level than Michigan, with the spending gap widening nearly every year and most dramatically over the past five. These substantial disparities in financial support are clearly reflected in teacher salary trends and working conditions. Figure 6.2 compares average teacher salaries in Massachusetts and Michigan since 2002–2003.

The average salary, a function of both teacher experience and education level, was actually higher in Michigan in the first two years of this 16-year history. But Michigan teacher salaries fell below those of their Massachusetts counterparts in 2004–2005 and have trailed the Bay State levels ever since, with the difference becoming more pronounced in recent years. By 2017–2018, the average teacher salary in the Bay State exceeded Michigan's average by fully 30 percent.

The trend in pupil-teacher ratios, depicted in Figure 6.3, is equally clear and perhaps even more telling when comparing the work of public school teachers in the two states. In every year since 2003–2004, the period for which consistent data are available, pupil-teacher ratios have been lower in Massachusetts, and the differences have not been trivial.

Figure 6.3 Number of Students per Teacher in Massachusetts and Michigan

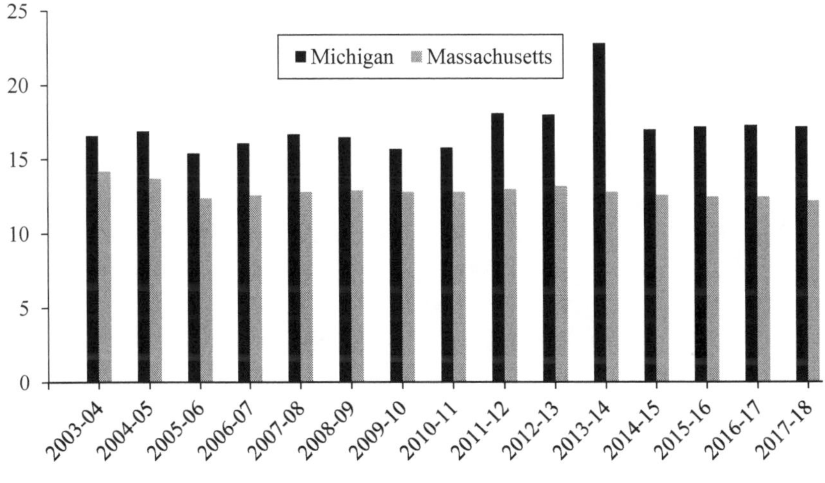

SOURCE: National Education Association.

In 2017–2018, the most recent year for which data are available, the difference is fully five students per teacher (Box 6.3).

Massachusetts and Michigan Teacher Labor Markets: A Seaworthy Vessel and a Leaky Bucket

As discussed in Chapter 2, a teacher shortage arises when teacher demand exceeds supply. Demand depends on student enrollment. Michigan's K–12 enrollments have declined steadily over the past dozen years, falling from just over 1.7 million students in the fall of 2005 to slightly more than 1.5 million in the fall of 2015, roughly a 12 percent decline. Over this same period, the Michigan teaching force shrank by about 16 percent, from almost 118,000 to just over 99,100 (Citizens Research Council of Michigan 2019, p. vi). At the same time, however, the number of students identified as economically disadvantaged and the number of non-English-speaking students have increased. Those students generally require enhanced instructional support, including specially trained teachers and smaller classes.

Box 6.3 The Slide in Starting Salaries for Michigan Teachers

Seventeen states impose salary schedules for public school teachers, but Massachusetts and Michigan do not. Teacher compensation issues in both states are settled at the district level.[1] While each state maintains teacher salary databases and reports average teacher salaries across districts, average starting salaries are not tracked and published. However, consistent data on average starting salaries for Michigan Education Association bargaining units, obtained for the years 1992–1993 through 2017–2018, reveal little nominal growth over this extended period and a substantial decline in real terms. These data are depicted in the figure below.

Over the entire 23-year period, real average starting salaries for Michigan teachers fell by more than 11 percent. Recent history has been particularly dire for new teachers, with real starting salaries falling in 12 of the last 14 years and declining more than 15 percent over this period.

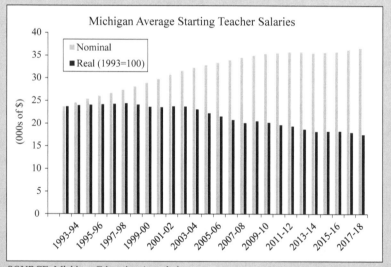

SOURCE: Michigan Education Association.

1. Contrary to popular belief, statewide salary schedules do not dictate what teachers in the state will earn. Rather, the schedules merely set minimum salaries that districts may pay their teachers, typically based on a teacher's education and years of experience. In the 17 states that used salary schedules in 2016, districts often paid teachers more than the schedule required. If not updated regularly, a state salary schedule can become irrelevant. In Illinois, for example, where the schedule had not been revised since 1980, the 2016 minimum starting salary was $10,000. See Griffith (2016).

Figure 6.4 Michigan Teacher Turnover

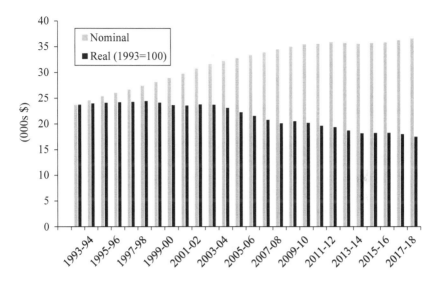

SOURCE: Citizens Research Council of Michigan (2019), p. 19; reproduced from 2017 Michigan Department of Education report, *Teacher Turnover in Michigan*.

Turnover and attrition

A study by the Michigan Department of Education found that average teacher turnover across the public schools was 19.8 percent between the 2012–2013 and 2013–2014 school years—much higher than the national average of 15.7 percent. And the rate for Michigan has remained high, registering at 19.3 percent in 2016–2017 (Citizens Research Council of Michigan 2019, pp. vii–viii). Turnover rates for selected years are depicted in Figure 6.4.

This higher-than-average turnover rate (movers plus leavers) is not reflected in the estimate of a statewide teacher shortage. One district's loss is another's gain. The rate does, however, signal local shortages. On average, about 16 percent of public school teaching positions must be filled each year because of "leavers" (career exits) or "movers" (job changers). The percentage of leavers has remained fairly stable in recent years at about 8 percent. Movers, however, have increased from 9.5 percent in 2004–2005 to 11.4 percent in 2016–2017, well above the national rate of 8.1 percent.

Turnover rates are particularly high in Michigan's urban districts and in charter schools, reflecting in part increased student mobility stemming from Michigan's expansive charter school and cross-district choice programs. Research published by the Michigan Department of Education found more than 24 percent turnover in urban districts over the three-year period from 2014–2015 through 2016–2017; by comparison, rural and suburban districts had annual rates of 16 percent and 15 percent, respectively. And school governance was found to matter, as teacher turnover for 2016–2017 was fully 30 percent, more than twice the rate for traditional public schools of 14 percent (Stackhouse and Lloyd 2018). The turnover rate for charter schools in the Detroit metropolitan area, where such schools are highly concentrated, is particularly alarming: at 36 percent, it is more than double the rate for the region's traditional public schools. In summary, the recent Michigan Department of Education and Citizens Research Council studies confirm that Michigan's teacher workforce is markedly less stable than the national workforce as a whole (Box 6.4).

These findings for Michigan contrast starkly with conditions found in Massachusetts, where, according to a 2016 report by the Learning Policy Institute (LPI), the attrition rate (i.e., leavers) was less than one-third the Michigan rate in 2013 (3 percent vs. 10 percent). Key determinants of teacher supply and demand reported in the national LPI study for our two subject states are presented in Table 6.1.

As the LPI study shows, teachers in the Bay State enjoy substantially lower pupil-teacher ratios than their Michigan counterparts, along

Table 6.1 Teacher Labor Market Indicators

Indicator	Massachusetts	Michigan
Average starting salary, 2013 ($)	40,600	35,901
% teacher attrition (leavers), 2013	3	10
% planning to leave ASAP, 2012	3.5	6.5
Pupil-teacher ratio, 2014	13.6	18.1
% of teachers worried about job security because of testing	7	18
% of teachers who feel supported by their administrator	45	44

SOURCE: Sutcher, Darling-Hammond, and Carver-Thomas (2016).

Box 6.4 Anatomy of a Teacher Shortage: The Rise of Long-Term Subs in Michigan

A teacher shortage does not reveal itself in the form of leaderless or overcrowded classrooms. Rather, the classrooms appear as ones headed by unqualified or poorly prepared instructors. In recent years, Michigan public schools have increasingly staffed their classrooms with long-term substitutes with as little as 60 college credits and no formal educational training. An investigative report by *Bridge Michigan* (Wilkinson and French 2019) revealed that the number of such teachers, intended to fill a few slots during times of statewide teacher shortages, had increased tenfold over the past six years:

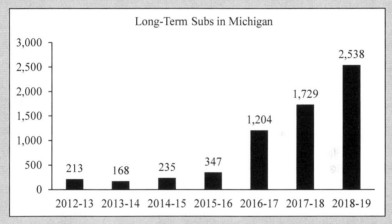

SOURCE: Michigan Department of Education, Office of Educator Excellence (Wilkinson and French 2019).

As expected, these subs are not randomly distributed across Michigan schools. The Bridge investigation revealed that students attending low-income school districts and charter schools were three times more likely to learn under a long-term sub than other districts. Furthermore, charter school students were four times more likely to have a long-term substitute than students in traditional public schools. Finally, students in the lowest-performing school districts and charter schools were more than three times as likely to have long-term substitutes instead of certified teachers.

Box 6.4 (continued)

The magnitude of the state's teacher shortage may have caught Michigan policymakers off guard. In any event, in 2018, the Michigan legislature lowered state standards for substitute teacher permits from 90 hours of college credit to 60.

---

with much less anxiety about job security associated with student testing. The survey reveals little difference between the two groups regarding perceived support by their building administrator. The vast differences revealed in the LPI study stem from divergences in state law and policy regarding school funding and teacher accountability.

The Learning Policy Institute reported an overall teacher surplus for Massachusetts for 2015. In April of that year, the Massachusetts Department of Elementary and Secondary Education (ESE) commissioned a study by the American Institutes for Research (AIR) to develop a comprehensive set of 10-year projections of teacher supply and demand. This study confirmed the finding of an overall teacher surplus in the Bay State. Specifically, the AIR study projected student enrollment to decline over the next 10 years by just under 6 percent, while the annual supply of teachers fell by slightly less than 2 percent, creating a teacher surplus of about 4 percent by 2023–2024. The study did forecast a decline in new entrants to the teacher labor market—something not unexpected in light of the looming surplus.

The study projected a decline in teacher demand in all four program areas: 1) general education, 2) special education, 3) English language learners, and 4) career/technical education, with expected declines of more than 10 percent in all but general education. At the same time, while AIR projects an increase in the supply of general education teachers, resulting in a statewide surplus, the study projects a decline of more than 20 percent in English language learning (ELL) and special education teachers, outpacing expected declines in demand and yielding teacher shortages in these areas (Levin et al. 2015, pp. 31–36).

Teacher demographic groups

AIR projects an increase in the demand for minority teachers, while projecting little change in their supply. Consequently, a shortage of minority teachers is expected in the Bay State by the end of the projection period, 2023–2024. In contrast, while the supply of white teachers is expected to decline, the corresponding demand is projected to fall more rapidly, leading to a small surplus by the end of the projection period (Levin et al. 2015, pp. 41–46). The "under 26" age group is the only group for which supply is projected to fall short of demand. This group, of course, makes up the greatest portion of new entrants to the profession.

Collaboration or Confrontation: Contrasting Approaches to Teacher Evaluation

As illustrated in Table 6.1, teachers in Michigan appear to worry much more than their Bay State colleagues about job security and student testing. While it is difficult to trace the precise origins of these diverging sentiments, a look at teacher evaluation law and practice in the two states is enlightening. A comparative analysis of teacher evaluation laws across the states was published by the National Council on Teacher Quality (NCTQ) in 2015. The analysis examines each state's laws and regulations in terms of a comprehensive set of personnel policies, including those relating to the use of student test scores in teacher evaluation and the linkage of teacher evaluations and teacher compensation. Key findings of the 2015 NCTQ study are presented in Table 6.2.

As the comparison shows, the two states are aligned with respect to the first six policies. Both states adopted the first five policies in following the majority of states regarding professional development, improvement plans, and teacher dismissals. And both Massachusetts and Michigan join a near majority ($n = 23$) of states in considering teacher performance in tenure decisions. Both are also among the great majority of states that reject teacher merit pay. But the Bay State differs from Michigan on two policies of fundamental importance to classroom teachers. First, unlike Michigan and the great majority of states ($n = 35$), Massachusetts does not use student growth as a significant or preponderant metric when evaluating teachers. Second, while Michigan

Table 6.2 Teacher Evaluation in Massachusetts and Michigan

Policy	Massachusetts	Michigan	No. of states adopting policy
Teacher performance considered in tenure decisions	Yes	Yes	23
Professional development designed based on individual teacher evaluations	Yes	Yes	31
Teachers rated ineffective must have improvement plan	Yes	Yes	35
Teachers rated ineffective are eligible for dismissal	Yes	Yes	28
Layoff decisions consider teacher performance	Yes	Yes	19
Teachers can receive merit pay based on student achievement results	No	No	9
Student growth is significant or preponderant evaluation criterion	No	Yes	35
Teacher evaluations impact compensation	No	Yes	16

SOURCE: National Council on Teacher Quality (2015), Figure 25.

is among a minority of states ($n = 16$) that link teacher evaluations to compensation, Massachusetts does not.

Conclusion: The Importance of Vision and Leadership

Public school policy, including finance and personnel issues, while one would hope it is informed by sound research, is fundamentally political, with decisions and outcomes stemming from the vision and leadership of those in charge. That vision may be broadly informed and nuanced and the leadership broad and bipartisan, or the vision narrow and leadership insular and partisan. With Massachusetts and Michigan, we have an example of each, with outcomes diverging accordingly.

In the Bay State, a diverse and bipartisan coalition of business, political, and educational leaders focused their efforts on a singular goal: the educational achievement of all children. The business leaders learned about public education by forming partnerships with schools and educators. And these leaders were concerned about more than the availability of a skilled workforce. They viewed the public schools as the means for enhancing citizenship, bolstering the civic as well as economic health of local communities across the Commonwealth.

Business leadership was critical to the success of the reform movement. The agenda of the Massachusetts Business Alliance for Education (MBAE) was crystalized in the organization's manifesto, "Every Child a Winner," with its emphasis on providing educational opportunities for all children in the state. Their report became the blueprint for the Bay State's landmark bipartisan 1993 legislation, which was shaped in part by the education community. Most importantly, leadership's attention to public education did not end with passage of these bills. Business involvement has been ongoing and persistent. Writing in 2014, Paul Reville, former Massachusetts Secretary of Education and current professor at Harvard University's Graduate School of Education, observes the following:

> Governors, the legislature, business groups, education advocacy groups, the media, urban superintendents, and many others maintained long-term commitments to implementing the work of education reform. Legal pressure also came from the state's highest court, the Supreme Judicial Court, which accepted the reforms as a remedy to a long-running equity finance case while demanding consistent, long-term commitment by the state to the reforms.

> Now, 21 years after the 1993 education reform policy victory and deep into successful implementation, it is all too readily apparent that although Massachusetts has done very well, comparatively speaking, we are a long way from achieving our original goal of closing pernicious, persistent achievement gaps. (Reville 2015, pp. 189–190)

Michigan's reform movement, which began about the same time and was perhaps more widely heralded because it entailed the sudden and unexpected dismantling and subsequent rebuilding of the school funding system, was less focused on educational standards and equity goals and proved far less enduring as a state priority. Perhaps most importantly, leadership of the Michigan reforms was far less inclusive and enduring than in Massachusetts, with little voice from Michigan educators and relentless turnover in the legislature. The initial motivation of the reform effort was property tax relief, not school improvement, and the absence of an adverse court ruling on school funding (or the credible threat of such a challenge) muted any serious calls for equal educational opportunities or the narrowing of achievement gaps based on race or class.

While Michigan's basic foundation allowance rose by nearly 3 percent annually between 1994–1995 and 2002–2003, outpacing the average annual inflation rate over this period even as enrollments rose steadily, Michigan's leaders have drastically cut their support for public schools since then. As Arsen, Delpier, and Nagel (2019) report, inflation-adjusted funding for Michigan schools declined an astounding 30 percent between 2002 and 2015. Unlike Massachusetts, where the adequacy of school funding has been studied, monitored, and addressed in state appropriations decisions for decades, thus assuring decent compensation, class sizes, and support staff for the state's classroom teachers, the financial support of schools and teachers in Michigan has taken a back seat to tax cuts, school choice, and charter school expansion.

The enduring bipartisan alliance of political, business, and educational leaders that has been so productive in Massachusetts has never been achieved in Michigan. Whether a function of the strict term limits, which triggered rapid turnover and loss of institutional memory and policy expertise among Michigan legislators, or a more general change in the state's political culture, Michigan has long since abandoned the promises made in the early 1990s by the architects of the Proposal A foundation formula. As a result, while Massachusetts enjoys a healthy surplus of classroom teachers and exceptionally strong levels of student achievement, Michigan's education fortunes have declined precipitously over the past two decades, with chronic and rising teacher shortages and steadily declining student achievement.

Notes

1. In the 1970s, the Bay State (then home for a time to the author) was often referred to as "Taxachusetts," a state where residents faced the second-highest combined state and local tax burden in the nation and where per capita property taxes were nearly twice the national average (Zabel 2014).
2. For a good discussion of the purpose and alternative methodologies of adequacy studies, see Rebell (2006).
3. For a vivid and detailed account of the process and politics of the Massachusetts reforms, see Gabor (2018), Chapter 3.

4. This brief summary is based on Gabor (2018). See Chapter 3 of that book for a more complete discussion.

5. The rollout of the high-stakes MCAS CD was gradual and transparent. The test was first given in 1998 but was not required for graduation until 2001. And the test was "open," allowing the schools full access to all questions and students' answers.

6. Horace Mann charter schools, in which traditional district school committees participate in the application process, were created under subsequent legislation, beginning in 1997. See Chester (2014).

7. For a more complete account of this history, see Addonizio and Kearney (2012), Chapter 2.

8. For more detail on these alternative plans, see Addonizio, Kearney, and Prince (1995).

9. Although small amounts are still transferred from the GF to the SAF, in recent years more than $600 million in SAF revenues have been allocated annually to Michigan public universities and community colleges. See Ruark (2018).

10. In per pupil terms, Michigan ranked 48th among the states, with a 13 percent decline (Arsen, Delpier, and Nagel 2019).

7

Blue Collar or White?
Who Decides?

It is . . . advisable that the teacher should understand, and even be able to criticize, the general principles upon which the whole educational system is formed and administered. He is not like a private soldier in an army, expected merely to obey, or like a cog in a wheel, expected merely to respond to and transmit external energy; he must be an intelligent medium of action.

—John Dewey (1964)

A professional is a person who is an expert, and by virtue of that expertise is permitted to operate fairly independently, to make decisions, to exercise discretion, to be free of most direct supervision.

—Albert Shanker (1986)

In April 1985, two years after the release of *A Nation at Risk*, then–American Federation of Teachers President Al Shanker issued a stunning call for a new era of professionalism in public school teaching. In an address at the OFIA Educational Conference, a teacher convention held each year in Niagara Falls, he said the following:

> We have not been able to achieve all that we had hoped for through the bargaining process, and it is time to go beyond it to something additional and quite different. . . . We can continue working away only at collective bargaining. But if that is our decision, I predict that in 10 to 15 years we will find we've been on a treadmill. Unless we go beyond collective bargaining to teacher professionalism, we will fail in our major objectives: to preserve public education in the United States and to improve the status of teachers economically, socially, and politically. (Toch 1991, p. 141)

Shanker conceded that the industrial-style unionism embraced by teachers contributed to the public's view of classroom teachers as less than professional: "We tend to be viewed today as though we are acting only in our own self-interest. . . . That image is standing in the way of our achieving professional status" (Shanker 1985, p. 12; Toch 1991, p. 141).

Shanker's address reinforced recommendations made in *A Nation at Risk* that teacher salaries be made "professionally competitive, market-sensitive, and performance-based" and that salary, promotion, tenure, and retention decisions "be tied to an effective evaluation system that includes peer review so that superior teachers can be rewarded, average ones encouraged, and poor ones either improved or terminated" (National Commission on Excellence in Education 1983, p. 25). But he also called for "professionalizing" teaching through internal accountability and leadership within the ranks, both of which are distinguishing characteristics of more esteemed professions such as law and medicine.

Shanker sharpened his conception of teacher professionalism in his 1988 speech at the National Press Club, where he proposed that small groups of teachers be empowered to create their own "schools within schools." These teacher-led "empowered" (or "charter") schools would adopt such specific reforms as peer assistance and review, performance-based pay, and explicit sharing of responsibility for school performance by teachers and administrators. As the standards-based school reform movement proceeded through the 1990s, other union leaders voiced support for Shanker's vision of an evolution from industrial-style to professional unionism. NEA President Bob Chase, in a 1997 National Press Club address, called on his members to abandon their traditional defensive, self-serving posture and assume responsibility for school quality:

> The fact is that, in some instances, we have used our power to block uncomfortable changes...to protect the narrow interest of our members, and not to advance the interests of students and schools. . . .
>
> The fact is that while the vast majority of teachers are capable and dedicated...there are indeed some bad teachers in America's schools. And it is our job as a union to improve these teachers or—failing that—to get them out of the classroom.
>
> The fact is that while NEA does not control curriculum, set funding levels, or hire and fire, we cannot go on denying responsibility for school quality. We cannot wash our hands of it and say "that's management's job." School quality—the quality of the environment where students learn and where our members work—must be our responsibility as a union.

The fact is that, too often, NEA has sat on the sidelines of change . . . naysaying . . . quick to say what won't work and slow to say what will. (Chase, p. 3)

THE CARNEGIE CORPORATION AND THE PROFESSIONALIZATION CAMPAIGN

The call for the professionalization of classroom teaching was given a prominent voice in 1985, when the Carnegie Corporation of New York established the Carnegie Forum on Education and the Economy to examine the link between economic growth and education. In May 1986, the Carnegie Foundation's Task Force on Teaching as a Profession released its report *A Nation Prepared: Teaching for the 21st Century.*[1] The report sought to detail the "pay and conditions of work" needed to attract talented newcomers into teaching. The task force argued that, in addition to higher salaries, the teaching profession would need to be "restructured" to provide greater autonomy and career opportunities in order to recruit and retain able and ambitious candidates. Specific recommendations included teacher participation in decisions about student and staff assignments, organization of the school day, school budgeting, and even the hiring and firing of staff and administrators (Carnegie Forum on Education and the Economy 1986; Toch 1991).

A central theme of the Carnegie report, adopted by Shanker a few years later in his advocacy of "empowered schools," was the need to abandon the traditional hierarchical control that fully subordinated teachers to administrators and empower them with greater professional discretion. The authors noted that teaching had retained the vestiges of its historical roots as a part-time occupation for women, burdened by conditions that "more nearly resemble those of semi-skilled workers on the assembly line rather than those of professionals" (Carnegie Forum on Education and the Economy 1986, p. 36, quoted in Mehta 2013b, p. 131). In order to attract talent to classroom teaching, the job would need to ensure the autonomy and empowerment enjoyed by true professions:

Professional work is characterized by the assumption that the job of a professional is to bring special expertise and judgment to bear on the work at hand. Because their expertise and judgment [are] respected and they alone are presumed to have it, professionals enjoy a high degree of autonomy in carrying out their work. (Carnegie Forum on Education and the Economy 1986, p. 36)

The authors emphasized the need for educators to define and elevate the standards of the profession. They called on teachers to take control of their certification process in the manner in which other, more highly respected professions establish their quality standards:

> Virtually every occupation regarded by the public as a true profession has codified the knowledge, the specific expertise, required by its practitioners, and has required that those who wish to practice that profession . . . demonstrate that they have a command of the needed knowledge and the ability to apply it. . . . They capture that knowledge in an assessment or examination and administer that examination to people who want a certificate saying they passed the assessment. (Carnegie Forum on Education and the Economy 1986, p. 65)

In the years following publication of the Carnegie report *A Nation Prepared*, professionalization advocates crafted a three-pronged strategy to take control of teaching training and licensure. The first prong addressed the task of defining excellence in the teaching profession. To do this, the Task Force called for the creation of a National Board for Professional Teaching Standards (NBPTS). This independent, non-profit board, described in Chapter 1, was established in 1987 to certify successful candidates from the ranks of the current teaching force as highly qualified on the basis of a rigorous, teacher-designed evaluation process. Unlike initial licensure for new teachers, which is governed by state law and typically requires coursework in pedagogy and subject matter along with student teaching and a written exam, the NBPTS certifies accomplished teaching by analyzing detailed portfolios, including videos of classroom practice and a standardized written exam. As such, the program does not directly address the need for entry-level talent but seeks to enhance the professional status of classroom teaching by recognizing demonstrated teaching excellence according to rigorous standards and compelling evidence.

The first National Board–certified teachers earned their certificate in 1994. By the end of 2012, more than 100,000 teachers had earned National Board certification. Also by that time, 49 states had recognized or assisted with National Board certification, either by paying participation costs or awarding higher status or pay for successful participants. The program appears to have been well received by the profession. Studies have found that National Board–certified teachers (NBCTs) believe that participation has improved their classroom practice and that NBCTs are more likely to ascend to teacher leader and mentoring roles (Cannata et al. 2010). Research evidence also indicates that NBCTs have generally improved student achievement (Harris and Sass 2009). Nevertheless, they represent a mere 3 percent of teachers nationwide, far too small a movement to materially impact the profession as a whole.

New Standards for Beginning Teachers

NBPTS sought to create a new high tier for classroom teachers, bestowing enhanced status, responsibility, opportunities, and compensation on successful candidates and elevating the status of the profession in the process. As such, however, the National Board program did not address an essential gatekeeping function: standards setting and enforcement for new entrants into the profession. To elevate standards for beginning teachers, the Interstate New Teacher Assessment and Support Consortium (INTASC) was created in 1987, the same year NBPTS was launched.[2] In 1992, INTASC released *Model Standards for Beginning Teacher Licensing and Development: A Resource for State Dialogue*, which outlined what beginning teachers should know and be able to do respecting pedagogy and particular subject areas.

Recognizing that the great majority of veteran teachers would never achieve National Board certification, the consortium, which is affiliated with the Council of Chief State School Officers, widened its focus to include all classroom teachers. In 2011, the organization published *InTASC Model Core Teaching Standards: A Resource for State Dialogue*. The document explicitly addresses the new, wider focus on the teaching profession (Council of Chief State School Officers 2011, p. 6):

> These standards differ from the original standards in one key respect: These standards are no longer intended only for "beginning" teachers but as professional practice standards, setting one standard for performance that will look different at different developmental stages of the teacher's career. What distinguishes the beginning from the accomplished teacher is the degree of sophis-

tication in the application of the knowledge and skills. To reflect this change in emphasis, InTASC removed "new" from its name and now is called the Interstate Teacher Assessment and Support Consortium (InTASC).

The consortium seeks to translate these standards into professional rubrics that can be used to assess performance at key points along a teacher's career. In so doing, the consortium aims to develop the sort of codified, shared knowledge base and accompanying professional infra-structure that guide work in other fields (Cohen 2011). To do this, the consortium faces the daunting task of navigating the highly decentral-ized structure of U.S. public education, including states and national education organizations, to achieve consensus around a common core of teaching standards and putting these standards into practice (Council of Chief State School Officers 2011, p. 7).

New Standards for Teacher Preparation

The third prong of the professionalization agenda involved rais-ing standards for teacher preparation programs. This would be accom-plished through a rejuvenated National Council on Accreditation of Teacher Education (NCATE), founded as a nonprofit, nongovernmental accrediting body in 1954. Their work and mission achieved greater influ-ence and notoriety in the 1990s as the educational standards movement gained momentum and the notion of *teacher quality* assumed greater prominence in education policy debates. In 1997, a rival organization was founded: the Teacher Education Accreditation Council (TEAC), like NCATE a nonprofit organization, would work toward "improving academic degree programs for professional educators, those who will teach and lead in schools, pre-K through grade 12. TEAC's goal is to support the preparation of competent, caring, and qualified professional educators" (TEAC 2014).

In October of 2014, the boards of NCATE and TEAC met in Wash-ington, D.C., and voted unanimously to consolidate educator accredita-tion under a new agency, the Council for the Accreditation of Educator Preparation (CAEP). As with both founding organizations, the stated goal of the new, consolidated entity was to raise the quality and burnish the image of the teaching profession:

CAEP goals are to raise the performance of candidates as practitioners in the nation's P–12 schools and to raise standards for
the evidence the field relies on to support its claims of quality. By
meeting these goals, NCATE and TEAC leaders believe they will
raise the stature of the profession. (TEAC 2014)

The CAEP standards for teacher preparation programs address
teacher candidates' understanding of their discipline, the quality of their
preservice clinical experience, the quality of the candidates themselves,
and the impact of program completers on P–12 (preschool through
twelfth grade) student learning. The impact on learning is to be verified
by an evidence-based "quality assurance" evaluation system, a mandate
clearly designed to align the accreditation program with the broader
standards movement and shed the traditional image of such accreditation programs as mere compliance exercises having little impact on
outcomes that matter. As this is written, 34 states and the District of
Columbia have established partnerships with CAEP. Each partner state
maintains its particular policies regarding teacher preparation program
approvals while seeking to meet CAEP's national standards (CAEP
2020).

Seeking a Professional Knowledge Base

A defining attribute of any professional is the expectation that she
will discharge routine responsibilities in accordance with the standards
of her field. Such consistency is not found in classroom teaching. As
Dan Lortie observed in his classic work *Schoolteacher: A Sociological
Study*, in the absence of such standards, the teaching profession has
acquired a defensiveness that emphasizes an individualism that "leads
to distrust of the concept of shared knowledge" and militates against
the more mature professionalism of other fields where shared expertise
guides practice (Lortie 1975, p. 240).

The NBPTS, INTASC, and CAEP initiatives are intended to establish just such a shared and vetted knowledge base for classroom teaching. Mehta (2013a) underscores the importance of this element for any
profession:

At their core, professions rest on their respective knowledge bases.
In the absence of specialized expertise, there is no basis for the
claim for professional licensing. Research suggests that there are

three kinds of knowledge most relevant for classroom teaching: content knowledge about the subject matter, pedagogical knowledge about how to teach, and pedagogical content knowledge about how to teach particular subjects (Shulman 1987). Expert teachers not only possess these kinds of knowledge, but also [know] how to integrate them in real situations; like experts in other domains, they are able to quickly diagnose situations and draw on a wide repertoire of techniques in response (Chi, Glaser, and Farr 1988; Cimino 1999; Livingston and Borko 1989). (Mehta 2013a, p. 481)

At the same time, however, we should not underestimate the complexity of the teacher's challenge in applying pedagogical knowledge to particular classrooms and students. Given the great diversity of students across our public schools in terms of maturity, cognitive ability, life experiences, and levels of motivation and interest, the knowledge base for classroom teaching can never be expected to attain the degree of precision and standardization found in most professions. Judgment and discretion will always remain essential elements of the teacher's craft.

TEACHER UNIONS VS. DEREGULATORS: THE WAR OVER TEACHER STANDARDS

The teacher standards movement of the late 1980s and 1990s clearly coincided with the student achievement standards movement prompted by *A Nation at Risk* and emphasized in 2001 with the passage of No Child Left Behind. More recently, advocates of teacher professionalism have sought to position themselves favorably within the school and teacher accountability debates, with teacher preparation institutions and their accrediting bodies shifting their focus from program inputs (e.g., course requirements, program resources) to measured impacts on student learning. This linkage of the teacher professionalization initiative with the broader educational standards and accountability movement has succeeded in persuading states to adopt the educator-led InTASC/CAEP agenda.

But another, perhaps more powerful reason for teacher support of the professionalization agenda, with its emphasis on new teacher licensure and standards for teacher preparation institutions and for advanced teaching practice, has been the influence of the NEA and AFT, both key authors of the 2011 InTASC report. As Mehta (2013b) notes, teachers' unions represent 90 percent of the nation's teachers and make up the largest single block of delegates to the Democratic National Convention. They are joined in support of this agenda by other state-level participants in the educator licensing and accreditation arena, including governors, legislatures, state boards of education, state education agencies, and professional standards boards, which often include teachers and administrators in their memberships. Indeed, it is the substantial influence of teachers' unions in this standards movement and regulatory process that has prompted critics' charges of educators' capture and monopolistic control of the process itself (Rotherdam and Mead 2004). Citing a lack of evidence that traditional teacher preparation programs are more effective in improving measured student achievement than alternative routes into the profession, critics characterize these professionalization efforts as nothing more than self-serving attempts to monopolize and restrict entry into the profession by piling on licensing requirements that contribute little or nothing to teaching effectiveness and only exacerbate teacher shortage problems, especially in chronically short fields like math and science.

In place of this educator-driven and standards-based model for professional preparation and licensing of classroom teachers, critics call for a deregulated intake process which would effectively cast a wider net for new entrants into the profession. The rationale for such deregulation was concisely summarized by the conservative Fordham Foundation (1999, p. 2), as quoted in Mehta (2013b, p. 141):

> We conclude that the regulatory strategy being pursued today to boost teacher quality is seriously flawed. Every additional requirement for prospective teachers—every additional pedagogical course, every new hoop or hurdle—will have a predictable and inexorable effect: it will limit the potential supply of teachers by narrowing the pipeline while having no bearing whatever on the quality or effectiveness of those in the pipeline.

By 2001, proponents of the deregulatory approach to teacher licensure created a program to rival the InTASC and National Board certification programs. In response to perceived barriers to entry posed by both initial licensure for new teachers and the NBPTS certification of experienced teachers, the George W. Bush administration founded the American Board for Certification of Teacher Excellence (ABCTE), a less teacher-driven process with the express purpose of assisting schools in meeting the new No Child Left Behind mandate that every classroom have a "highly qualified" teacher. With a stated mission of increasing teacher supply by providing a less costly and time-consuming alternative to traditional, generally state-specific licensure programs, ABCTE dispenses with portfolios or teaching experiences, relying almost entirely on a series of exams on subject matter and teaching knowledge to license new candidates. The program is particularly focused on those who have changed careers to enter teaching, and it offers two certificates: 1) the Passport to Teaching ("Passport") and 2) a Master Teacher certificate which supplements the "Passport" exams with evidence of candidate effectiveness as documented through value-added assessments.

ABCTE represents a market-driven supply response to our nation's substantial demand for classroom teachers. It is also a clear repudiation of the educator-led InTASC/NBPTS efforts to professionalize classroom teaching. This repudiation rests on two explicit premises: 1) that the craft of classroom teaching lacks a scientific knowledge base and 2) that the sheer demand for teachers undermines the profession's call for more stringent licensing requirements. But implicit in some of these criticisms is the presumption that classroom teaching is less than a profession and that teachers are motivated more by self-interest than by concerns for students and the public good. According to the critics, the professionalism agenda is nothing more than a facade erected by union leadership to conceal their bid for monopoly control over entry to the field.

Classroom Teaching: A Profession Controlled by Outsiders

Classroom teaching is a unique occupation. First, it is a public profession, serving every community in the nation. Second, it employs more people than any other professional field, outnumbering law and medicine combined by a 10-to-1 margin.[3] Third, as a vast and diffuse public profession permeating every political subdivision in the United States, teaching is the subject of close and constant oversight by locally elected officials, many of whom remain skeptical of the profession's interest in or capability of raising educational outcomes. Teaching is seen by many critics as less an art than a trade. Consequently, classroom teaching is the sole profession in the U.S. that is expected to justify its public support and very existence by demonstrating a positive impact on client outcomes through government-specified metrics, with value-added measures currently in vogue (Neville, Sherman, and Cohen 2005, cited in Cochran-Smith 2005).

This narrow view of teacher (and school) performance, which glosses over such daunting challenges as the substantial discrepancies in educational resources, needs, and capacity across local communities and relies on performance measures beset by demonstrated problems of validity and reliability, has created two major problems for those seeking to elevate the status of the teaching profession. First, by attributing the problems of our public education system to deficits in the quality of our classroom teachers, policymakers fail to address deficits in both school resources and in the lives of many students outside school that impair student learning, including deficiencies in nutrition, health care, housing, and household income. Second, the decline in real resources for our nation's public schools and the steady erosion of job protections for classroom teachers have made unions' traditional role of protecting membership interests more important in a political environment that has grown demonstrably more hostile in recent years. These concerns were clearly articulated by four Wisconsin teacher union locals in a 1997 letter to then–NEA President Chase following his "new unionism" address:

> You must understand our reality. We have a governor and legislature committed to wiping out the rights of our members, curtailing collective bargaining rights, attempting to shift precious resources from our schools to private and religious schools. . . . It is, at best, naive to believe the people who are attempting to destroy our union for ideological and economic gain will be assuaged because of your pledge to get "the bad teachers out of the classroom." Because you were a social studies teacher before you became president of NEA, you should understand the results of appeasement in Eastern Europe in the '30s and '40s.[4]

Cause for concerns such as these expressed by teachers in Wisconsin more than 20 years ago has been evident across the states ever since. In many states, real cuts in education spending and teacher pay have persisted since well before the Great Recession and throughout the ensuing and enduring economic recovery. Nationally, the sharp economic downturn following the collapse of the housing market, commencing in 2008 and continuing through the 2010 Tea Party wave, gave state policymakers a platform from which to lecture our public schools on their need to do more with less. What followed was a widespread political assault on public school funding and teacher compensation that persists to the present day. The Center on Budget and Policy Priorities reports that, in 2015, fully 29 states were still providing less total state and local funding per pupil than they had in 2008 (Leachman, Masterson, and Figueroa 2017). And the state-level cuts to K–12 funding reflected a clear partisan divide. By 2016, more than half of states controlled by Democrats had restored per pupil spending to 2009 levels, but only 5 of 22 Republican-controlled states had done the same (Gebeloff 2018).

Teachers represent the most important investment we make in education, with teacher salaries and benefits accounting for about 70 percent of school operating expenditures (Monk, Roelke, and Brent 1996). Given the large share of public education funding allocated to teacher compensation, these draconian school funding cuts of the post-recession era have inevitably led to real teacher pay cuts and layoffs. School districts began cutting teachers and other school staff in mid-2008, and by mid-2012 they had eliminated 351,000 jobs. By 2017, some jobs had been restored, but the total number of teachers employed was still 135,000 below the 2008 level, despite the number of students having risen by 1,419,000 since that Great Recession year. In 39 states, the average teacher's salary declined in real terms between 2010 and 2016 (Leachman, Masterson, and Figueroa 2017). And these declines were not the result of teacher turnover, with retiring and relatively well-paid baby boomers being replaced by new entry-level millennials. A 2018 Brookings study found that teachers were more qualified in 2016 than in 2007. Teachers in 2016 were older, on average, and possessed significantly higher levels of formal education, with a greater proportion of them holding master's and doctoral degrees (Hansen 2018). As a consequence, every state headed into the 2017–2018 school year with shortages in qualified teachers, and these shortages have continued to the present day (Garcia and Weiss 2020). And they have only been heightened by the pandemic. An analysis of data from the Current Population Survey by the Economic Policy Institute shows that the number of people reporting that they worked in public K–12 schools declined by

4.7 percent from Fall 2019 to Fall 2021. The number of teachers fell by 6.8 percent during this same period (Cooper and Hickey 2022).

As Allegretto and Mishel (2020) document in their latest in a series of teacher-pay studies, the average weekly, inflation-adjusted wages of public school teachers decreased from 1996 to 2017, from $1,164 to $1,137 in 2017 dollars, while weekly wages of other college graduates rose from $1,339 to $1,476 over the same period.[5] Put another way, the "relative wage gap," which measures the difference between teacher wages and wages of other college graduates, adjusted for education, experience, and other factors known to impact earnings, has grown substantially since the mid-1990s, rising from 1.8 percent in 1994 to 11.8 percent by 2000 and reaching a record 22.0 percent in 2018 before falling back to a still substantial 19.2 percent in 2019. Classroom teaching, while never a way to riches, has traditionally placed its practitioners solidly in the middle class, with respectable salaries and benefits. Now, in many districts, this is no longer the case, and the concerns expressed by Wisconsin union members back in 1997 have come to pass in many states. Indeed, in some states, teachers earn so little they qualify for public assistance. In 2014, midcareer teachers in Arizona, Colorado, Maine, Minnesota, Montana, North Carolina, North Dakota, and South Dakota qualified for as many as seven benefit programs, including the Children's Health Insurance Program and the National School Lunch Program (Boser and Straus 2014).

New Public Support for a Beleaguered Profession

In the spring of 2018, tens of thousands of public school teachers walked out of their classrooms in a half-dozen states, protesting low salaries, rising class sizes, and cuts to school budgets that have prompted many teachers to purchase their own classroom materials.[6] In West Virginia, a right-to-work state, more than 10,000 teachers walked off their jobs on February 22, 2018, and flooded the state capital, demanding action on five issues: 1) a check on charter school expansion, 2) protection of teachers' seniority rights, 3) eliminating the payroll deduction for union dues, 4) addressing rising health insurance costs, and 5) rectifying eight years with no pay raise. The strike shut down every school in the state, compelling Governor Jim Justice to promise a veto of anti-union bills and to support a 5 percent raise for not only the state's 20,000 classroom teachers but its 14,000 support staff as well. He also agreed to create a task force on health care that included organized labor.[7] The union continued the strike, however, until Republican legislators also signed on. After nine days on the picket line, teachers returned to their classes on March 6.[8]

Additional teacher actions, including district-level strikes in Washington state and California and a teacher-led hunger strike in Georgia, followed the opening of schools in the fall. In December 2018, more than 500 teachers at the UNO/Acero charter school network in Chicago went on strike, demanding higher pay and smaller classes. This action canceled classes for about 7,500 students across 15 schools and marked the first strike by charter school teachers in U.S. history. A month later, in January 2019, more than 30,000 teachers in Los Angeles Unified District (LAUD), the nation's second largest district with more than 640,000 students, walked off their jobs, after nearly two years of failed contract negotiations centering on the rapid expansion of charter schools and the consequent impact on traditional school budgets, teacher pay, class sizes, and support staff.[9]

These statewide teacher walkouts, along with the heralded LAUD strike, won considerable public support, in large part because they were viewed as a fight on behalf of students and traditional public schools. In addition to better pay, teachers demanded better facilities, more support staff, smaller classes, and updated classroom resources, all of which can benefit students. At the same time, the walkouts were also aimed at restoring union power in a post-*Janus* world, where unions can no longer collect "agency" fees from nonmembers to defray the costs of negotiating and enforcing contracts. In particular, the successful demands for hiring more classroom teachers and support staff illustrate the effectiveness of teacher mobilization. And because only union members can vote to authorize a walkout, union leadership can use strike votes to recruit new members. For example, the Los Angeles union reports adding more than 1,000 members during its strike vote, while the Denver union reports a membership increase of 250 during its vote (*Conversation* 2019). The union victory in Los Angeles is a particularly telling case study of the power of professional organizing efforts, as Box 7.1 illustrates.

While the interests of teachers and students have often diverged, the concessions achieved by the teacher unions in this recent and dra-

Box 7.1 Los Angeles District Teachers Organize to Fight and Win

In January 2019, 34,000 Los Angeles teachers walked off their jobs and picketed outside their schools in drenching rain day after day. During their six-day strike, they were joined by tens of thousands of parents, students, and other supporters. Taco trucks arrived to feed the striking teachers.

The teachers' union, United Teachers Los Angeles (UTLA), presented an ambitious list of demands that extended beyond wages and class sizes: more nurses, librarians, and school counselors, less standardized testing, fewer "random" student searches, and a moratorium on charter expansion. They also demanded more green space on school campuses for student recreation.

By the fourth day of the walkout, the L.A. mayor and other political leaders summoned both sides to city hall to forge an agreement and get 600,000 kids back to classes. Two days later, the district got the teachers to end the strike by pledging to hire 300 more nurses and 82 more librarians, assuring a full-time nurse in every school and a librarian in every middle and high school. The teachers also won commitments to lower class size in grades 4 through 12 by four students per class over three years, to reduce random searches in 28 schools and to create 30 "community schools" with wraparound services, including after-school programs, health care, and adult education. The union also secured a board commitment to lobby the state for a moratorium on new charter schools in the city until a study was completed on their effects on district schools.

How did UTLA achieve such a big win? According to labor organizer and author Jane McAlevey, the teachers came to realize that they had to be prepared to strike, and that would require assembling a full-time union staff with successful strike experience. In her notable book *A Collective Bargain: Unions, Organizing, and the Fight for Democracy*, McAlevey (2020) traces the origins of ULTA's breakthrough to an April 2014 election, when a diverse and representative slate of seven teachers swept every union leadership post on a campaign pledge to rebuild union power. Specifically, the "Union Power" slate promised to build a union organizing department, a parent-community organizing

Box 7.1 (continued)

unit, and a research department that would scrutinize the district budget and the antiunion privatizers who had been successfully promoting privately managed charter schools in the city. The slate also pledged to rebuild the union's communications department to proactively shape the public narrative of the teachers' efforts to restore public education in the city following years of budget cuts and privatization efforts.

In early 2015, following a citywide rally where 15,000 teachers gathered outside City Hall, the new union leadership won a 10 percent raise for the teachers, their first pay hike since 2006. This victory gave union leaders the momentum to add professional staff, strengthen ties to parents and the community, and, in July, launch a plan to build their war chest by asking teachers to raise their dues. The campaign succeeded. In February 2016, more than half of the district's 34,000 teachers participated in a vote on membership dues, with 83 percent supporting the increase. This vote was soon followed by a new round of contract negotiations over health insurance for all LAUSD employees, including janitors, bus drivers, cafeteria workers, and administrators as well as teachers.

In spring 2017, the union was challenged when a well-financed, antiunion, pro–charter school candidate slate won a majority on the LAUSD board. (The procharter forces spent $9.7 million on these elections, with $7 million coming from a single donor: Netflix founder Reed Hastings.) In response, union leaders formed a contract action team of school-site leaders to prepare all 900 UTLA schools to fight a board effort to cut employee health benefits. These efforts, including Fall 2017 rallies, helped the union win a favorable health care proposal in January 2018. As teachers held school-by-school ratification votes on the proposed health care deal, however, national media coverage began of the U.S. Supreme Court case *Janus v. AFSME*. Union leaders responded by launching an "All In" campaign, asking every teacher, concurrently with the health care ratification vote, to sign new membership cards that union lawyers believed would satisfy the new requirements about dues and membership that would be imposed by an antiunion decision in *Janus*. Over just several days, more than 20,000 UTLA members would sign these cards.

> **Box 7.1 (continued)**
>
> Another challenge for the union arose in early 2018, when LAUSD Superintendent Michele King, a widely respected African American educator who had been a student and then parent, teacher, and principal in the district, resigned for health reasons. The new board quickly hired a procharter, antiunion hedge fund manager with no education experience. By August 2018, with teacher negotiations stalled, the union began planning for a strike authorization vote. Over seven days in late August, teachers voted school by school, with 84 percent of the district's 34,000 teachers participating and a whopping 98 percent of voters authorizing a strike if necessary. The school board managed to forestall a strike that fall with a series of legal filings, but by early January 2019 the courts had rejected each management claim, paving the way for the union's successful and historic six-day strike.

matic wave of walkouts will undoubtedly benefit both groups. How the walkouts will ultimately be interpreted by the public, and how they will influence public education policy and teacher union strength, remains to be seen. But in the near term, the jobs and working conditions of classroom teachers in these walkout states and districts should improve, as both teacher compensation levels and school policies on class sizes and school support staff are changed in their favor.

New Support for Teachers and Unions. These recent teacher strikes are part of a broader surge in strike activity across both the private and public sectors. Whether this surge portends a new and enduring labor movement or is a mere blip in labor's long-term decline remains to be seen. But much of the public now appears to be siding with the teachers, not in their capacity as union reformers, but as members of a traditional, blue-collar-style union. Following the spring strikes and walkouts, a poll conducted annually by *Education Next* found that 63 percent of respondents favored raising teacher pay, fully 16 percentage points above the prior year's figure. Moreover, across the nation, nearly half (49 percent) of respondents who had been provided with information on average teacher salaries in their state called for increased teacher pay, 13 points higher than the previous year. Support for teacher pay raises rose among both Democrats and Republicans, although such support is 21 points higher among Democrats (Cheng et al. 2019). A 2018 *New York Times* poll was even more decisive, finding that nearly three-fourths of U.S. adults believe that teacher pay is too low, and that two-thirds support increasing taxes to raise public school teacher salaries (Goldstein and Casselman 2018). The *Education Next* survey also found that 53 percent of the public supports teachers' having the right to strike, despite the fact that such strikes are legal in only 12 states. The survey revealed a partisan divide on this issue as well, with about two-thirds of Democrats and 38 percent of Republicans supporting teachers' right to strike. Antistrike laws, however, are rarely enforced.

Support for public school teachers and their unions is particularly evident among the millennial generation, who came of age during our current time of intensified testing, accountability, and austere public-school budgets. A September 2018 poll conducted by the GenForward Survey Project at the University of Chicago's Center for the Study of Race, Politics, and Culture and involving a nationally representative sample of nearly 2,000 respondents revealed strong support for public schools and teachers. Asked whether strengthening or weakening teachers' unions would do more to improve public education, more than three-quarters of the respondents supported stronger unions. This finding is consistent with a 2017 Pew study that found that fully 75 percent of 18- to 29-year-olds hold a favorable view of labor unions (Weingarten 2018).

The appeal of unions to our millennial generation, defined as those aged 21 to 36 in 2017, is quite understandable. Many are underemployed, enduring stagnant wages, poor or nonexistent benefits, and unsteady work in a growing gig economy that leaves them far behind their parents' economic circumstances. Analyzing data from the Federal Reserve, the advocacy group Young Invincibles concluded that millennials earn 20 percent less than baby boomers did at the same stage of life. They have half the net worth, lower rates of home ownership, and drastically higher student debt. And they are a potentially potent political force, comprising fully 35 percent of U.S. workers according to the Pew Research Center (Fry 2018). Some will choose to become teachers themselves, while many others will become parents of public-school students. And both groups will be natural constituents of the teachers' movement, likely to support teachers in their efforts to improve their pay and working conditions and generally increase their influence over the profession.

BLUE COLLAR OR WHITE? WHO DECIDES?

To a great extent, the professional status of our public-school teachers is determined not by the teachers themselves, but by the public they serve. The status of our classroom teachers is largely driven by our notions of the purposes of public education. Since publication of *A Nation at Risk* in 1983, discourse about our public schools has been dramatically narrowed from a focus on the values and knowledge needed for an enlightened democratic citizenry to the proclaimed needs of firms engaged in economic competition, domestic and international. This legacy of *A Nation at Risk*, which elevates skill building and student performance on standardized reading and math tests over such traditional school values as critical thinking, personal growth, and social justice, has greatly diminished the influence of progressive educators on school policy. Progressive values such as student creativity, teacher autonomy, and the idea that knowledge is constructed—that is, linked to students' experience, perceptions, and understandings and achieved through hands-on learning and exploration—has been supplanted by "skill development," acquired through scripted drill and practice.

In the process, influence over education policy and, indeed, the very work of teachers, has been shifted away from teachers, school administrators, school board members, and parents to state and federal legislators and business leaders who see schools primarily as tools serving economic ends. As a result, the broader goals of public education, such as equality of opportunity and support for democratic institutions, have been devalued. "Citizens" have been demoted to "customers," and our public schools, once both products and creators of values foundational to our democracy, have been largely reduced to instruments of commerce. In the process, teachers, now tasked with the narrow job of raising student scores on a few standardized tests, have seen their true purpose subverted and their autonomy and security undermined.

As Dan Lortie observed more than four decades ago, teachers cite as their greatest professional satisfaction and reward the witnessing of their students' intellectual and personal growth (Lortie 1975). This hasn't changed. Writing more than 20 years later, David Tyack and Larry Cuban, in their notable 1995 book *Tinkering toward Utopia: A Century of Public School Reform*, report on their talks with civic groups about those persons' best memories as public school students: "Almost always they remember the influence of a teacher who challenged them to develop their potential, who made a subject come alive, or who gave caring advice at a stressful time" (Tyack and Cuban 1995, p. 136). Neither teachers nor students cite high scores on standardized tests as compelling goals. Rather, they speak of inspired interactions between teacher and student that serve to engender and sustain in students a life-long desire to pursue knowledge and individual growth.

But for such inspired interactions to occur, schools must be organized with the needs of both students *and teachers* in mind. And this will happen only when policymakers and school leaders collaborate with teachers to address their classroom challenges and provide opportunities for teachers' own continued learning and professional growth. As we saw in the preceding chapter, Massachusetts is an example of such a collaboration of school, business, and political leaders that has largely succeeded in adequately funding the state's public schools and providing its teachers with the resources and autonomy to work effectively.

The issue of teacher autonomy is intertwined with the nature of teachers' work and holds enormous implications for teachers' effectiveness, the desirability of teaching as a career, and the quality of the teacher workforce. It is also among the most contentious issues in K–12 education. The basic argument for teacher autonomy arises from the core technology of the work itself. Unlike other professions such as medicine, law, and accounting, there are no generally accepted, standard procedures for teaching. Vast differences across students, including cognitive abilities and out-of-school experience, render standardized teaching procedures virtually useless. Effective teaching is highly contextual, varying with student, subject, grade level, and other factors. And the teaching task is multifaceted, including the development of cognitive abilities, interpersonal skills, moral sensibilities, and civic participation. Given the differences across schools, classrooms, and students, coupled with teachers' firsthand views and understanding of these differences—an understanding clearly superior to that of a principal, district administrator, or legislator—teachers have traditionally enjoyed considerable latitude in deciding how to teach their classes. Substantial research evidence confirms that, as teachers gain classroom experience, they are increasingly able to differentiate and refine their instruction and improve their effectiveness.

Autonomy also strengthens the profession. As with other professions, teaching requires specialized training and certification. It also generally involves membership in professional associations, where standards for training, licensing, evaluation, and career paths are debated and refined. But, without autonomy to make decisions about practices and standards, teachers are less than professional and the occupation struggles to attract well-educated, creative, and committed candidates.

Schools have traditionally been organized in accordance with teacher autonomy. In his classic 1976 article, Karl Weick characterizes schools as unique among organizations. In his taxonomy, most organizations are "tightly coupled" systems, with four defining characteristics: 1) rules, 2) agreement on the rules, 3) systematic inspection to see if the rules are followed, and 4) feedback to improve compliance. With a clear and agreed-upon technology, an organization can establish rules, and then the other elements of "tight coupling" will follow accordingly. The organizational task is seen essentially as an engineering problem amenable to a straight-line solution to optimize a bottom-line metric. This approach works well in a manufacturing setting, but not in a diverse human enterprise like teaching and learning. When there are no specific rules governing an organization's core activity, as is the case for schools' core technology of teaching, "loose coupling" offers several advantages:

> A loosely coupled system may be a good system for localized adaptation. If all of the elements in a large system are loosely coupled to one another, then any one element can adjust to and modify a local unique contingency without affecting the whole system. These local adaptations can be swift, relatively economical, and substantial. By definition, the antithesis of localized adaptation is standardization. (Weick 1976, p. 7)

Standardization, in the form of student achievement standards and standardized testing, as initiated among the states in the 1990s and mandated nationally by NCLB in 2001, necessarily restricts teacher autonomy by proscribing curriculum, standardizing instruction, and incentivizing teaching to the test. This standards movement, the origins of which can be traced to the National Commission's 1983 report *A Nation at Risk*, has proven a challenge to the teaching profession. Union leadership has largely embraced the core logic of the movement—that a strong curriculum will protect students from educational malpractice and its consequences—but fiercely resists the attendant loss of teacher autonomy, as tech and publishing giants increasingly influence classroom activity with scripted curricula and standardized testing materials. Can the profession regain its traditional autonomy, along with compensation levels and job security, while continuing to embrace and shape the standards movement going forward?

The near-term prospects for such success appear exceedingly dim. While much of the public currently views teachers as beleaguered union workers, who need and deserve increased support after their compensation and job security have been severely diminished by policymakers, particularly at the state level, teachers currently lack the political leverage to achieve professional empowerment by themselves. They need demonstrated support from their communities, parents, and other constituents in order to convince policymakers that we all benefit when teachers are empowered to advance beyond the levels of income and job security they enjoyed in the mid-1990s and become full participants in education decision making as envisioned by union leaders like Al Shanker and Bob Chase. Shanker's vision of teacher-led charter public schools is a particularly appealing model for professionalizing the teacher force, with its emphasis on teacher autonomy and peer support and evaluation. The charter school movement, however, was an inadequate vehicle for its realization. Nationally, the movement was never more than a peripheral phenomenon, accounting for no more than 6 percent of our public-school students at its peak (National Center for Education Statistics 2021a). And while Shanker's charter-school experiment might have spawned a wider application across our public schools, the charter program was quickly hijacked in many states by school privatizers and union critics, who viewed teachers as less than professional and largely expendable, easily replaced with new and more obedient candidates or by instructional technology.

How likely is it that proponents of change could compel public support for not merely restored salary levels and job security but for a professionalized and more empowered teaching force in the near term? The rise of conservative politics across many states and the dogmatic belief of many state lawmakers in the power of tax cuts to broadly benefit society despite overwhelming evidence to the contrary have amounted to a war on public schools and teachers. The best and brightest are most likely to exit the profession because they have the best alternatives, particularly during periods of job growth and rising wages in the private sector. During the first 10 months of 2018, public educators, including teachers, community-college faculty, and school psychologists, quit their jobs at a rate of 83 per 10,000, according to the U.S. Department of Labor statistics. That is the highest rate since the government began collecting these data in 2001, and nearly twice the rate for 2009 (Reisinger 2018).[10] And while the public support for teachers who have recently staged walkouts over pay and working conditions may be encouraging in the near term, it colors the occupation as more blue collar than white.

PROSPECTS FOR THE PROFESSION

A certain level of dysfunction is baked into education policymaking in the U.S. by virtue of its decentralized, public, and politically volatile nature, and teachers must contend with the considerable power of nonschool institutions and actors over teachers' work. Progress toward a more professional and secure teaching force, if any is to be made, is sure to be halting and uneven across the states and local districts. It will depend crucially on the way two key policy issues are addressed. The first and more immediate is the funding of our public schools. Will the public and their elected leaders summon the political will to restore school funding levels to pre–Great Recession levels adequate to provide teachers with a middle-class income and decent working conditions, including manageable class sizes and teaching loads, and student and staff supports (e.g., guidance counselors, social workers, psychologists, attendance officers, nurses, etc.) sufficient to give all students and teachers a reasonable chance to succeed?

The second relates to school accountability and teacher evaluation. Specifically, with the new flexibility provided by ESSA, how will educators and policymakers construe and measure educational outcomes and gauge teacher performance in light of that construction? Nearly all states, responding to federal incentives like RTT and waivers from NCLB mandates, took a narrow and reductionist approach that sought to evaluate individual teachers, at least in part, on the basis of student test-score growth measures. Now, however, in response to implementation problems (e.g., not all grades and subjects are tested), adverse public opinion, serious criticism from the research community, and challenges in the courts, Congress has changed course. ESSA not only discontinues the focus on student growth, it omits any requirement that states have a teacher evaluation system.[11] In this new, decentralized environment, will states and local districts continue with this reductionist approach, or will policymakers engage with classroom teachers to embrace a broader conception of the purposes of education and teaching, one that focuses on preparing students to engage in personally rewarding work and lifelong learning that will help them navigate a changing and increasingly global society?

The education and research communities have expressed grave concerns over the reductionist approach. Richard Elmore was an early critic, writing in 2002 that this narrow approach is "accelerating the worst trend of the current accountability movement: that performance-based accountability has come to mean testing alone" (Elmore 2002). He reasoned that such a narrowly conceived accountability system would not only fail to increase test scores in low-performing schools, but would likely widen the achievement gap between high- and low-performing schools and districts. His apprehensions, shared by many educators and researchers, have been confirmed, most recently by a 2018 report by the Rand Corporation. Its multiyear evaluation concluded that a $500 million investment in teacher evaluation that heavily weighted student growth measures not only failed to improve student outcomes but, in some cases, actually exacerbated the unequal access to effective teachers for low-income students and students of color. Furthermore, the new evaluation systems were found to suffer from the same problems afflicting their predecessors: very few teachers were deemed ineffective, and effective teachers were no more likely to be retained than they were prior to the reform (Stecher et al. 2018).

State law and policy may now be catching up with this research. Since passage of ESSA in December 2015, we have seen a deemphasis on student growth and, in some states, the introduction of legislation removing teacher evaluation systems altogether (Croft, Guffy, and Vitale 2018). What role will teachers play, if any, across the states as new accountability systems are designed and installed at the state or local levels? Will classroom teachers be active contributors in the remaking of these systems, or mere objects of the new designs?

Classroom teaching has never enjoyed the prestige or compensation levels of much smaller and more elite professions like law and medicine. For a long time, however, the profession did offer notable advantages, including economic security, professional autonomy, and an appealing work schedule unavailable in other occupations. Those advantages have been severely eroded over the past several decades, and restoring the profession's appeal will require material improvements in both teachers' compensation and their ability to define and control the terms of their own work. As always, the public and its elected representatives will determine the levels of school funding and, indirectly, teacher compensation across the states and school districts. It is less clear who will define educational outcomes and teacher performance going forward and what role teachers will play in those decisions.

These issues reflect a central paradox of the teaching profession: classroom teachers in the U.S. are often viewed as both the root cause of the problems in our educational system and the key to their solution. As shown in this book and in other works, the first premise of this paradox collapses under close scrutiny. A wealth of evidence compiled since (at least) the 1968 Coleman Report makes clear that educational outcomes are jointly produced by schools, families, and communities. But the second part of the paradox does hold a kernel of truth. Teachers are the most important school resource and an essential element of school improvement. But their educational contribution and the quality of their ranks have been increasingly hindered by the erosion of their status and autonomy. This trend can be reversed, but it will take the support of principals, parents, community leaders, and, finally, elected officials. If critical decisions about public school organization and operations can be motivated by the aspirations, knowledge, and expertise of skilled and experienced teachers, teaching and learning can be enhanced across our public schools, and the unique and vital craft of classroom teaching can rise to the status of a true profession.

Notes

1. The Task Force was chaired by Lewis Branscomb, chief scientist at IBM and included Shanker, NEA President Mary Futrell, California State Superintendent Bill Honig, former North Carolina Governor James Hunt, and New Jersey Governor Thomas Kean.
2. This discussion follows Mehta (2013b), Chapter 6.
3. In the 2015–2016 school year, U.S. public schools employed 3.8 million full- and part-time teachers, including 1.9 million elementary school teachers and 1.9 million secondary school teachers (National Center for Education Statistics 2019a).
4. Letter to Bob Chase, "Teacher Unionism: Bob Chase Is Attacked," *Rethinking Schools*, vol. 11(4), 1977; cited in Mehta (2013b), p. 152.
5. Allegretto and Mishel (2018), Appendix B, pp. 19–20. The authors use weekly wages to sidestep measurement issues related to the number of weeks worked annually (e.g., teachers' "summers off") and hours worked per week.
6. The six states are West Virginia, Oklahoma, Arizona, North Carolina, Kentucky, and Colorado. At least four are "red" states with right-to-work laws.
7. This summary draws upon a more detailed account in McAlevey (2020).
8. West Virginia educators flexed their rediscovered muscles again a year later, shutting down schools across the state in protest of the Senate's passage of a school voucher bill. This two-day walkout killed the bill.
9. On the sixth day of the walkout, a deal was struck that included a 6 percent pay raise for teachers, class-size reductions that would be phased in over four years, and more school nurses, counselors, and librarians. The district also agreed to create 30 community schools offering wraparound social services for students and established an "immigrant defense fund" to protect immigrant students and families (Will 2019).
10. The threat of extensive teacher turnover arising from pandemic-era working conditions is addressed in the Epilogue.
11. Every Student Succeeds Act of 2015, Sec. 1111(e)(1)(B)(iii)(IX) and (X).

Epilogue
The Pandemic and Beyond

For most school-age children in America, the 2019–2020 school year effectively ended in March, as schools and much of the U.S. economy shut down in an effort to mitigate the spread of the coronavirus. The year 2020 may prove pivotal in the history of U.S. public education, as many children went missing from school completely, and millions more struggled with wholly inadequate remote learning experiences.

While many school districts sought to substitute, as best they could, online exercises and homework packets for children's classroom interactions with skilled teachers, educators and parents alike came to more fully appreciate the teacher's craft. Parents trying to work from home while teaching their children math, reading, social studies, and other subjects have undoubtedly come away with a deeper understanding of the energy, skill, and patience needed to hold their children's attention and teach effectively. And it is increasingly clear that the educational costs of the school shutdowns have been greatest for low-income kids, whose households often lack the technology, skills, and even the physical space to support their children's learning when school is closed.

As the pandemic gradually comes to an end, many more educational resources will be needed to restore the educational, social, and emotional deficits of these children, many of whom checked out during their schools' long spells with remote learning.

The Toll on Teachers

Teacher wellness is essential for the restoration and revitalization of our public schools following the extended disruptions and challenges of the pandemic—for the children, their families, and their communities. We gain some insight from the RAND Corporation's 2021 State of the U.S. Teacher Survey, conducted in January and February 2021 with a nationally representative sample of 1,006 teachers. In the survey, nearly one in four teachers said they were likely to leave their jobs by the end of the 2020–2021 school year, compared with one in six teachers who were likely to leave prior to the pandemic.

The problem appears to be more acute among black teachers, nearly half of whom said they were likely to leave their jobs in this time frame. This is particularly concerning because, as noted earlier, teaching is a profession populated predominantly by whites (NCES 2021a). A decline in teachers of color would have adverse educational effects on students. Studies have found that all students, especially students of color, benefit from having teachers of color (Carver-Thomas 2018; Cherng and Halpin 2016). These benefits can be substantial. A 2017 study found that low-income black students who have at least one black teacher in elementary school are significantly more likely to graduate and consider attending college: having at least one black teacher in grades 3 to 5 reduced the likelihood that a black student would drop out of school by 29 percent. And for black boys from very-low-income families, the drop-out rate fell by 39 percent (Gershenson et al. 2017). Research has identified five specific practices of teachers of color that help explain their beneficial effects of teachers of color for all students. Teachers of color tend to 1) hold high expectations for students, 2) employ culturally relevant teaching that relates to students' lives, 3) develop trusting relationships with their students, 4) confront racism in teaching, and 5) serve as effective liaisons between students' schools and homes (Villegas and Irvine 2010).

Teaching, already a high-stress profession, has been made more so by the pandemic, exacerbating the problems of low salaries and difficult working conditions. Before the pandemic, nearly 20 percent of teachers cited finances as the most important factor in their decision to leave the profession (Carver-Thomas and Darling-Hammond 2017), and 20 percent of teachers who left the profession because of the pandemic cited "insufficient pay to merit the risks or stress" among their top reasons for leaving (Dilberti, Schwartz, and Grant 2021).

Fully three out of four teachers reported that their work since the start of the 2020–2021 school year had frequently been stressful (Steiner and Woo 2021). The RAND survey found that the most prevalent sources of job-related stress mentioned by teachers were engaging students, dealing with changes to their schools' instructional models, teaching remotely, making or maintaining contact with students' families, and supporting students' social and emotional learning. Teachers cited hybrid instruction—defined broadly as some in-person instruction combined with some remote instruction—as being particularly stressful. Teachers also cited concerns about their own health and the health of loved ones in the survey.

Of course, higher stress levels among teachers will not necessarily lead to higher attrition rates or general teacher shortages. Teachers' sentiments and plans may change as school buildings reopen and normalcy is gradually restored. Their decision to leave current jobs likely rests on multiple factors, including vaccination rates in their schools, the abundance or scarcity of support staff (e.g., psychologists, teacher aides, social workers, cafeteria workers, guidance counselors, librarians, and nurses), and their districts' use of the substantial emergency aid from three federal programs: 1) March 2020's CARES Act, 2) December 2020's Coronavirus Response and Relief Supplemental Appropriations Act (CRRSA), and 3) the American Rescue Plan (ARP), by far the largest of the three, signed into law in March 2021.

Effective use of this emergency aid, which totals nearly $200 billion across the three programs, is essential for our public schools. These one-time federal dollars come with deadlines for their commitment but relatively few restrictions on their use. The ARP funds must be obligated by September 2024, with the sole restriction that at least 20 percent of the money must address "learning loss." School leaders need to work *with teachers* to develop spending plans that avoid a fiscal cliff when the emergency funds run out. Educators recognize the importance of targeting investment to low-income and minority children who have been particularly hard hit by the pandemic, which has exposed and exacerbated deep inequities across our public schools. Targeted approaches like individual or small-group tutoring, summer learning or enrichment, or comprehensive after-school programs will help struggling students get back on track.

Teachers will be at the center of these recovery efforts. Of course, many district plans will undoubtedly address school infrastructure improvements, including HVAC systems upgrades, roof repairs, windows, and broadband Internet access. Such needed capital investments sidestep the mistake of baking one-time money into school operating budgets without solid plans for reliable replacement revenue. However, a variety of staffing initiatives may also make sense for many districts. Possibilities include teacher stipends for tutoring or summer school, one-time bonuses to attract or retain staff whose regular compensation is covered with recurring operating revenue, and social work and mental health services to address student and staff trauma triggered by the pandemic.

Smart use of these federal dollars, flowing mostly to districts with large concentrations of poor and special-needs children through the federal Title I formula, will be a great help in addressing our schools' COVID-related challenges. But the problems of inadequate funding and staffing shortages that plagued our schools prior to the pandemic will require long-term state responses. Merely restoring school budgets to their prepandemic levels will not be enough to mitigate the deep inequities, particularly in the distribution of teaching talent, that afflict many of our public schools. Lasting support must come from the states, which provide, on average, 47 percent of school revenue. Local districts raise 45 percent, with the remaining 8 percent coming from the federal government. Local districts, however, vary enormously in their capacity to raise school revenue from local property taxes. In the long run, only the states can address the inequities across local districts.

Teacher Shortages Remain Local

The pandemic has exacerbated inequities in the distribution of teaching talent across local school districts, worsening teacher shortages in particular subjects, grade levels, and schools, with many large urban districts facing more widespread shortages as they navigate their third school year with COVID. Many states have already used emergency funds and higher-than-expected state revenues to avert significant staffing reductions (Jacobs 2021). Bureau of Labor Statistics (BLS) data from July 2021 show 33,000 new hires in state and local government education over June and July as schools geared up for the 2021–2022 school year (U.S. Bureau of Labor Statistics 2021).

Nevertheless, localized shortages of school support staff exert increased pressure on teachers. Fully 40 percent of school district leaders and school principals describe their current staff shortages as "severe" or "very severe," according to a survey conducted from September 29 to October 8 by the EdWeek Research Center. Another 30 percent characterized their current staffing shortage as "moderate," while only 5 percent said their schools are not experiencing staffing issues (Lieberman 2021).

Schools' difficulties in filling vacancies for bus drivers, custodians, school nutrition workers, and other support staff are part of a broader national phenomenon conventionally termed a "labor shortage" but perhaps more accurately characterized as a shortage of adequately compensated jobs. Not only are organized strikes popping up across the country—from workers at John Deere, Nabisco, and Kellogg; Alabama coal miners; nurses in California; health-care workers in Buffalo; and others—but job openings in general hit a record high with the U.S. Department of Labor's October 2021 jobs report. Our public schools are part of this nationwide labor movement.

In response, school leaders are raising wages, enhancing benefits, and stepping up recruitment efforts. But the most common response to school staff shortages is to ask more of those working in the schools, particularly the teachers. Nearly two-thirds of the school leaders responding to the October 2021 EdWeek Research Center survey said they have asked their teachers to shoulder additional responsibilities this school year.

Will Recent History Repeat Itself?

The greatest cost of the pandemic will, of course, be measured in terms of suffering and loss of life. But the pandemic has also heightened long-standing concerns of classroom teachers. The relative wage gap, challenging work environments, and contentious political disputes, often centered on teacher unions, are now combined with aggravated shortages of support personnel, burdensome pandemic protocols, new controversies regarding vaccinations, mask mandates, and the teaching of history and race relations in the U.S., all of which makes the current school year particularly chaotic and difficult for teachers.

As discussed above, the substantial federal emergency aid will certainly help schools with large concentrations of low-income children through these short-term challenges. However, the danger for public schools lies not only in our current period of acute, localized staff shortages, but also in the uncertain economic and political period to follow. That is, will the public and our elected leaders view the recovering economy as an opportunity to reinvest in our public schools and their teachers, or to lower tax rates and continue, if not accelerate, cuts in real school spending? The Great Recession of 2007–2009 and the long expansion following are particularly instructive here. Average state and local funding for school districts, adjusted for labor costs, fell precipitously starting in 2008 and bottomed out in 2011 at about 6 percent below prerecession levels. And as expected, the impacts on school budgets were most severe in high-poverty districts (Baker and Di Carlo 2020).

How were teachers affected during that time? Interestingly, the "teacher wage gap," or the shortfall in teacher salaries compared with nonteacher wages, actually shrank slightly during the Great Recession as teacher salaries, propped up by temporary emergency federal aid, remained flat while salaries of nonteachers declined. But the gap quickly resumed its prerecession widening as federal emergency aid ended and the economy recovered. Indeed, despite the emergency aid provided as part of the federal American Recovery and Reinvestment Act, a sum that totaled $48.6 billion over two years, most states never fully restored school funding to prerecession levels after the emergency aid ran out. As Baker and Di Carlo (2020) observe: "Fiscal effort in virtually every state was lower in 2017 than in 2009, and tax cuts and austerity in many states caused revenue to keep dropping even after the economy recovered" (p. 28).

Looking Ahead

Predictions about this pandemic are particularly difficult to make because the virus is new and not yet fully understood, and outcomes depend at least as much on our behavior as on the plague itself. But one outcome is readily apparent: the impact of the coronavirus recession is greater in our poor districts. And it will be up to federal and state government to save them. The federal government has responded forcefully, providing our public schools with nearly $200 billion in three tranches of emergency aid. But this aid, while quite substantial, will run out by 2025, and the enduring circumstances of our schools and teachers will depend upon the states, where revenues have generally held up better than expected since the economic shutdown in early 2020.

More importantly, in the longer run, will states summon the political will to restore their fiscal effort for public schools to the levels maintained prior to the Great Recession? Or will states repeat the general pullback of support for public schools, and public services in general, that followed the Great Recession, a pullback that saw teacher salaries plummet in real terms while their working conditions, including school facilities, generally deteriorated (Addonizio 2021).

Without a return to such historical levels of state school support, overall school funding will decline, educational inequality—particularly in the distribution of teaching talent—will rise, and classroom teachers in many districts will bear the brunt. Affluent districts will have the option to tap local revenues to recruit and retain teachers, maintain and improve facilities, and support rich educational programs. But without increased support across the states, many districts will struggle with shrinking support staff, larger classes, deterioriating facilities, greater use of inferior online instruction, and continued disinvestment in our most important and proven school resource—our classroom teachers.

References

Aaronson, Daniel, Lisa Barrow, and William Sander. 2007. "Teachers and Student Achievement in the Chicago Public High Schools." *Journal of Labor Economics* 25(1): 95–135.

Abrams, Samuel E. 2016. *Education and the Commercial Mindset.* Cambridge, MA: Harvard University Press.

Addonizio, Michael F. 2014. "A Nation at Risk." In *Encyclopedia of Education Economics and Finance*, Dominic J. Brewer and Lawrence O. Picus, eds. Thousand Oaks, CA: Sage, pp. 463–467.

———. 2021. "America Gets a D+ for School Infrastructure—but Federal COVID Relief Could Pay for Many Repairs." *The Conversation*, April 2. Waltham, MA: *The Conversation*. https://theconversation.com/america-gets -a-d-for-school-infrastructure-but-federal-covid-relief-could-pay-for-many -repairs-156831 (accessed February 4, 2022).

Addonizio, Michael F., and Douglas Drake. 2005. *Revolution and Evolution: Michigan's Proposal A School Finance Reform: A Retrospective Analysis.* Okemos, MI: Michigan Prospect.

Addonizio, Michael F., and C. Philip Kearney. 2012. *Education Reform and the Limits of Policy: Lessons from Michigan.* Kalamazoo, MI: W.E. Upjohn Institute for Employment Research.

Addonizio, Michael F., C. Philip Kearney, and Marytza A. Gawlik. 2015. "Teacher Quality and Sorting across Traditional Public and Charter Schools in the Detroit Metropolitan Region." *Educational Considerations* 42(2): 20–34.

Addonizio, Michael F., C. Philip Kearney, and Henry J. Prince. 1995. "Michigan's High Wire Act." *Journal of Education Finance* 20(3): 235–269.

Akerlof, George A., and Rachel E. Kranton. 2010. *Identity Economics: How Our Identities Shape Our Work, Wages, and Well-Being.* Princeton, NJ: Princeton University Press.

Aldeman, Chad. 2017. "The Teacher Evaluation Revamp, in Hindsight." *EducationNext* 17(2): 61–68.

Allegretto, Sylvia A., Sean P. Corcoran, and Lawrence Mishel. 2008. *The Teaching Penalty: Teacher Pay Losing Ground.* Washington, DC: Economic Policy Institute.

Allegretto, Sylvia A., and Lawrence Mishel. 2016. *The Teacher Pay Gap Is Wider than Ever: Teachers' Pay Continues to Fall Further Behind Pay of Comparable Workers.* Washington, DC: Economic Policy Institute.

———. 2018. *The Teacher Pay Penalty Has Hit a New High: Trends in the Teacher Wage and Compensation Gaps through 2017.* Washington, DC: Economic Policy Institute.

————. 2019. *The Teacher Weekly Wage Penalty Hit 21.4 Percent in 2018, a Record High*. Report. Washington, DC: Economic Policy Institute.

————. 2020. *Teacher Pay Penalty Dips but Persists in 2019: Public School Teachers Earn about 20% Less in Weekly Wages than Nonteacher College Graduates*. Washington, DC: Economic Policy Institute; and Berkeley, CA: Center on Wage and Employment Dynamics.

Alliance for Excellent Education. 2005. "Teacher Attrition: A Costly Loss to the Nation and to the States." Issue brief. Washington, DC: Alliance for Excellent Education.

American College Testing (ACT). 2015. *The Condition of Future Educators 2014*. Iowa City, IA: American College Testing. https://www.act.org/content/dam/act/unsecured/documents/CCCR-2014-FutureEducators.pdf (accessed February 7, 2022).

Archambault, Reginald D., ed. 1964. *John Dewey on Education: Selected Writings*. New York: Modern Library.

Arsen, David, Tanner Delpier, and Jesse Nagel. 2019. *Michigan School Finance at the Crossroads: A Quarter Century of State Control*. MSU Education Policy Report. East Lansing: College of Education, Michigan State University.

Bacolod, Marigee. 2007. "Who Teaches and Where They Choose to Teach: College Graduates of the 1990s." *Educational Evaluation and Policy Analysis* 29(3): 155–168.

Baker, A. Paige, Dengke Xu, and Ethel Detch. 1995. *The Measure of Education: A Review of the Tennessee Value Added Assessment System*. Nashville, TN: Office of Education Accountability, Department of Education.

Baker, Bruce D. 2016a. *Does Money Matter in Education?* 2nd ed. Washington, DC: Albert Shanker Institute.

————. 2016b. *Exploring the Consequences of Charter School Expansion in U.S. Cities*. Washington, DC: Economic Policy Institute.

Baker, Bruce D., and Matthew Di Carlo. 2020. *The Coronavirus Pandemic and K–12 Education Funding*. Washington, DC: Albert Shanker Institute.

Baker, Bruce D., and Jill L. Dickerson. 2006. "Charter Schools, Teacher Labor Market Deregulation, and Teacher Quality: Evidence from the Schools and Staffing Survey." *Educational Policy* 20(5): 752–778.

Baker, Bruce D., and Gary Miron. 2015. *The Business of Charter Schooling: Understanding the Policies That Charter Operators Use for Financial Benefit*. Boulder, CO: National Education Policy Center.

Balch, Ryan, and Matthew G. Springer. 2015. "Performance Pay, Test Scores, and Student Learning Objectives." *Economics of Education Review* 44(C): 114–125.

Barr, Arvil S. 1948. "The Measurement and Prediction of Teaching Efficiency:

A Summary of Investigations." *Journal of Experimental Education* 16(4): 203–283.

Barrett, Nathan, Deven Carlson, Douglas N. Harris, and Jane Arnold Lincove. 2020. *When the Walls Come Down: Evidence on Charter Schools' Ability to Keep Their Best Teachers without Unions and Certification Rules.* New Orleans, LA: National Center for Research on Education Access and Choice (REACH).

Barron's Educational Series. 1998. *Barron's Profiles of American Colleges.* 23rd ed. Hauppauge, NY: Barron's Educational Series.

Baumol, William J. 1967. "Macroeconomics of Unbalanced Growth: The Anatomy of the Urban Crisis." *American Economic Review* 62(June): 415–426.

———. 2012. *The Cost Disease: Why Computers Get Cheaper and Health Care Doesn't.* New Haven, CT: Yale University Press.

Bedortha, Darcy. 2014. "15 Months in Virtual Charter Hell: A Teacher's Tale." Guest post, Opinion section, *Education Week*, January 6. https://www.edweek.org/leadership/opinion-15-months-in-virtual-charter-hell-a-teachers-tale/2014/01 (accessed February 7, 2022).

Berends, Mark, Samuel R. Lucas, and Roberto V. Penaloza. 2008. "How Changes in Families and Schools Are Related to Trends in Black-White Test Scores." *Sociology of Education* 81(4): 313–344.

Berube, Maurice R., and Marilyn Gittell, eds. 1969. *The New York School Strikes of 1968.* New York: Frederick A. Praeger.

Betts, Juliann R., Kim Rueben, and Anne Danenberg. 2000. *Equal Resources, Equal Outcomes? The Distribution of School Resources and Student Achievement in California.* San Francisco: Public Policy Institute of California.

Bifulco, Robert, and Helen F. Ladd. 2006. "The Impacts of Charter Schools on Student Achievement: Evidence from North Carolina." *Education Finance and Policy* 1(1): 50–90.

Bitler, Marianne, Sean Corcoran, Thurston Domina, and Emily Penner. 2019. "Teacher Effects on Student Achievement and Height: A Cautionary Tale." NBER Working Paper No. 26480. Cambridge, MA: National Bureau of Economic Research. http://www.nber.org/papers/w26480 (accessed September 7, 2021).

Bivens, Josh, and Lawrence Mishel. 2015. "Understanding the Historic Divergence between Productivity and a Typical Worker's Pay: Why It Matters and Why It's Real." EPI Briefing Paper No. 406. Washington, DC: Economic Policy Institute.

Blinder, Alan S. 1987. *Hard Heads, Soft Hearts: Tough-Minded Economics for a Just Society.* Reading, MA: Addison-Wesley.

Bobbitt, Franklin. 1913. "The Supervision of City Schools: Some General Principles of Management Applied to the Problems of City-School Systems." In *Twelfth Yearbook of the National Society for the Study of Education*. Bloomington, IL: National Society for the Study of Education, pp. 54–55.

Booker, Kevin, Scott M. Gilpatric, Timothy Gronberg, and Dennis Jansen. 2007. "The Impact of Charter School Student Attendance on Student Performance." *Journal of Public Economics* 91(5–6): 849–876.

Boser, Ulrich, and Chelsea Straus. 2014. "Mid- and Late-Career Teachers Struggle with Paltry Incomes." News release, July 23. Washington, DC: Center for American Progress. https://www.americanprogress.org/issues/education-k-12/reports/2014/07/23/94168/ (accessed September 7, 2021).

Boyd, Donald, Pamela Grossman, Hamilton Lankford, Susanna Loeb, and James Wyckoff. 2006. "How Changes in Entry Requirements Alter the Teacher Workforce and Affect Student Achievement." *Education Finance and Policy* 1(2): 176–216.

———. 2009. "Teacher Preparation and Student Achievement." *Educational Evaluation and Policy Analysis* 31(4): 416–440.

Boyd, Donald, Hamilton Lankford, Susanna Loeb, and James Wyckoff. 2005. "The Draw of Home: How Teachers' Preferences for Proximity Disadvantage Urban Schools." *Journal of Policy Analysis and Management* 24(1): 113–132.

———. 2008. "The Narrowing Gap in New York City Teacher Qualifications and Its Implications for Student Achievement in High-Poverty Schools." *Journal of Policy Analysis and Management* 227(4): 793–818.

Brill, Steven. 2009. "The Rubber Room: The Battle over New York City's Worst Teachers." *New Yorker*, August 31.

Brown, Charles, and James L. Medoff. 1988. "Employer Size, Pay, and the Ability to Pay in the Public Sector." In *When Public Sector Workers Unionize*, Richard Freeman and Casey Ichniowski, eds. Chicago: University of Chicago Press, pp. 195–216.

Brunner, Eric, and Tim Squires. 2013. "The Bargaining Power of Teachers' Unions and the Allocation of School Resources." *Journal of Urban Economics* 76(C): 15–27.

Bryk, Anthony, and Barbara Schneider. 2002. *Trust in Schools: A Core Resource for Improvement*. New York: Russell Sage Foundation.

Buddin, Richard, and Gema Zamarro. 2009. "Teacher Qualifications and Student Achievement in Urban Elementary Schools." *Journal of Urban Economics* 66(2): 103–115.

Burian-Fitzgerald, Marisa, and Debbi Harris. 2004. *Teacher Recruitment and Teacher Quality? Are Charter Schools Different?* East Lansing: Education Policy Center at Michigan State University.

Callahan, Raymond E. 1962. *Education and the Cult of Efficiency*. Chicago: University of Chicago Press.

Campbell, Donald T. 1976. "Assessing the Impact of Planned Social Change." *Journal of Multidisciplinary Evaluation* 7(15): 3–45.

Cannata, Marisa, Raven McCrory, Gary Sykes, Dorothea Anagnostopoulos, and Kenneth A. Frank. 2010. "Exploring the Influence of National Board Certified Teachers in Their Schools and Beyond." *Educational Administration Quarterly* 46(4): 463–490.

Cannata, Marisa, and Roberto Penaloza. 2012. "Who Are Charter School Teachers? Comparing Teacher Characteristics, Job Choices, and Job Preferences." *Education Policy Analysis Archives* 20(29): 1–21.

Carey, Kevin. 2017. "The Little-Known Statistician Who Taught Us to Measure Teachers." *New York Times*, May 19.

Carnegie Forum on Education and the Economy. 1986. *A Nation Prepared: Teachers for the 21st Century.* The Report of the Task Force on Teaching as a Profession. New York: Carnegie Corporation.

Carver-Thomas, Desiree. 2018. *Diversifying the Teaching Profession: How to Recruit and Retain Teachers of Color.* Palo Alto, CA: Learning Policy Institute. https://learningpolicyinstitute.org/sites/default/files/product-files/ Diversifying_Teaching_Profession_REPORT_0.pdf (accessed February 4, 2022).

Carver-Thomas, Desiree, and Linda Darling-Hammond. 2017. *Teacher Turnover: Why It Matters and What We Can Do about It.* Palo Alto, CA: Learning Policy Institute. https://learningpolicyinstitute.org/sites/default/files/ product-files/Teacher_Turnover_REPORT.pdf (accessed February 4, 2022).

Center for Research on Education Outcomes (CREDO). 2009. *National Charter School Study*. Palo Alto, CA: Stanford University.

———. 2013. *Charter School Growth and Replication.* Palo Alto, CA: Stanford University.

Century Foundation. 2019. *The Benefits of Socioeconomically and Racially Integrated Schools and Classrooms*. Washington, DC: Century Foundation. https://tcf.org/content/facts/the-benefits-of-socioeconomically-and -racially-integrated-schools-and-classrooms/ (accessed March 2, 2022).

Chase, Bob. 1997. "The New NEA: Reinventing Teacher Unions for a NEW ERA." Address to the National Press Club, Washington, DC, February 5.

Cheng, Albert, Michael B. Henderson, Paul E. Peterson, and Martin R. West. 2019. "Public Support Climbs for Teacher Pay, School Expenditures, Charter Schools, and Universal Vouchers: Results from the 2018 *EdNext* Poll." *Education Next* 19(1): 8–26.

Cherng, Hua-Yu Sebastian, and Peter F. Halpin. 2016. "The Importance of Minority Teachers: Student Perceptions of Minority versus White Teachers." *Educational Researcher* 45(7): 407–420.

Chester, Mitchell D. 2014. *Building on 20 Years of Massachusetts Education*

Reform. Malden, MA: Massachusetts Department of Elementary and Secondary Education. https://www.doe.mass.edu/commissioner/BuildingOn Reform.pdf (accessed September 15, 2021).

Chetty, Raj, John N. Friedman, Nathaniel Hilger, Emmanuel Saez, Diane Whitmore Schanzenbach, and Danny Yagan. 2011. "How Does Your Kindergarten Classroom Affect Your Earnings? Evidence from Project Star." *Quarterly Journal of Economics* 126(4): 1593–1660.

Chetty, Raj, John N. Friedman, and Jonah E. Rockoff. 2014. "Measuring the Impacts of Teachers II: Teacher Value-Added and Student Outcomes in Adulthood." *American Economic Review* 109(9): 2633–2679.

Chevalier, Arnaud, Peter Dolton, and Steven McIntosh. 2002. *Recruiting and Retaining Teachers in the UK: An Analysis of Graduate Occupation Choice from the 1960s to the 1990s.* London: Centre for the Economics of Education.

Chi, Michelene T. H., Robert Glaser, and Marshall J. Farr, eds. 1988. *The Nature of Expertise.* Hillsdale, NJ: Erlbaum.

Cimino, James. 1999. "Development of Expertise in Medical Practice." In *Tacit Knowledge in Professional Practice: Researcher and Practitioner Perspectives,* Robert J. Sternberg and Joseph A. Horvath, eds. Mahwah, NJ: Erlbaum, pp. 101–119.

Citizens League. 1988. *Chartered Schools = Choices for Educators + Quality for All Students.* Minneapolis, MN: Citizens League.

Citizens Research Council of Michigan. 1992. "State Ballot Proposals A and C—Proposed Property Tax Amendments." Council Comments No. 1012. Lansing, MI: Citizens Research Council of Michigan.

———. 2003. "A Recap of the FY04 Budget and a Look Ahead to FY05 and Beyond." *State Budget Notes* 2003(10): 1–10.

———. 2019. *Michigan's Leaky Teacher Pipeline.* Report No. 404. Lansing, MI: Citizens Research Council of Michigan.

Clark, Melissa A., Hanley S. Chiang, Tim Silve, Sheena McConnell, Kathy Sonnenfeld, Anastasia Erbe, and Michael Puma. 2013. *The Effectiveness of Secondary Math Teachers from Teach for America and the Teaching Fellows Programs.* NCEE Report No. 2013-4015. Washington, DC: U.S. Department of Education, National Center for Education Evaluation and Regional Assistance, Institute of Education Sciences.

Clark, Robert L. 2008. "Financing Retiree Health Benefits in the Public Sector." Unpublished paper, University of North Carolina.

———. 2009. "Will Public Sector Retiree Health Benefit Plans Survive? Economic and Policy Implications of Unfunded Liabilities." *American Economic Review* 99(2): 533–537.

———. 2010. "Retiree Health Plans for Public School Teachers after GASB 43 and 45." *Education Finance and Policy* 5(4): 438–462.

Clark, Robert L., Lee A. Craig, and Jack W. Wilson. 2003. *A History of Public Sector Pensions in the United States*. Philadelphia: University of Pennsylvania Press.

Close, Kevin, Audrey Amrein-Beardsley, and Clarin Collins. 2018. *State-Level Assessments and Teacher Evaluation Systems after the Passage of the Every Student Succeeds Act*. Boulder, CO: National Education Policy Center.

Clotfelter, Charles T., Elizabeth Glennie, Helen F. Ladd, and Jacob L. Vigdor. 2008. "Would Higher Salaries Keep Teachers in High-Poverty Schools? Evidence from a Policy Intervention in North Carolina." *Journal of Public Economics* 92(5–6): 1352–1370.

Clotfelter, Charles T., Helen F. Ladd, and Jacob L. Vigdor. 2005. "Who Teaches Whom? Race and the Distribution of Novice Teachers." *Economics of Education Review* 24(4): 377–392.

———. 2006. "Teacher-Student Matching and the Assessment of Teacher Effectiveness." *Journal of Human Resources* 41(4): 778–820.

———. 2007. "Teacher Credentials and Student Achievement: Longitudinal Analysis with Student Fixed Effects." *Economics of Education Review* 26(6): 673–682.

Cochran-Smith, Marilyn. 2005. "Teacher Education and the Outcomes Trap." *Journal of Teacher Education* 56(5): 411–417.

Cohen, David K. 2011. *Teaching and Its Predicaments*. Cambridge, MA: Harvard University Press.

Constantine, Jill, Daniel Player, Tim Silver, Kristan Hallgren, Mary Grider, and John Deke. 2009. *An Evaluation of Teachers Trained through Different Routes to Certification*. Washington, DC: U.S. Department of Education.

Conversation, The. 2019. "Teacher Unions Say They're Fighting for Students and Schools—What They Really Want Is More Members." *The Conversation*, March 4. https://theconversation.com/teacher-unions-say-they're -fighting-for-students-and-schools-what-they-really-want-is-more -members-112735 (accessed September 15, 2021).

Cooper, David, and Sebastian Martinez Hickey. 2022. *Raising Pay in Public K–12 Schools Is Critical to Solving Staffing Shortages*. Washington, DC: Economic Policy Institute.

Corcoran, Sean P. 2009. "Human Capital Policy and the Quality of the Teacher Workforce." In *Creating a New Teaching Profession*, Dan Goldhaber and Jane Hannaway, eds. Washington, DC: Urban Institute Press, pp. 29–52.

Corcoran, Sean P., and William N. Evans. 2008. "The Role of Inequality in Teacher Quality." In *Steady Gains and Stalled Progress: Inequality and the Black-White Test Score Gap*, Katherine Magnuson and Jane Waldfogel, eds. New York: Russell Sage Foundation, pp. 212–249.

Corcoran, Sean P., William N. Evans, and Robert M. Schwab. 2004. "Women, the Labor Market, and the Declining Relative Quality of Teachers." *Journal of Policy Analysis and Management* 23(3): 449–470.

Costrell, Robert M., and Michael Podgursky. 2010. "Distribution of Benefits in Teacher Retirement Systems and Their Implications for Mobility." *Education Finance and Policy* 5(4): 519–557.

Council for the Accreditation of Educator Preparation (CAEP). 2020. *State Partnership Agreements*. Washington, DC: Council for the Accreditation of Educator Preparation. http://www.caepnet.org/working-together/state -partners (accessed September 15, 2021).

Council of Chief State School Officers (CCSO). 2011. *(InTASC) Model Core Teaching Standards: A Resource for State Dialogue*. Washington, DC: CCSO.

Croft, Michelle, Gretchen Guffy, and Dan Vitale. 2018. "The Shrinking Use of Growth: Teacher Evaluation Legislation since ESSA." ACT Research and Policy Brief, July. Iowa City, IA: American College Testing.

Cubberley, Elwood. 1916. *Public School Administration*. Boston, MA: Houghton Mifflin.

Curto, Vilsa E., and Roland G. Fryer Jr. 2011. "Estimating the Returns to Urban Boarding Schools: Evidence from SEED." NBER Working Paper No. 16746. Cambridge, MA: National Board of Economic Research.

Darby, Derrick, and John L. Rury. 2018. *The Color of Mind*. Chicago, IL: University of Chicago Press.

Darling-Hammond, Linda. 1989. "Accountability for Professional Practice." *Teachers College Record* 91(1): 59–80.

———. 2010. *The Flat World and Education: How America's Commitment to Equity Will Determine Our Future*. New York: Teachers College Press.

Dee, Thomas S. 2004. "Teachers, Race, and Student Achievement in a Randomized Experiment." *Review of Economics and Statistics* 86(1): 195–210.

Dee, Thomas S., and James Wyckoff. 2015. "Incentives, Selection, and Teacher Performance: Evidence from IMPACT." *Journal of Policy Analysis and Management* 34(2): 267–297.

Dewey, John. 1964. *John Dewey on Education: Selected Writings*, Reginald D. Archambault, ed. New York: Modern Library.

Dickens, William, and Jonathan Leonard. 1985. "Accounting for the Decline in Union Membership, 1950–1980." *Industrial and Labor Relations Review* 38(3): 323–334.

Diliberti, Melissa Kay, Heather L. Schwartz, and David Grant. 2021. *Stress Topped the Reasons Why Public School Teachers Quit, Even before COVID-19*. Santa Monica, CA: RAND Corporation. https://www.rand.org/pubs/ research_reports/RRA1121-2.html (accessed February 4, 2022).

Dunn, Joshua. 2017. "Hands Off My Tenure! Unions Challenge Constitutionality of Reforms." *Education Next* 17(2): 7.

Eagan, Kevin, Ellen Bara Stolzenberg, Hilary B. Zimmerman, Melissa C. Aragon, Hannah Whang Sayson, and Cecilia Rios-Aguilar. 2017. *The American Freshman: National Norms Fall 2016*. Los Angeles: Cooperative Institutional Research Program at the Higher Education Research Institute at UCLA. https://www.heri.ucla.edu/monographs/TheAmerican Freshman2016.pdf (accessed February 7, 2022).

Eberts, Randall W. 2007. "Teachers Unions and Student Performance: Help or Hindrance?" *Future of Children* 17(1): 175–200.

Eberts, Randall W., and Joe A. Stone. 1987. "Teachers Unions and the Productivity of Public Schools." *Industrial and Labor Relations Review* 40(3): 354–363.

Education Commission of the States. 2014. *50-State Comparison: Teacher Employment Contract Policies*. Denver, CO: Education Commission of the States. https://www.ecs.org/50-state-comparison-teacher-employment -contract-policies/ (accessed March 2, 2022).

———. 2020. *50-State-Comparison: Charter School Policies—Does the State Have a Charter School Law?* Denver, CO: Education Commission of the States.

Ellerson, Noelle M. 2012. "Weathering the Storm: How Economic Recession Continues to Impact School Districts." Alexandria, VA: American Association of School Administrators.

Elmore, Richard. 2002. "The Testing Trap." *Harvard Magazine* 105(1): 35–37.

Engel, Mimi, Brian A. Jacob, and F. Chris Curran. 2014. "New Evidence on Teacher Labor Supply." *American Educational Research Journal* 51(1): 36–72. https://doi.org/10.3102/0002831213503031 (accessed March 1, 2022).

Epple, Dennis R., Richard Romano, and Ron Zimmer. 2015. "Charter Schools: A Survey of Research on Their Characteristics and Effectiveness." NBER Working Paper No. 21256. Cambridge, MA: National Bureau of Economic Research. http://www.nber.org/papers/w21256 (accessed March 6, 2022).

Exstrom, Michelle. 2012. *Teaching in Charter Schools*. Washington, DC: National Conference of State Legislatures.

Farber, Henry. 1990. "The Decline of Unionization in the United States." *Journal of Labor Economics* 8(1): S75–S105.

Feistritzer, C. Emily. 2011. *Profile of Teachers in the U.S.* Washington, DC: National Center for Education Information.

Fensterwald, John. 2016. "California High Court Lets Rulings Stand on Teacher Tenure, School Funding Lawsuits." *EdSource*, April 22. https://edsource.org/2016/state-supreme-court-declines-to-hear-vergara -inadequate-funding-cases/568350 (accessed February 23, 2022).

Figlio, David, and Susanna Loeb. 2011. "School Accountability." In *Handbook* in *Economics: Economics of Education*, Eric A. Hanushek, Stephen Machin, and Ludger Woessman, eds. Amsterdam, Netherlands: North-Holland, pp. 383–421.

Fordham Foundation. 1999. "The Teachers We Need and How to Get More of Them: A Manifesto." In *Better Teachers, Better Schools*, Marci Kanstoroom and Chester E. Finn Jr., eds. Washington, DC: Thomas B. Fordham Foundation, pp. 1–18.

Fox, Sylvan. 1968. "Some Hostility Marks Return of 83 Teachers to Ocean Hill." *New York Times*, October 1.

Freeman, Richard B. 1986. "Unionism Comes to the Public Sector." *Journal of Economic Literature* 24(March): 41–86.

Freeman, Richard B., and Morris Kleiner. 1990. "Employer Behavior in the Face of Union Organizing Drives." *Industrial and Labor Relations Review* 43(4): 351–365.

Friedman, Milton. 1962. *Capitalism and Freedom*. Chicago: University of Chicago Press.

Frumkin, Peter, Bruno Manno, and Nell Edgington. 2011. *The Strategic Management of Charter Schools*. Cambridge, MA: Harvard Education Press.

Fry, Richard. 2018. "Millennials Are the Largest Generation in the U.S. Labor Force." *Facttank*, April 11. Washington, DC: Pew Research Center. https://www.pewresearch.org/fact-tank/2018/04/11/millennials-largest-generation-us-labor-force/ (accessed March 6, 2022).

Fryer, Roland G., Steven D. Levitt, John List, and Sally Sadoff. 2012. "Enhancing the Efficiency of Teacher Incentives through Loss Aversion: A Field Experiment." NBER Working Paper No. w18237. Cambridge, MA: National Bureau of Economic Research.

Gabor, Andrea. 2018. *After the Education Wars: How Smart Schools Upend the Business of Reform*. New York: New Press.

Garcia, Emma, and Elaine Weiss. 2020. *Examining the Factors That Play a Role in the Teacher Shortage Crisis: Key Findings from EPI's "Perfect Storm in the Teacher Labor Market" Series*. Washington, DC: Economic Policy Institute.

Gebeloff, Robert. 2018. "The Numbers That Explain Why Teachers Are in Revolt." *New York Times*, June 4. https://www.nytimes.com/2018/06/04/upshot/school-funding-still-lags-after-recession-ended.html (accessed March 6, 2022).

Gershenson, Seth, Cassandra M. D. Hart, Constance A. Lindsay, and Nicholas W. Papageorge. 2017. *The Long-Run Impacts of Same-Race Teachers*. IZA Discussion Paper No. 10630. Bonn, Germany: Institute of Labor Economics).

Glazerman, Steven, and Allison Seifullah. 2010. *An Evaluation of the Teacher*

Advancement Program (TAP) in Chicago: Year Two Impact Report. Princeton, NJ: Mathematica Policy Research.

Gleason, Philip, Melissa Clark, Christina Clark Tuttle, Emily Dwoyer. 2010. *The Evaluation of Charter School Impacts*. Washington, DC: U.S. Department of Education, National Center for Education Evaluation and Regional Assistance.

Goldhaber, Dan. 2008. "Teachers Matter, but Effective Teacher Quality Policies Are Elusive." In *Handbook of Research in Education Finance and Policy*, H. F. Ladd and E. B. Fiske, eds. New York: Routledge, pp. 146–165.

Goldhaber, Dan, Lesley Lavery, and Roddy Theobald. 2015. "Uneven Playing Field? Assessing the Teacher Quality Gap between Advantaged and Disadvantaged Students." *Educational Researcher* 44(5): 293–307.

Goldhaber, Dan, and Joe Walch. 2013. "Gains in Teacher Quality." *EducationNext* 14(1): 38–45.

Goldring, Rebecca, Lucinda Gray, and Amy Bitterman. 2013. *Characteristics of Public and Private Elementary and Secondary School Teachers in the U.S.: Results from the 2011–12 Schools and Staffing Survey, First Look*. National Center for Education Statistics 2013-314. Washington, DC: U.S. Department of Education.

Goldstein, Dana. 2014. *The Teacher Wars: A History of America's Most Embattled Profession*. New York: Doubleday.

Goldstein, Dana, and Ben Casselman. 2018. "Teachers Find Public Support as Campaign for Higher Pay Goes to Voters." *New York Times*, May 31. https://www.nytimes.com/2018/05/31/us/politics/teachers-campaign.html (accessed March 6, 2022).

Gordon, Robert, Thomas J. Kane, and Douglas O. Staiger. 2006. "Identifying Effective Teachers Using Performance on the Job." Hamilton Project White Paper No. 2006-01. Washington, DC: Brookings Institution.

Graebner, William. 1980. *A History of Retirement: The Meaning and Function of an American Institution, 1885–1978*. New Haven, CT: Yale University Press.

Gray, Lucinda, and Soheyla Taie. 2015. *Public School Teacher Attrition and Mobility in the First Five Years: Results from the First through Fifth Waves of the 2007–08 Beginning Teacher Longitudinal Study*. NCES 2015-337. Washington, DC: U.S. Department of Education, National Center for Education Statistics.

Green, Max. 1996. *Epitaph for American Labor: How Union Leaders Lost Touch with America*. Washington, DC: American Enterprise Institute Press.

Griffith, Michael. 2016. *Policy Analysis: State Teacher Salary Schedules*. Denver, CO: Education Commission of the States.

Grissmer, David, and Sheila Nataraj Kirby. 1997. "Teacher Turnover and Teacher Quality." *Teachers College Record* 99(1): 45–56.

Grissom, Jason A., Susanna Loeb, and Nathaniel A. Nakashima. 2014. "Strategic Involuntary Teacher Transfers and Teacher Performance: Examining Equity and Efficiency." *Journal of Policy Analysis and Management* 33(1): 112–140.

Han, Eunice S. 2016. "The Myth of Unions' Overprotection of Bad Teachers: Evidence from the District-Teacher Matched Panel Data on Teacher Turnover." Unpublished manuscript, Wellesley College.

Hansen, Janet S. 2010. "An Introduction to Teacher Retirement Benefits." *Education Finance and Policy* 5(4): 402–437.

Hansen, Michael. 2018. "Teachers Aren't Getting Younger, We're Just Paying Them Less." Washington, DC: Brookings Institution, Brown Center on Education Policy. https://www.brookings.edu/blog/brown-center-chalkboard/2018/09/05/teachers-arent-getting-younger-were-just-paying-them-less/ (accessed March 6, 2022).

Hanushek, Eric A. 1994. *Making Schools Work: Improving Performance and Controlling Costs*. Washington, DC: Brookings Institution.

———. 2006. "Alternative School Policies and the Benefits of General Cognitive Skills." *Economics of Education Review* 25(4): 447–462.

———. 2020. "The Unavoidable: Tomorrow's Teacher Compensation." Hoover Institution Policy Paper. Stanford, CA: Stanford University.

Hanushek, Eric A., John F. Kain, Daniel M. O'Brien, and Steven G. Rivkin. 2005. "The Market for Teacher Quality." NBER Working Paper No. 11154. Cambridge, MA: National Bureau of Economic Research.

Hanushek, Eric A., John F. Kain, and Steven G. Rivkin. 2004. "Why Public Schools Lose Teachers." *Journal of Human Resources* 39(2): 326–354.

Hanushek, Eric A., John F. Kain, Steven G. Rivkin, and Gregory F. Branch. 2007. "Charter School Quality and Parental Decision Making with School Choice." *Journal of Public Economics* 91(5): 823–848.

Hanushek, Eric A., and Steven G. Rivkin. 2004. "How to Improve the Supply of High-Quality Teachers." In *Brookings Papers on Education Policy*, Diane Ravitch, ed. Washington, DC: Brookings Institution, pp. 7–25.

Hanushek, Eric A., Steven G. Rivkin, and Jeffrey C. Schiman. 2016. "Dynamic Effects of Teacher Turnover on the Quality of Instruction." *Economics of Education Review* 55(1): 132–148.

Harris, Douglas N., and Tim R. Sass. 2009. "The Effects of NBPTS-Certified Teachers on Student Achievement." *Journal of Policy Analysis and Management* 28(1): 55–80.

———. 2011. "Teacher Training, Teacher Quality and Student Achievement." *Journal of Public Economics* 95(7): 798–812.

Hart, Cassandra M. D., and Aaron Sojourner. 2014. "Unionization and Productivity: Evidence from Charter Schools." IZA Discussion Paper No. 7887. Bonn, Germany: Institute of Labor Economics.

Hendricks, Matthew D. 2015a. "Public Schools Are Hemorrhaging Talented Teachers: Can Higher Salaries Function as a Tourniquet?" Working paper, University of Tulsa. http://papers.ssrn.com/sol3/papers.cfm?abstract_id =2564703 (accessed March 6, 2022).

———. 2015b. "Towards an Optimal Teacher Salary Schedule: Designing Base Salary to Attract and Retain Effective Teachers." *Economics of Education Review* 47(August): 143–167.

Henry, Gary T., and Christopher Redding. 2018. "The Consequences of Leaving School Early: The Effects of Within-Year and End-of-Year Teacher Turnover." *Education Finance and Policy* 15(2): 332–356.

Hodgkinson, Harold L. 1985. *All One System: Demographics of Education— Kindergarten through Graduate School*. Washington, DC: Institute of Educational Leadership.

Howell, William G. 2015. "Results of President Obama's Race to the Top." *EducationNext* 15(4): 58–66.

Hoxby, Caroline M. 1996. "How Teachers Unions Affect Education Production." *Quarterly Journal of Economics* 111(3): 671–718.

Hoxby, Caroline M., and Andrew Leigh. 2004. "Pulled Away or Pushed Out? Explaining the Decline of Teacher Aptitude in the United States." *American Economic Review* 94(2): 236–240.

Hoxby, Caroline M., Sonali Murarka, and Jenny Kang. 2009. *How New York City's Charter Schools Affect Achievement*. Cambridge, MA: New York City Charter Schools Evaluation Project.

Hoyt, William H. 1999. "Leviathan, Local Governments, Expenditures, and Capitalization." *Regional Science and Urban Economics* 29(2): 155–171.

Illinois General Assembly. 2022. *Illinois Compiled Statutes*. 105 ILCS 5/Article 27A: Charter Schools. Springfield, IL: Illinois General Assembly.

Imberman, Scott. 2011. "The Effect of Charter Schools on Achievement and Behavior of Public School Students." *Journal of Public Economics* 95(7): 850–863.

Ingersoll, Richard M. 2003. *Who Controls Teachers' Work? Power and Accountability in America's Schools*. Cambridge, MA: Harvard University.

———. 2011. "Do We Produce Enough Mathematics and Science Teachers?" *Phi Delta Kappan* 92(6): 37–41.

Ingersoll, Richard M., Lisa Merrill, and Daniel Stuckey. 2014. *Seven Trends: The Transformation of the Teaching Force*. CPRE Research Report No. RR-80. Philadelphia: Consortium for Policy Research in Education, University of Pennsylvania.

Ingersoll, Richard M., Elizabeth Merrill, Daniel Stuckey, Gregory Collins, and Brandon Harrison. 2021. "The Demographic Transformation of the Teaching Force in the United States. *Education Sciences* 11(5): 234–264.

Ingersoll, Richard M., and David Perda. 2010. "Is the Supply of Mathematics and Science Teachers Sufficient?" *American Educational Research Journal* 20(3): 1–32.

———. 2012. *How High Is Teacher Turnover, and Is It a Problem?* Philadelphia: Consortium for Policy Research in Education, University of Pennsylvania.

Ingersoll, Richard, and Thomas M. Smith. 2003. "The Wrong Solution to the Teacher Shortage." *Educational Leadership* 60(8): 30—33.

Jacob, Brian A. 2007. "The Challenges of Staffing Urban Schools with Effective Teachers." *Future of Children* 17(1): 129–153.

———. 2017. *How the U.S. Department of Education Can Foster Education Reform in the Era of Trump and ESSA.* Evidence Speaks Reports, Vol. 2, No. 7. Washington, DC: Brookings. https://www.brookings.edu/research/how-the-u-s-department-of-education-can-foster-education-reform-in-the-era-of-trump-and-essa/ (accessed March 6, 2022).

Jacob, Brian, and Lars Lefgren. 2005. "Principals as Agents: Subjective Performance Measurement in Education." NBER Working Paper No. 11463. Cambridge, MA: National Bureau of Economic Research.

———. 2008. "Can Principals Identify Effective Teachers? Evidence on Subjective Performance Evaluation in Education." *Journal of Labor Economics* 26(1): 101–136.

Jacob, Brian, Jonah E. Rockoff, Eric S. Taylor, Benjamin Lindy, and Rachel Rosen. 2016. "Teacher Applicant Hiring and Teacher Performance: Evidence from D.C. Public Schools." NBER Working Paper No. 22054. Cambridge, MA: National Bureau of Economic Research.

Jacobs, Sandi. 2021. *In Demand: The Real Teacher Shortages and How to Solve Them.* Washington, DC: FutureEd. https://www.future-ed.org/wp-content/uploads/2021/10/FutureEd_EdCounsel_Teacher_Shortages.pdf (accessed February 4, 2022).

Jencks, Christopher, and Meredith Phillips, eds. 1998. *The Black-White Test Score Gap.* Washington, DC: Brookings Institution.

Johnson, Rucker. 2015. "Long-Run Impacts of School Desegregation and School Quality on Adult Attainments." NBER Working Paper No. 16664. Cambridge, MA: National Bureau of Economic Research. https://gsppi.berkeley.edu/~ruckerj/johnson_schooldesegregation_NBERw16664.pdf (accessed March 6, 2022).

Junge, Ember Reichgott. 2012. "Reclaiming the Origins of Chartered Schools." *Education Week,* June 11.

Kahlenberg, Richard D. 2007. *Tough Liberal: Albert Shanker and the Battles over Schools, Unions, Race, and Democracy.* New York: Columbia University Press.

Kahlenberg, Richard D., and Halley Potter. 2014. *A Smarter Charter*. New York: Teachers College Press.

Kane, Thomas J., Jonah E. Rockoff, and Douglas O. Staiger. 2008. "What Does Teacher Certification Tell Us about Teacher Effectiveness? Evidence from New York City." *Economics of Education Review* 27(6): 615–631.

Kane, Thomas J., and Douglas O. Staiger. 2008. "Estimating Teacher Impacts on Student Achievement: An Experimental Evaluation." NBER Working Paper No. 14607. Cambridge, MA: National Bureau of Economic Research.

Kardaras, Nicholas. 2016. "Screens in Schools Are a $60 Billion Hoax." *Time*, August 31. http://time.com/4474496/screen-in-school-hoax/ (accessed September 19, 2021).

Kearney, C. Philip, and Addonizio, Michael F. 2002. *A Primer on Michigan School Finance*. 4th ed. Detroit, MI: Wayne State University Press.

Kirp, David L. 2014. "Teaching Is Not a Business." *New York Times*, August 17, p. SR4.

Kolderie, Ted. 2005. "Ray Budde and the Origins of the 'Charter Concept.'" Memo. St. Paul, MN: Education Evolving.

Kraft, Matthew A., and Allison F. Gilmour. 2017. "Revisiting *The Widget Effect*: Teacher Evaluation Reforms and the Distribution of Teacher Effectiveness." *Educational Researcher* 46(5): 234–249.

Kwak, James. 2017. *Economism*. New York: Pantheon.

Ladd, Helen F. 2007. "Teacher Labor Markets in Developed Countries." *Future of Children* 17(1): 201–217.

Ladd, Helen F., and Lucy C. Sorensen. 2017. "Returns to Teacher Experience: Student Achievement and Motivation in Middle School." *Education Finance and Policy* 12(2): 241–279.

Lafer, Gordon. 2017. *The One Percent Solution*. Ithaca, NY: Cornell University Press.

Lankford, Hamilton, Susanna Loeb, Andrew McEachin, Luke C. Miller, and James H. Wyckoff. 2014. "Who Enters Teaching? Encouraging Evidence That the Status of Teaching Is Improving." Working paper. Charottesville, VA: Curry School of Education, Center for Education Policy and Workforce Competitiveness, University of Virginia.

Lankford, Hamilton, Susanna Loeb, and James H. Wyckoff. 2002. "Teacher Sorting and the Plight of Urban Schools: A Descriptive Analysis." *Educational Evaluation and Policy Analysis* 24(1): 37–62.

Leachman, Michael L., Kathleen Masterson, and Eric Figueroa. 2017. *A Punishing Decade for School Funding*. Washington, DC: Center on Budget and Policy Priorities.

Leigh, Andrew. 2005. *Teacher Pay and Teacher Aptitude*. Canberra: Australian National University, Social Policy Evaluation, Analysis and Research Centre.

Levin, Jesse, Alex Berg-Jacobson, Drew Atchison, Katelyn Lee, and Emily Vontsolos. 2015. *Massachusetts Study of Teacher Supply and Demand: Trends and Projections*. Washington, DC: American Institutes for Research.

Lieberman, Mark. 2021. "How Bad Are School Staffing Shortages? What We Learned by Asking Administrators." *Education Week*, October 12. https://www.edweek.org/leadership/how-bad-are-school-staffing-shortages-what-we-learned-by-asking-administrators/2021/10 (accessed February 4, 2022).

Livingston, Carol, and Hilda Borko. 1989. "Expert-Novice Differences in Teaching: A Cognitive Analysis and Implications for Teacher Education." *Journal of Teacher Education* 40(4): 36–42.

Lortie, Dan C. 1975. *Schoolteacher: A Sociological Study*. Chicago: University of Chicago Press.

Losen, Daniel, Cherl Hodson, Michael A. Keith, Katrina Morrison, and Shatki Belway. 2015. *Are We Closing the School Discipline Gap?* Los Angeles, CA: Center for Civil Rights Remedies, the Civil Rights Project at UCLA. http://civiltightsproject.ucla.edu/resources/projects/center-for-civil-rights-remedies/school-to-prison-folder/federal-reports/are-we-closing-the-school-discipline-gap/ (accessed March 6, 2022).

Lovenheim, Michael F. 2009. "The Effect of Teachers' Unions on Education Production: Evidence from Union Election Certifications in Three Midwestern States." *Journal of Labor Economics* 27(4): 527–587.

Lovenheim, Michael F., and Alexander Willen. 2019. "The Long-Run Effects of Teacher Collective Bargaining." *American Economic Journal: Economic Policy* 11(3): 292–324.

Malloy, Courtney L., and Priscilla Wohlstetter. 2003. "Working Conditions in Charter Schools: What's the Appeal for Teachers?" Education and Urban Policy 35(2): 219–241.

Marsh, Julie A., Matthew G. Springer, Daniel F. McCaffrey, Kun Yuan, Scott Epstein, Julia Koppich, Nidhi Kalra, Catherine DiMartino, and Art Peng. 2011. *A Big Apple for Educators: New York City's Experiment with School-wide Performance Bonuses, Final Evaluation Report*. Santa Monica, CA: RAND Education.

Massachusetts Business Alliance for Education (MBAE). 1991. *Every Child a Winner! A Proposal for a Legislative Action Plan for Systematic Reform of Massachusetts' Public Primary and Secondary Education System*. Boston: Massachusetts Business Alliance for Education.

Mayer, Gerald. 2004. *Union Membership Trends in the United States*. Appendix A: Annual Data. CRS Report for Congress. Washington, DC: Congressional Research Service.

McAlevey, Jane. 2020. *A Collective Bargain: Unions, Organizing, and the Fight for Democracy*. New York: HarperCollins.

Mehta, Jal. 2013a. "From Bureaucracy to Profession: Remaking the Educational Sector for the Twenty-First Century." *Harvard Educational Review* 83(3): 463–488.

———. 2013b. *The Allure of Order*. New York: Oxford University Press.

Miron, Gary, and Brooks Applegate. 2007. *Teacher Attrition in Charter Schools*. East Lansing, MI: Great Lakes Center for Education Research and Practice.

Miron, Gary, and Charisse Gulosino. 2013. *Profiles of For-Profit and Nonprofit Education Management Organizations: Fourteenth Edition—2011–12.* Boulder, CO: National Education Policy Center. http://nepc.colorado.edu/publication/EMO-profiles-11-12 (accessed March 6, 2022).

Miron, Gary, and Jessica L. Urschel. 2012. *Understanding and Improving Full-Time Virtual Schools: A Study of Student Characteristics, School Finance, and School Performance in Schools Operated by K12 Inc.* Boulder, CO: National Education Policy Center.

Moe, Terry M. 2005 "Teachers Unions and School Board Elections." In *Beseiged: School Boards and the Future of Education Politics*, William G. Howell, ed. Washington, DC: Brookings Institution, pp. 254–287.

———. 2011. *Special Interest: Teachers Unions and America's Public Schools.* Washington, DC: Brookings Institution.

Molnar, Michele. 2013. "K12 Inc. Learning Hard Management, Financial Lessons." *Education Week*, Oct. 23.

Monk, David H., Christopher F. Roelke, and Brian O. Brent. 1996. *What Education Dollars Buy: An Examination of Resource Allocation Patterns in New York Public School Systems*. Madison, WI: Consortium for Policy Research in Education.

Muller, Jerry Z. 2018. *The Tyranny of Metrics*. Princeton, NJ: Princeton University Press.

Murnane, Richard J. 1988. "Education and the Productivity of the Workforce: Looking Ahead." In *American Living Standards: Threats and Challenges*, Robert E. Litan, Robert Z. Lawrence, and Charles L. Schultze, eds. Washington, DC: Brookings Institution, pp. 215–244.

Murnane, Richard J., and Barbara R. Phillips. 1981. "What Do Effective Teachers of Inner City Children Have in Common?" *Social Science Research* 10(1): 83–100.

Murnane, Richard J., Judith D. Singer, John B. Willett, James J. Kemple, and Randall J. Olsen. 1991. *Who Will Teach? Policies That Matter*. Cambridge, MA: Harvard University Press.

Murnane, Richard J., and Jennifer L. Steele. 2007. "What Is the Problem? The Challenge of Providing Effective Teachers for All Children." *Future of Children* 17(1): 15–43.

Murphy, Marjorie. 1990. *Blackboard Unions: The AFT and the NEA, 1900–1980.* Ithaca, NY: Cornell University Press.

National Alliance for Public Charter Schools. 2014. *Measuring Up: A Tool for Comparing State Charter School Laws and Movements.* Washington, DC: National Alliance for Public Charter Schools. https://www.publiccharters.org/get-the-facts/law-database (accessed March 6, 2022).

———. 2016. *A Call to Action to Improve the Quality of Full-Time Virtual Charter Public Schools.* Washington, DC: National Alliance for Public Charter Schools.

National Association of Charter School Authorizers and Public Impact. 2015. *Study of Virtual School Performance and Impact: Presentation of Findings.* Atlanta: State Charter Schools Commission of Georgia.

National Board for Professional Teaching Standards (NBPTS). 1989. *Toward High and Rigorous Standards for the Teaching Profession: Initial Policies and Perspectives of the National Board for Professional Teaching Standards.* Arlington, VA: National Board for Professional Teaching Standards.

———. 2021a. *In Your State.* Arlington, VA: National Board for Professional Teaching Standards. https://www.nbpts.org/support/in-your-state/ (accessed November 19, 2021).

———. 2021b. *More than 2,570 Teachers Earn National Board Certification; National Total Exceeds 128,500 Despite Extraordinary Year for Educators.* Arlington, VA: National Board for Professional Teaching Standards. https://www.nbpts.org/newsroom/more-than-2570-teachers-earn-national-board-certification-national-total-exceeds-128500-despite-extraordinary-year-for-educators-2/ (accessed November 19, 2021).

National Center for Education Statistics (NCES). 2012. "Percentage Distribution of Public School Districts, by Type of Agreement with Teachers' Associations or Unions and Selected Public School District Characteristics: 2011–12." Washington, DC: National Center for Education Statistics, Schools and Staffing Survey. https://nces.ed.gov/surveys/sass/tables/sass1112_2013311_d1n_007.asp (accessed October 20, 2021).

———. 2015. *Digest of Education Statistics: Table 210.30, Mobility of Public Elementary and Secondary Teachers, by Selected Teacher and School Characteristics: Selected Years, 1987–88 through 2012–13.* Washington, DC: National Center for Education Statistics. https://nces.ed.gov/programs/digest/d18/tables/dt18_210.30.asp (accessed February 25, 2022).

———. 2019a. *The Condition of Education 2019.* Washington, DC: National Center for Education Statistics. https://nces.ed.gov/programs/coe/indicator/cga (accessed December 9, 2021).

———. 2019b. *Status and Trends in the Education of Racial and Ethnic Groups: Indicator 4: Children Living in Poverty.* Washington, DC:

National Center for Education Statistics. https://nces.ed.gov/programs/raceindicators/indicator_RAD.asp (accessed September 14, 2021).

———. 2021a. *The Condition of Education 2021*. Washington, DC: U.S. Department of Education.

———. 2021b. *Fast Facts: Charter Schools*. Washington, DC: National Center for Education Statistics. https://nces.ed.gov/fastfacts/display.asp?id=30 (accessed September 15, 2021).

National Commission on Excellence in Education. 1983. *A Nation at Risk: The Imperative for Educational Reform*. A Report to the Nation and the Secretary of Education, United States Department of Education. Washington, DC: U.S. Department of Education.

National Council on Teacher Quality (NCTQ). 2012. *State of the States 2012: Teacher Effectiveness Policies—Area 3: Identifying Effective Teachers*. Washington, DC: National Council on Teacher Quality.

———. 2015. *State of the States 2015: Evaluating Teaching, Leading, and Learning*. Washington, DC: National Council on Teacher Quality.

National Education Association (NEA). 2008. *Characteristics of Large Public Education Pension Plans*. Washington, DC: National Education Association.

National Research Council. 2008. *Assessing Accomplished Teaching: Advanced-Level Certification Programs*. Washington, DC: National Academies Press.

Neal, Derek. 2005. "How Families and Schools Shape the Achievement Gap." In *Generational Change: Closing the Test Score Gap*, Paul E. Peterson, ed. Lanham, MD: Rowman and Littlefield, pp. 26-46.

Neumann, George, and Ellen Rissman. 1984. "Where Have All the Union Members Gone?" *Journal of Labor Economics* 2(2): 175–192.

Neville, Katherine S., Rachel H. Sherman, and Carol E. Cohen. 2005. *Preparing and Training Professionals: Comparing Education to Six Other Fields*. New York: The Finance Project.

Ni, Yongmei, and Andrea K. Rorrer. 2012. "Twice Considered: Charter Schools and Student Achievement in Utah." *Economics of Education Review* 31(5): 835–849.

O'Leary, Brian. 2020. "Backgrounds and Beliefs of College Freshmen." *Chronicle of Higher Education*, August 12.

Ost, Ben. 2014. "How Do Teachers Improve? The Relative Importance of Specified General Human Capital." *American Economic Journal: Applied Economics* 6(2): 127–151.

Papay, John P., and Matthew A. Kraft. 2015. "Productivity Returns to Experience in the Teacher Labor Market: Methodological Challenges and New Evidence on Long-Term Career Improvement." *Journal of Public Economics* 130(1): 105–119.

Passantino, George, and Adam Summers. 2005. *The Gathering Pension Storm:*

How Government Pension Plans Are Breaking the Bank and Strategies for Reform. Los Angeles: Reason Public Policy Institute.

Patten, Simon. 1911. "An Economic Measure of School Efficiency." *Educational Review* 41(May): 467–469.

Perda, David. 2013. "Transitions into and out of Teaching: A Longitudinal Analysis of Early Career Teacher Turnover." Dissertation, University of Pennsylvania.

Peterson, Paul E. 2010. *Saving Schools: From Horace Mann to Virtual Learning*. Cambridge, MA: Harvard University Press.

Pew Center on the States. 2007. *Promises with a Price: Public Sector Retirement Benefits*. Philadelphia, PA: Pew Charitable Trusts.

Piketty, Thomas. 2014. *Capital in the Twenty-First Century*. Cambridge, MA: Belknap Press, Harvard University.

Public Fund Survey. 2009. *Public Fund Survey Summary of Findings for FY 2008*. Washington, DC: National Association of State Retirement Administrators.

Ravitch, Diane. 2010. *The Death and Life of the Great American School System*. New York: Basic Books.

———. 2013. *Reign of Error*. New York: Alfred A. Knopf.

Rebell, Michael A. 2006. "Adequacy Cost Studies: Perspectives on the State of the Art." *Education Finance and Policy* 1(4): 465–483.

Reisinger, Don. 2018. "America Is Losing Its Teachers at a Record Rate." *Fortune*, December 28. http://fortune.com/2018/12/28/american-teachers -quitting/ (accessed September 15, 2021).

Reville, Paul. 2015. "The Journey toward Equity and Excellence: The Massachusetts Experience." In *Excellence through Equity: Five Principles of Courageous Leadership to Guide Achievement for Every Student*, Alan M. Blankstein and Pedro Noguera, eds. Alexandria, VA: ASCD, pp. 185–202.

Rivkin, Steven G. 2009. "The Estimation of Teacher Value Added as a Determinant of Performance Pay." In *Creating a New Teaching Profession*, Dan Goldhaber and Jane Hannaway, eds. Washington, DC: Urban Institute, pp. 181–193.

Rivkin, Steven G., Eric Hanushek, and John F. Kain. 2005. "Teachers, Schools, and Academic Achievement." *Econometrica* 73(2): 417–458.

Rockoff, Jonah E. 2004. "The Impact of Individual Teachers on Student Achievement: Evidence from Panel Data." *American Economic Review Papers and Proceedings* 94(2): 247–252.

Ronfeldt, Matthew. 2012. "Where Should Student Teachers Learn to Teach? Effects of Field Placement School Characteristics on Teacher Retention and Effectiveness." *Educational Evaluation and Policy Analysis* 34(1): 3–26.

Ronfeldt, Matthew, Susanna Loeb, and James Wyckoff. 2013. "How Teacher

Turnover Harms Student Achievement." *American Educational Research Journal* 50(1): 4–36.

Rose, Heather, and Jon Sonstelie. 2010. "School Board Politics, School District Size, and the Bargaining Power of Teachers' Unions." *Journal of Urban Economics* 67(3): 438–450.

Rotherdam, Andrew J., and Sara Mead. 2004. "Back to the Future: The History and Politics of State Teacher Licensure and Certification." In *A Qualified Teacher in Every Classroom? Appraising Old Answers and New Ideas*, Frederick M. Hess, Andrew J. Rotherdam, and Kate Burke Walsh, eds. Cambridge, MA: Harvard Education Press, pp. 11–47.

Rothstein, Jesse. 2010. "Teacher Quality in Educational Production: Tracking, Decay, and Student Achievement." *Quarterly Journal of Economics* 125(1): 175–214.

Ruark, Peter. 2018. *A Hard Habit to Break: The Raiding of K–12 Funds for Postsecondary Education*. Lansing: Michigan League for Public Policy.

Sanders, William L. 2000. "Value-Added Assessment from Student Achievement Data: Opportunities and Hurdles." *Journal of Personnel Evaluation in Education* 14(December): 329–339.

Sass, Tim R. 2006. "Charter Schools and Student Achievement in Florida." *Education Finance and Policy* 1(1): 91–122.

Scafidi, Benjamin, David L. Sjoquist, and Todd R. Stinebrickner. 2007. "Race, Poverty, and Teacher Mobility." *Economics of Education Review* 26(2): 145–159.

Schochet, Peter Z., and Hanley S. Chiang. 2010. *Error Rates in Measuring Teacher and School Performance Based on Student Test Score Gains*. Institute of Education Sciences/Mathematica report. Washington, DC: National Center for Education Evaluation and Regional Assistance; Institute of Education Sciences, U.S. Department of Education.

Scott, James C. 1998. *Seeing like a State: How Certain Schemes to Improve the Human Condition Have Failed*. New Haven, CT: Yale University Press.

Selvers, Lana C. 2005. *Tennessee Plan for Implementing the Teacher and Paraprofessional Quality Provisions of the No Child Left Behind Act of 2001*. Nashville, TN: Tennessee State Department of Education.

Shanker, Albert. 1985. "The Making of a Profession." *American Educator* 9(3): 10–17, 46, 48.

———. 1986. "The Making of a Profession." *Journal of Negro Education* 55(3): 405–421.

———. 1988. "National Press Club Speech." Detroit, MI: Walter P. Reuther Library.

Shulman, Lee. 1987. "Knowledge and Teaching: Foundations of the New Reform." *Harvard Educational Review* 57(1): 1–22.

Smith, Thomas M., and Richard M. Ingersoll. 2004. *Do Teacher Induction and Mentoring Matter?* Philadelphia: University of Pennsylvania Press.

Snyder, Thomas D., Cristobal de Brey, and Sally A. Dillow. 2019. *Digest of Education Statistics 2017*. 53rd ed. National Center for Education Statistics 2018-070. Washington, DC: U.S. Department of Education. https://nces .ed.gov/pubs2018/2018070.pdf (accessed March 26, 2022).

Sorensen, Lucy C., and Helen F. Ladd. 2019. "The Hidden Costs of Teacher Turnover." Working Paper No. 19-63. Providence, RI: Annenberg Institute at Brown University.

Springer, Matthew G., Dale Ballou, Laura S. Hamilton, Vi-Nhuan Le, J. R. Lockwood, Daniel M. McCaffrey, Matthew Pepper, and Brian Stecher. 2010. *Teacher Pay for Performance: Experimental Evidence from the Project on Incentives in Teaching*. Rockville, MD: Society for Research on Educational Effectiveness.

Stackhouse, Shannon, and Brian Lloyd. 2018. "Michigan Teacher Mobility by Geographic Location and Locale." White Paper. Lansing: Michigan Department of Education https://www.michigan.gov/documents/mde/Michigan _Teacher_Mobility_White_Paper_639846_7.pdf (accessed July 21, 2021).

Stecher, Brian M., Deborah J. Holtzman, Michael S. Garet, Laura S. Hamilton, John Engberg. Elizabeth D. Steiner, and Jay Chambers. 2018. *Improving Teaching Effectiveness: Final Report*. Santa Monica, CA: RAND Corporation.

Steiner, Elizabeth D., and Ashley Woo. 2021. *Job-Related Stress Threatens the Teacher Supply: Key Findings from the 2021 State of the U.S. Teacher Survey*. Santa Monica, CA: RAND Corporation.

Strunk, Katharine O., and Jason A. Grissom. 2010. "Do Strong Unions Shape District Policies? Collective Bargaining, Teacher Contract Restrictiveness, and the Political Power of Teachers' Unions." *Educational Evaluation and Policy Analysis* 32(3): 389–406.

Stuit, David A., and Thomas M. Smith. 2009. "Teacher Turnover in Charter Schools." Nashville, TN: Vanderbilt University.

———. 2012. "Explaining the Gap in Charter and Traditional Public School Teacher Turnover Rates." *Economics of Education Review* 31(2): 268–279.

Sutcher, Leib, Linda Darling-Hammond, and Desiree Carver-Thomas. 2016. *A Coming Crisis in Teaching? Teacher Supply, Demand, and Shortages in the U.S.* Palo Alto, CA: Learning Policy Institute, Stanford University.

Synar, Edwyna, and Jeffrey Maiden. 2012. "A Comprehensive Model for Estimating the Financial Impact of Teacher Turnover." *Journal of Education Finance* 38(2): 130–144.

Taylor, Frederick Winslow. 1911. *The Principles of Scientific Management*. Norwood, MA: Plimpton Press.

Taylor, Joseph S. 1912. "Measurement of Educational Efficiency." *Educational Review* 44(November): 350–351.

Teacher Education Accreditation Council (TEAC). 2014. *Council for the Accreditation of Educator Preparation (CAEP)*. New York: Teacher Education Accreditation Council. http://www.teac.org/news-events/caep/ (accessed September 15, 2021).

Temin, Peter. 2017. *The Vanishing Middle Class*. Cambridge, MA: MIT Press.

Toch, Thomas. 1991. *In the Name of Excellence*. New York: Oxford University Press.

Tuttle, Christina Clark, Brian Gill, Philip Gleason, Virginia Knechtel, Ira Nichols-Barrer, and Alexandra Resch. 2013. *KIPP Middle Schools: Impacts on Achievement and Other Outcomes*. Washington, DC: Mathematica Policy Research.

Tyack, David, and Larry Cuban. 1995. *Tinkering toward Utopia: A Century of Public School Reform*. Cambridge, MA: Harvard University Press.

U.S. Bureau of Labor Statistics (BLS). 2016. "Union Members—2015." News release, January 28. Washington, DC: Bureau of Labor Statistics. https://www.bls.gov/news.release/archives/union2_01282016.pdf (accessed March 2, 2022).

U.S. Bureau of Labor Statistics. 2021a. *Labor Force Statistics from the Current Population Survey*. Washington, DC: U.S. Bureau of Labor Statistics. https://www.bls.gov/cps/cpsaat11.htm (accessed on April 15, 2022).

———. 2021b. *Impact of Coronavirus (COVID-19) Pandemic on Job Openings and Labor Turnover Data for July 2021*. Washington, DC: U.S. Bureau of Labor Statistics. https://www.bls.gov/covid19/job-openings-and-labor-turnover-covid19-july-2021.htm (accessed February 4, 2022).

U.S. Government Accountability Office (USGAO). 2008. *State and Local Government Retiree Benefits: Current Funded Status of Pension and Health Benefits*. GAO-08-223. Washington, DC: USGAO.

Vergari, Sandra. 2007. "The Politics of Charter Schools." *Education Policy* 21(1): 15–39.

Villegas, Ana María, and Jacqueline Jordan Irvine. 2010. "Diversifying the Teaching Force: An Examination of Major Arguments." *Urban Review* 42(3): 175–192.

Watson, John, Amy Murin, Lauren Vashaw, Butch Germin, and Chris Rapp. 2011. *Keeping Pace with K–12 Online Learning: A Review of State-Level Policy and Practice*. Evergreen, CO: Evergreen Education Group. https://kpk12.com/cms/wp-content/uploads/KeepingPace2011.pdf (accessed March 6, 2022).

Weick, Karl E. 1976. "Educational Organizations as Loosely Coupled Systems." *Administrative Science Quarterly* 21(1): 1–19.

Weil, David. 2014. *The Fissured Workplace.* Cambridge, MA: Harvard University Press.

Weingarten, Randi. 2018. "Commentary: Millennials Support Teachers' Unions. Politicians Should Take Heed." *Education Week*, Oct. 29.

Weisberg, Daniel, Susan Sexton, Jennifer Mulhern, and David Keeling. 2009. *The Widget Effect.* New York: New Teacher Project.

Wilkinson, Mike, and Ron French. 2019. "Michigan Leans on Long-Term Substitutes as Its Schools Struggle." *Bridge Michigan*, August 7. https://www .bridgemi.com/talent-education/michigan-leans-long-term-substitutes-its -schools-struggle (accessed March 6, 2022).

Will, Madeline. 2019. "Los Angeles School District and Teachers' Union Reach 'Historic' Deal to End Strike." *Education Week*, January 22. https:// www.edweek.org/teaching-learning/los-angeles-school-district-and -teachers-union-reach-historic-deal-to-end-strike/2019/01 (accessed September 15, 2021).

Wise, Arthur. 1988. "The Two Conflicting Trends in School Reform: Legislated Learning Revisited." *Phi Delta Kappan* 69(5): 328–333.

———. 2016. "Why Can't Teachers Cross State Lines?" *Education Week*, Sept. 13. http://www.edweek.org/ew/articles/2016/09/14 (accessed September 15, 2016).

Woodworth, James, Margaret Raymond, Kurt Chirbas, Maribel Gonzalez, Yohannes Negassi, Will Snow, and Christine Van Donge. 2015. *Online Charter School Study.* Stanford, CA: Stanford University, Center on Education Outcomes.

Xu, Zeyu, Jane Hannaway, and Colin Taylor. 2008. "Making a Difference? The Effects of Teach for America in High School." CALDER Working Paper No. 17. Washington, DC: Urban Institute.

Zabel, Jeffrey. 2014. "Unintended Consequences: The Impact of Proposition 2½ Overrides on School Segregation in Massachusetts." *Education Finance and Policy* 9(4): 481–514.

Zimmer, Ron, Richard Buddin, Sarah Ausmus Smith, and Danielle Duffy 2019. "Nearly Three Decades into the Charter School Movement, What Has Research Told Us about Charter Schools?" Working Paper No. 19-156. Providence, RI: Annenberg Institute at Brown University. https://www .edworkingpapers.com/ai19-156 (accessed March 8, 2022).

Zimmer, Ron, Richard Buddin, Derrick Chan, Brian Gill, Cassandra Guarino, Laura Hamilton, Cathy Krop, Dan McCaffrey, Melinda Sandler, and Dominic Brewer. 2003. *Charter School Operations and Performance: Evidence from California.* Santa Monica, CA: RAND.

Zimmer, Ron, Brian Gill, Kevin Booker, Stéphane Lavertu, and John Witte. 2012. "Examining Charter School Achievement in Seven States." *Economics of Education Review* 31(2): 213–224.

Author

Michael F. Addonizio is Charles H. Gershenson Distinguished Faculty Fellow and professor emeritus of Educational Leadership and Policy Studies at the College of Education at Wayne State University in Detroit, Michigan, and a member of the Kaplan Collaborative for Urban Education. He earned a bachelor's degree in English from College of the Holy Cross, a master's degree in Public Policy from the University of Michigan, and a PhD in Economics from Michigan State University. His academic interests encompass the economics of education, public school finance, and program evaluation, with a particular interest in the topics of teacher quality and teacher labor markets, charter schools and school choice, and public school finance. Before joining the faculty at Wayne State's College of Education, he served as assistant state superintendent for research and policy in the Michigan Department of Education. This is his second book for the Upjohn Institute; in 2012 he coauthored, with C. Philip Kearney, *Education Reform and the Limits of Policy: Lessons from Michigan.*

Index

Note: The italic letters *b, f, n,* or *t* following a page number indicate a box, figure, note, or table on that page. Double letters mean there is more than one such item on a single page.

About the Institute

The W.E. Upjohn Institute for Employment Research is a nonprofit research organization devoted to finding and promoting solutions to employment-related problems at the national, state, and local levels. It is an activity of the W.E. Upjohn Unemployment Trustee Corporation, which was established in 1932 to administer a fund set aside by Dr. W.E. Upjohn, founder of The Upjohn Company, to seek ways to counteract the loss of employment income during economic downturns.

The Institute is funded largely by income from the W.E. Upjohn Unemployment Trust, supplemented by outside grants, contracts, and sales of publications. Activities of the Institute comprise the following elements: 1) a research program conducted by a resident staff of professional social scientists; 2) the Early Career Research Award program, which provides funding for emerging scholars to complete policy-relevant research on labor-market issues; 3) a publications program and online research repository, which provide vehicles for disseminating the research of staff and outside scholars; 4) a regional team that conducts analyses for local economic and workforce development; and 5) the Employment Management Services Division, which administers publicly funded employment and training services as Michigan Works! Southwest in the Institute's local four-county area.

The broad objectives of the Institute's activities are to 1) promote scholarship and evidence-based practices on issues of employment and unemployment policy, and 2) make knowledge and scholarship relevant and useful to policymakers in their pursuit of solutions related to employment and unemployment.

Current areas of concentration for these programs include the causes, consequences, and measures to alleviate unemployment; social insurance and income maintenance programs; compensation and benefits; workforce skills; nonstandard work arrangements; and place-based policy initiatives for strengthening regional economic development and local labor markets.